The Wine and Food
of Spain

The Wine and Food of Spain

Jan Read

Maite Manjón

Hugh Johnson

Little, Brown and Company
Boston   Toronto

First American Edition
Library of Congress Catalog Card No. 86-82286

Designed by Simon Bell and Joy FitzSimmons

Published simultaneously in Canada
by Little, Brown and Company (Canada) Limited

Printed in Italy

ENDPAPERS Vines and olive trees on the plains of central Spain.

HALF-TITLE PAGE *Arenques* (salt herrings) from Majorca.

FRONTISPIECE Harvesting Xarel-lo grapes.

Contents

Acknowledgements

The three great Spanish wine companies of Codorníu, S.A.,
Gonzalez Byass, S.A. and Vinos de los Herederos del Marqués de
Riscal have made a major contribution towards the book with the
object of interesting readers and visitors in the many fascinating
aspects of Spain, not least its wines and cuisine.

Picture Acknowledgements

The publishers are grateful to David and Susan Worth of
Line and Line who kindly supplied the maps. They would
also like to thank the following who very kindly supplied
photographs for reproduction in the book:

Ace Photo Agency   11 (photo Pamla Toler), 56 (photo
    Gabe Palmer), 175 (photo Bill Wassman), 201 (photo
    Barry Hall)
Anne Bolt   65, 120 right, 121, 136, 177, 199, 204
Derry Brabbs   endpapers, 62, 63, 70–1, 79, 80, 82–3
Thomas Chitty   65, 190 above
Codorníu S.A.   139, 141
Comer y Beber, Barcelona   111, 130
Daily Telegraph Colour Library   24 (photo Peter Tit-
    muss), 61 (photo Adam Woolfitt), 166 (photo Peter
    Keen), 189 (John Sims)

Robert Estall   72, 112, 173
Greg Evans Photo Library   54
Fotomas Index Barcelona   191 left, 192 left
Gonzalez Byass S.A.   27 below
Susan Griggs Agency   frontispiece, 163, 168, 176
    (photos Tor Eigeland), 38 (photo Adam Woolfitt), 190
    below (photo Rob Cousins), 205 below (photo Anthony
    Howarth)
Administración Turística Española   41, 85 right, 180,
    184, 192 right
Jan Read   13, 17, 18, 22, 23, 25, 26, 33, 37, 45, 47, 48, 50,
    53, 57, 67, 68, 85 left, 87, 92, 93, 94–5, 99, 100, 101, 102,
    103, 107, 110, 119, 120 below, 122, 133, 135, 140, 141,
    145, 149, 150, 152, 154–5, 157, 165, 178, 181, 182, 191
    right, 194, 200, 202
Sobremesa, Madrid   73, 78, 129, 183, 185
Ronald Traeger   half-title, 205 above
VS Photo Library   158 below
Wines from Spain   27 above

Introduction

*I*S THERE A COUNTRY that comes so clearly to the inward eye as Spain? Spain is a country of burning light and beckoning darkness. Its pictures are intense, full of dramas of the imagination, of distortions and strange chiaroscuros. You feel that the eyes of Goya, El Greco or Dali must have been sore from peering out of shadow into glare, or from brilliant sunlight into the depths of shadows.

English light is perfectly expressed in watercolours; northern French light in *pointillisme* or the pastel dabs of the Impressionists. Central Italy has a crystal brilliance. But Spain is scarlet and gold and black – and so, to stretch the point a little, are her wines: *claretes, finos* and *tintos*, each a sharply defined character that can be confused with the wines of no other country.

The wine traditions of Spain are so ancient that in some cases they can be said never to have changed since the first presses were installed by – who knows? – the Romans, Carthaginians, the Greeks or the Phoenicians. The amphora, in the form of the *tinaja*, is still in daily use in certain regions. The ancient practice of boiling the must to concentrate it is still found here and there. Grape varieties are in use whose origins are lost in antiquity. In much of Spain, moreover, wine is still regarded as a commodity of scarcely more interest than bread. Fine differentiation is a foreign idea – not practicable in a country where the standard storage vessel was either a gigantic vat or a wineskin (which added its own peculiarity to the contents).

It was in the areas where the barrel had been long in use that distinct characters and reputations for quality first developed. The barrel was associated with export, or at least with commerce and wealth, being far more expensive than its alternatives. Jerez was the first Spanish region that achieved prosperity by barrel-ageing its wine for export, although Catalonia was probably not far behind. Rioja did not rise to prominence until the second half of the nineteenth century, but when it did it became Spain's national luxury table wine, on every good restaurant wine list throughout the land.

One may say, in fact, that it was specifically the taste of oak-aged wine that the Spanish associated, and still do associate, with quality . . . memories of wineskins still lingering in the national consciousness. That, at least, is the old picture, which is only now, within the last decade or so, giving place to outward-looking, international attitudes.

Twenty years ago in London, the capital of the world's wine trade, representatives of the great table wines of Spain were few and far between. Business was lean. I believe that the most successful wine from the agent of one well-known bodega in Rioja went under the name of 'Chablis'. A great deal of bulk Spanish wine was shipped for blending and bottling in Britain, though the only Spanish wines universally known, respected and drunk were sherries; and these, too, were usually blended in a way that would have made them almost unrecognizable to a Spaniard.

Uncompromising Spanish character was not in demand. The British, well-supplied with French wines at reasonable prices, were not to be persuaded that Spain, or Italy either, had anything to offer them that France could not supply. So conservative were the times, indeed, that not even the 'lesser' wines of France – anything, that is, from outside the hallowed ground of Bordeaux, Burgundy and Champagne – could find a market. The Rhône, Alsace and the Loire were almost as contemptuously ignored, or at best produced with patronizing apologies.

We have come a long way in twenty years.

This book sets out to put the Spanish wine of today in perspective and in context. It is a leisurely tour of a country whose regions sometimes mean more to their inhabitants even than their nationality. In every region wine is moving forward into the modern world of scientific control, of emphasis on grape varieties and their individual flavours, on fruitiness and freshness rather than strength and maturity. But each region still holds dear its own approach to the table, its own resources and recipes. Food still dominates in Spanish gastronomy, as it does in Italian, with wine playing a vital but fundamentally subsidiary role. Thus this tour of Spain, wine-based though it is, defines the regions through their cookery as well as their wine. Recipes are central to a full understanding of the nature of the land – and so are the inns and restaurants in which regional character is most fully displayed.

These three elements, wine, food and restaurants, have permitted the authors to paint a much fuller picture of the country than a study of its wine alone would represent.

Spain is still hard to penetrate. To discover what truly lies behind its internationalized coastline, in the beckoning shadows beyond the glare, in the private patios of its people, the visitor needs both curiosity and persistence. Most of all he needs information. We hope this resumé of the resources of Spain will lead to happy discoveries and deeper acquaintance.

Hugh Johnson

Andalucía

IN AD 711 TARIQ IBN-SAYID crossed the Strait of Gibraltar with some seven thousand men, routing King Roderick and launching a Moorish occupation of southern Spain which was to last for some three centuries. The Moors named the conquered territory, extending at the heyday of the Córdoban Caliphate from the River Ebro in the north to the Mediterranean and southern Portugal, al-Andalus. Modern Andalucía occupies a much smaller, but still very considerable area in the south of Spain, divided from the Castilian plateau by the rugged heights of the Sierra Morena.

It is the part of the country which most visitors think of as typically Spanish, with its almond and olive groves, the sherry vineyards, the white houses and patios, the flamenco dancers, the Easter *feria* in Seville with its hooded penitents and processions – and above all the unfailing sunshine, the great attraction of the seaside resorts of Marbella, Torremolinos and Fuengirola along the Costa del Sol.

Many of its inhabitants are directly descended from the Moors, and not so long ago it was the custom for women to go veiled in the seaside villages near Cádiz. There is a tendency to think of the Andalucíans as dark-skinned, volatile and lazy, with a perpetual *mañana* on their lips, and to identify them with the *gitanos* of Sacramonte in Granada; but this of course is to underestimate them. It was a dynamic Andalucían who founded the vast Rumasa empire, whose tentacles at one time embraced half the Spanish wine industry, banks, hotels, heavy industry and a great deal more; and perhaps more typical of modern Andalucía are the irrigation schemes and the neat new villages built during the Franquist regime, from which men and women alike go out to a hard day's work in the cottonfields or to pick olives or grapes.

In the Moorish or Jewish quarter of a city like Córdoba, with the houses built close together against the dazzling sunshine and sometimes thrust apart across the narrow cobbled thoroughfare, time seems to have stood still. Córdoba, with its splendid mosque (now the cathedral) supported by myriads of horseshoe arches, was the heart of Muslim Spain. After 'Abd-al-Rahman I, exiled from his native Syria, founded the Umayyad emirate in Spain, it was Córdoba that he made his capital in 756, and so it remained until the dynasty came to an end in the early years of the eleventh century, when al-Andalus, split by internal dissensions, broke up into small 'party kingdoms' and lay prey to the advancing Christians from the north.

During this period the mantle of Córdoba descended on nearby Seville, and here the most interesting Moorish relics are the Alcázar (or royal palace) with its dazzling polychrome tiles and shaded gardens, and the Giralda, once the minaret of the mosque, which flanks the great Gothic cathedral and the Barrio de Santa Cruz, the old Jewish quarter. A reminder that Seville, which stands on the River Guadalquivir, was later the centre for the colonial trade with Spanish America, is the four-square Renaissance building housing the Archives of the Indies; while the suburb of Triana is famous both for its gypsies

PREVIOUS PAGE The walls of the Alhambra Palace in Granada, with the snow-covered peaks of the Sierra Nevada in the far distance.

and for being the venue of the Easter processions. Sightseeing in Seville is hot and thirsty work, and when you have seen enough, make your way to the Calle de las Sierpes in the centre. It is closed to traffic and cool even in summer thanks to the awnings stretched between the housetops overhead. Sit down at one of the tables, with its inviting white tablecloth, in the street outside any of its numerous restaurants; order a glass of chilled *fino* sherry, and then, if you are wise, more to drink through the meal, as do the Sevillanos themselves.

Two other great cities of Andalucía, Málaga and Granada, are closely linked with the Moors and both lie in the former kingdom of Granada to the south-east. When the caliphate broke up, Granada was not the largest of the small Moorish principalities formed from the ruins, but it was to prove the longest lived, and it was not until Castile and Aragón were united under the Catholic Monarchs that the Christians moved in for the kill. First to fall

RIGHT **Part of the Barrio de Santa Cruz, the old Jewish quarter of Seville.**

BELOW **A *mirador*, or balcony, with a decorative bay window overlooking a street in old Seville.**

was Málaga in 1487. The ruins of the great castle of Djabal Faro ('the hill of light', so-called because of its great beacon), where the Moors made their fierce last stand, lies close to the modern Parador of Gibralfaro. (Throughout Spain there are government-run establishments known as Paradors, which have been converted from ancient castles, monasteries and private houses into excellent hotels.) At Gibralfaro you may look across the castle's jagged silhouette from the terrace of the Parador which also overlooks the blue waters of the bay.

Now the centre of the flourishing tourist region of the Costa del Sol, Málaga, bustling and cheerful, is not particularly rich in historic buildings, but you may care to explore the old quarter behind the port with its colourful food market (spices in bulk are a particularly good buy), its narrow streets lined with shops and its old-fashioned bars, where Málaga wines in all their variety are drawn from the wood.

By 1491 King Ferdinand had overrun the whole of the kingdom of Granada except the city itself and established the great tented camp of Santa Fe beneath the walls of the Alhambra. The last of its Moorish sovereigns, the luckless Boabdil, delivered up the keys of the city in January 1492 and rode off into exile, pursued by his mother's ringing epitaph : 'Weep like a woman for what you could not defend like a man.'

Granada itself is now ringed by ugly motorways and high-rise buildings, and seems a world apart from the airy fantasies of the Alhambra Palace and the fountains and flowers of the Generalife gardens above the city. High in the Sierra Nevada, which forms a spectacular backdrop to the Alhambra and whose snows feed its pools and fountains, is the cheerful ski resort of Sol y Nieve with good facilities for winter sports.

At the other extreme of Andalucía, in the province of Huelva towards the Portuguese frontier, is another must for the visitor. The 600,000-acre nature reserve of the Coto Doñana, on the coast between Cádiz and Palos de la Frontera from where Columbus first sailed for America, is perhaps the most remarkable in Europe. It is situated in the swampy delta of the River Guadalquivir and its marshlands provide a resting place for great flocks of birds on their migrations between Africa and Europe and a more permanent home for wild animals of all sorts, such as red deer, foxes, lynx and eagles. To reach it, you must make a wide detour to the north, since there are no bridges across the Guadalquivir south of Seville, but the southern fringe of the *marismas* (or marshes) may clearly be seen across the estuary at Sanlúcar de Barrameda on the extreme west of the sherry country.

The other great city of Andalucía is the glittering, sea-girt port of Cádiz, connected to the mainland by a narrow causeway. It is a place which has often been destroyed and rebuilt, and it was founded by the Phoenicians near the legendary Tartessos of the ancient world. Its present elegant white buildings, domed churches, wide squares and encircling promenade with long views across the bay date from 1596, when the place was razed to the ground during a destructive raid by the English under the Earl of Essex.

In Cádiz, from whose port sherry is shipped all over the world, you are on the threshold of the sherry country, and it is only an hour's drive down a sun-baked motorway to Jerez de la Frontera.

The Wines

Sherry

Outside the modern shopping area Jerez de la Frontera is full of charm, with narrow alleyways, whitewashed houses and hidden patios ablaze with geraniums. It is at its best during May, before the summer heat descends, with the blossom of the jacarandas around the old *alcázar* even more brilliantly blue than the sky, and at its liveliest during the Fiesta de la Vendimia (the harvest festival) in early September. Starting with a procession through the streets led by the Queen of the Vintage accompanied by her maids of honour in white dresses and blue silk scarves, it continues with bullfights, music, dancing and flamenco, and reaches its climax with the blessing of the grapes on the steps of the Collegiate Church. The Queen throws a basket of grapes into an old press, treading begins, and as the first of the must emerges, a cloud of white doves is released and the bells ring out to announce the beginning of yet another vintage.

Jerez had been making wine long before the time of the Romans. It was probably founded by the Greeks or Carthaginians, and 'sherry' or 'Sherris sack' as Shakespeare called it, is an English corruption of the name. Wine-making survived the Koranic prohibition of the Moors and was given further impetus by demand from abroad. What that most perceptive of travellers, Richard Ford, wrote in 1846 remains largely true today:

Sherry is a foreign wine, and made and drunk by foreigners; nor do the generality of Spaniards like its strong flavour and still less its high price, although some now affect its use, because from its great vogue in England it argues civilization to adopt it.

Regular exports of sherry to England probably began during the reign of Henry VII (1485–1509), but with the expulsion of the Spanish Jews after the fall of Granada in 1492 foreign merchants stepped into their shoes, establishing communities in Jerez and nearby Sanlúcar de Barrameda. What cemented the popularity of 'sack' in England was Sir Francis Drake's raid on Cádiz in 1587, during which he seized some three thousand pipes (110-gallon barrels), so that Shakespeare's Falstaff could declaim:

A good sherris-sack hath a twofold operation in it. It ascends me into the brain; dries me there all the foolish, dull and crudy vapours which environ it; makes it apprehensive, quick, forgetive, full of nimble, fiery and delectable shapes; which, deliver'd o'er to the voice, the tongue, which is the birth, becomes excellent wit...

The great expansion of the bodegas in which the wine is made and matured, 'sherry cathedrals' as Ford called them because of their size and grandeur, took place in the latter years of the eighteenth century and the earlier part of the nineteenth. English, Scottish and Irish merchants, who had often entered the trade by selling the wines in Britain, arrived in force to supervise operations on the spot. They intermarried with their Spanish partners, but maintained their links with the 'old country' by sending their sons to school in England, forming polo teams and joining wholeheartedly in the Jerezanos' passion for horseflesh (while their wives and daughters foregathered for afternoon tea at the old Los Cisnes Hotel, though at the Spanish hour of 8 p.m.). Most of the large sherry firms are now Spanish-owned, but the names survive: Duff Gordon, Osborne, Byass, Terry, Burdon, Sandeman, Williams & Humbert, Wisdom & Warter, and the rest.

Growing and making sherry

You can get the best impression of the vineyards by approaching Jerez not from Cádiz to the south but from Seville. Take the motorway and branch off it at Las Cabezas, following the by-road through Lebrija and Trebujana. This will take you by way of the famous areas of Macharnudo and Carrascal, through rolling hills of whitish sun-baked clay densely carpeted with dark green vines and crowned with low white buildings bearing the name of famous bodegas or sherries.

The demarcated area, a rough triangle with its apex near Cádiz, lies between the Guadalete River to the east and the Guadalquivir and Atlantic to the west. Besides Jerez de la Frontera, it embraces the important sherry-making towns of Puerto de Sta María, from which much of the wine was formerly shipped, and Sanlúcar de Barrameda on the Guadalquivir estuary, famous for its bone-dry *manzanilla*. The best of the vineyards lie within twenty miles of Jerez to the north and west, and the soils are of three types: *albariza*, *barro* and *arena*. Of these the most highly rated is the white *albariza*, containing some forty per cent of chalk, together with sand and clay; it is this which retains moisture throughout the year, and on which the deep-rooted vines draw during the hot and rainless summers. *Barro* is a darker mud clay, producing less delicate wines, while the sandy *arena* is mostly used for growing Moscatel grapes.

Most important of the grapes is the white Palomino, used for all the different sherries and almost exclusively for the *finos*. Smaller amounts of Pedro Ximénez and Moscatel are used in making sweet wines and for this purpose they are sunned on *esparto* grass mats, shrivelling like raisins as the sugar is concentrated. The story goes that the Pedro Ximénez was a native of the Canaries, transplanted to the Rhine and brought thence to Jerez in the seventeenth century by Peter Siemens, a soldier in the service of the Emperor Charles v.

Unlike table wines, sherry is matured with access to the atmosphere, and it is a carefully controlled degree of oxidation which gives the wines their entirely individual nose and flavour (the technical description is 'maderized', derived from 'Madeira', whose wines smell and taste somewhat similar).

In essentials, sherry is still made as it has been for centuries, although modern technology allows for much stricter control of the process. Analysis of the grapes in the laboratory enables them to be picked at the optimum moment, so that the Palomino need no longer be sunned to produce the right amount of sugar in the must, but is picked into plastic containers holding some seventeen kilogrammes (instead of the larger and more picturesque wooden tubs where bruising might cause premature fermentation), and transported straight to the bodega. On a tour of the bodegas you will be shown the studded cowhide boots or *zapatos de pisar*, in which gangs of men used to tread the grapes in wooden troughs. The grapes are now pressed within an hour of being picked, so conserving all their freshness, in a press which works by squeezing the grapes against the side of a stainless steel cylinder by means of an inflatable rubber bag. This avoids the rupture of skins and pips which makes the wine too tannic and bitter. An even newer type of continuous press applies increasing pressure as the grapes progress along it, first extracting must for the *finos* and later for the heavier *olorosos*.

The must, or grape juice, was traditionally fermented in oak butts – and still is in some of the bodegas – but modern practice is to use large stainless steel tanks where strict control of temperature produces wine of exactly the required type. Once fermented the new wine (or 'must', as it is still called at this stage in Jerez) is now transferred in age-old fashion to butts of American oak to begin the long process of maturation. They are not completely filled and only loosely stoppered; with ordinary table wines this would result in rapid oxidation and spoilage, but in Jerez the new wine spontaneously grows a *flor* (or 'flower') on the surface. It consists of a thick, wrinkled layer of yeasts, serving the double purpose of eliminating harmful vinegar-producing bacteria and permitting a very slow oxidation which gives the wines their unmistakable fragrance and flavour.

Although with modern methods of pressing and vinification the development of the wine is more predictable than it once was, new wines can behave very differently in cask. Some, used

criaderas are not always arranged in order of age. The number of 'scales' depends upon the type of sherry, but is usually not less than five – and more in the case of *finos* and *manzanillas*. Everybody's picture of a sherry bodega is of mountains of barrels in a lofty cathedral-like building, and there is good reason for the spaciousness. Unlike table wines, which are matured in damp underground cellars, sherry matures best in cool, dry, airy surroundings, and the very height of the bodegas prevents them from becoming overheated in the scorching summer suns of Andalucía.

Few sherries, except for the most expensive *finos*, are straight *solera* wines, and the final stage is to blend them to meet the tastes of the customer. The lighter *finos* for export are usually fortified with a little *mitad y mitad*, a mixture of equal parts of alcohol and mature sherry, and slightly sweetened. The popular 'medium' sherries, on the other hand, may be prepared from a blend of a dozen or so different wines; and the sweet dessert cream sherry is a blend of the naturally dry *oloroso* with Pedro Ximénez wine and *vino de color*, which contains a dark *arrope* or syrup made by evaporating down unfermented must.

Styles and serving

After touring one of the bodegas and traversing the serried rows of butts (some of them laid down a couple of centuries ago and dedicated to famous historical figures, such as the Kings of Spain, the Duke of Wellington, William Pitt, General Franco and scores more) the final port of call is always the *salón de degustación*, a spacious, softly lit room with bottles of sherry of different types laid out on tables for tasting. These are:

FINO: A pale straw colour, light, dry, delicate and a little acidic, containing 15.5° to 17° (percentage by volume) of alcohol.

MANZANILLA: Usually used to describe the very pale, delicate and bone-dry *fina* of 15.5° to 17° strength, made only in Sanlúcar de Barrameda. There are, however, other more full-bodied styles of *manzanilla*, including the darker and fragrant *manzanilla pasada*, equivalent to a *fino-amontillado* from Jerez.

AMONTILLADO: Amber yellow, with a dry, walnut flavour and containing between 16° and 18° of alcohol. Genuine *amontillado* is made by allowing a *fino* to age without 'refreshment'.

MEDIUM: A sherry developed for foreign markets, akin to *amontillado* in style, but a little sweetened and made from a blend of wines rather than by ageing *fino*.

OLOROSO: The darkest, softest, fullest-bodied and most fragrant of sherries, completely dry in its natural state. It normally contains between 18° and 20° of alcohol, but because of transpiration of water through the pores of the cask and evaporation into the dry air of the bodega, old *olorosos* may attain strengths of up to 24°.

PALO CORTADO: Somewhat darker than *amontillado* and upwards of 17.5° in strength, this is a difficult wine to make and combines the nose of an *amontillado* with the flavour of an *oloroso*. It is labelled *dos*, *tres* or *cuatro cortados* according to age.

AMOROSO: From the Spanish word meaning 'loving', this is a name now not much used for a smooth, sweet *oloroso* made by adding Pedro Ximénez wine and *vino de color*. Good sweetened *olorosos*, such as the Gonzalez Byass 'Matusalem', improve in bottle, ending up with a finish that is almost dry.

CREAM: Developed for foreign markets, the dark mahogany-coloured variety, e.g. Harvey's 'Bristol Cream', is made by sweetening an *oloroso* with a sugary must prepared from Pedro Ximénez (and other grapes) left to dry in the sun.

PALE CREAM: Introduced comparatively recently for sherry drinkers with a taste for something lighter than the traditional cream, pale creams like 'Croft Original' are produced by sweetening a *fino* with *dulce apagado*, a wine made by arresting the final stages of fermentation with brandy, so leaving some of the grape sugar.

PEDRO XIMÉNEZ AND MOSCATEL: Made from the grapes of the same name, harvested when very ripe and sunned to concentrate the sugar, these are very sweet wines with low alcohol content. The Moscatel is particularly luscious.

The proper serving of sherry, especially of the delicate *fino*, is of crucial importance if it is to be enjoyed to the full. In the bodegas it is served under ideal conditions from chilled half bottles in *copitas*, narrow in-curving glasses, filled only a third or half full to allow for development of the bouquet. Only too often in bars and restaurants, in Spain as well as abroad, you will be given a small trumpet-shaped glass, filled to the brim from a lukewarm, half-full bottle. In this case, ask for it to be poured into a wine glass with a lump of ice. *Fino* begins to lose its freshness after some three months in bottle, and once opened the deterioration is noticeable after about three days. A good tip when keeping it at home is to pour what is left into a half bottle, cork it tightly and leave it in the door of the fridge. *Amontillados* and medium sherries should also be drunk cool, but not icy; *olorosos* and cream sherries taste best at room temperature and will keep for much longer.

The bodegas and their wines

The sherry bodegas welcome visitors. Visiting hours are normally from 9.30 to 13.00; at the larger ones, such as Gonzalez Byass, Pedro Domecq and Williams & Humbert, no prior appointment is necessary and you will be shown round by an English-speaking guide. With others, it is advisable to write or telephone beforehand – always a sensible precaution because of the many unsuspected public holidays – and a letter from a shipper is useful in the case of smaller establishments.

The notes which follow cover many of the famous names, but are by no means exhaustive: a full list of sherry exporters appears on p. 30.

OPPOSITE **Labels of sherry and other Andalucían wines.**

Until its expropriation by the government in 1983, the great Rumasa conglomerate controlled some thirty-five per cent of the bodegas in Jerez, including such well-known concerns as Zoilo Ruiz Mateos S.A., Williams & Humbert Ltd, Palomino & Vergara S.A., de Terry and Bodegas Internacionales. After the collapse of the Rumasa empire, which also had a stake in other wine-making concerns up and down the country and in banking, insurance and industry generally, the firms were taken over by the government, but most have since been regrouped and are again in private hands.

ANTONIO BARBADILLO, S.A.
Founded in 1821 by Don Benigno Barbadillo y Ortiguela, a Castilian from Burgos, Barbadillo is the largest of the *manzanilla* firms in Sanlúcar de Barrameda. It remains in the hands of the fifth generation of this now Andalucían family. The late Don Manuel Barbadillo was to Sanlúcar and *manzanilla* what Don Manuel Gonzalez Gordon and Don José Ignacio Domecq are to Jerez, and was not only the doyen of the wines but also a lively and imaginative poet and novelist.

Barbadillo possesses extensive vineyards in Balbaina, Carrascal, Campiz and San Julián, and in partnership with Harvey's has developed one thousand hectares of new vineyards in Gilbalbín further north and built the most modern vinification plant in the sherry region. Its offices in Sanlúcar are housed in the former bishop's palace and are surrounded by rambling and picturesque old bodegas dating to 1850 and before.

It makes a range of some four dozen different *manzanillas* and sherries, ranging from the driest and freshest of *fina manzanillas* to cream sherries, under such names as 'Solear', 'Don Benigno', 'Viña del Cuco', 'Tio Rio', 'Eva Cream' and 'Sanlúcar Cream'. 'Principe' is a particularly satisfying *manzanilla pasada*, combining the fresh elegance of *manzanilla* with the depth and nuttiness of a fine *amontillado*. Barbadillo was the first of the sherry firms to introduce a table wine made from Palomino grapes. The fresh young 'Castillo de San Diego' is a good attempt at a difficult task : the Palomino must be caught very young to make table wine crisp enough to be refreshing. Drink it *very* young.

BODEGAS INTERNACIONALES, S.A.

The last stupendous fling of José María Ruiz-Mateos's Rumasa was to build the largest single bodega in Jerez, adjoining Gonzalez Byass's new vinification plant on the Cádiz road. It was constructed not only to make the range of 'Duke of Wellington' sherries sold under its label, but to service another six old-established firms taken over by Rumasa: M. Misa, S.A.; J. Pemartín y Cia, S.A.; Bertola, S.A.; Varela, S.L.; Diestro, S.A.; and C. de Otao-Laurruchi.

The *manzanilla solera* of Antonio Barbadillo in Sanlúcar de Barrameda.

Under new management Bodegas Internacionales continues to market the well-made 'Duke of Wellington' sherries and also those sold under the labels of the other companies.

CROFT JEREZ, S.A.

Although Croft is one of the oldest names in the port trade, the company has been operating in Jerez only since 1970, when its parent firm, International Distillers and Vintners, fell heir to some old *soleras* belonging to the Gilbey family. Since then the company has acquired six hundred hectares of vineyards in the best *albariza* area and constructed a handsome modern bodega in Jerez housing fifty thousand butts with a capacity of twenty-five million litres of sherry.

With its 'Croft Original', now second in terms of world sales, Croft pioneered the increasingly popular pale cream sherry. To a

traditionalist 'Croft Original' may lack the distinguishing characteristics of any of the classic styles of sherry. But it is based on market research and its very popularity proves the force of the argument. Other Croft sherries particularly to be recommended are the 'Croft Delicado' *fino* and its excellent *palo cortado*.

DIÉZ-MÉRITO, S.A.

The company was founded in Bayonne in 1876 as Diéz Hermanos, with the object of importing sherry into France. It subsequently acquired bodegas in Jerez and grew steadily but unostentatiously by selling wine for buyers' 'own brands'. In 1979 it bought the old-established house of the Marqués de Mérito; the name was then changed to Diéz-Mérito, but the firm is still entirely owned by the Diéz family.

Expansion has been rapid in recent years. The large new complex outside Jerez is one of the most modern in the area, and Diéz-Mérito has now acquired the jewel in the crown of the fallen Rumasa empire, Zoilo Ruiz-Mateos, S.A., the wine company which was the springboard of the whole gigantic venture, whose offices in the handsome mansion of Atalaya were the headquarters of the whole wine division, and whose *soleras* were among the choicest in Jerez.

Apart from its own established wines, such as the old 'Fino Imperial' (in fact, a *fino-amontillado*) and the first-rate 'Oloroso Victoria Regina', Diéz-Mérito now offers the extremely fine 'Don Zoilo' *fino*, *amontillado* and cream. 'Don Zoilo' *fino* is quite unlike such very fresh top-level *finos* as 'Tio Pepe'. Long barrel-ageing under *flor* allows it to develop depth and smoothness of flavour without oxidation. The result is a velvety, singularly luxurious wine.

DUFF GORDON Y CÍA, S.A.

This old-established company was founded in 1768 by Sir James Duff, British Consul in Cádiz. Born in Ayrshire, he survived until the ripe old age of 81, dying in 1815 a few months after the Battle of Waterloo. Control then passed to his nephew, Sir William Gordon, who transferred operations to Puerto de Sta María.

Duff Gordon's bodega in Puerto de Sta María.

It remained in the hands of the Gordon family until 1872, when it was sold to Thomas Osborne, a partner in the firm. Osborne (see p. 28) continues to make sherry in the old bodegas and markets them abroad under the Duff Gordon label, but not in Spain.

The range includes 'Fino Feria', 'Club Dry' and 'El Cid' medium *amontillado* and 'Santa María' cream.

EMILIO LUSTAU, S.A.

Founded in 1896, Lustau is a large family-owned concern. One of its old bodegas, built against the city wall, is a domed building said to have been a headquarters of the Moors during their occupation of the city; more recently Lustau has constructed a large new bodega outside Jerez. The firm has prospered through supplying quality sherries for sale under the customer's own label; it also ships a complete range of sherries from *manzanilla* to cream labelled as 'Lustau'. Its 'Dry Oloroso' has broadened the appreciation of this pungent style of wine – which is scarcely for beginners. Lustau also ships, though necessarily in small amounts, some entirely individual Almacenista sherries from small private stockholders, and by pioneering Almacenista sales in Britain has undoubtedly captured the imagination of wine-lovers who (quite mistakenly) seem to believe that 'mere' brands are somehow not quite exclusive enough for them.

GARVEY, S.A.

William Garvey, a distant descendant of King Edward I of England, emigrated from Ireland in 1780, married a Spanish girl in Cádiz and set up as a general merchant in Sanlúcar de Barrameda. Wine was always his first interest and he was a man who did nothing by halves. Moving to Jerez, he constructed a bodega 558 ft long by 126 ft (which until fairly recently remained the largest in the place). An arcade housing the *oloroso solera* is some quarter of a mile long, and the family mansion, meticulously restored during Rumasa's ownership of the firm, is one of the most impressive in Jerez. A patriotic Irishman, Garvey named his bodega, his son and his *fino* sherry after St Patrick.

Garvey owns vineyards in the best *albariza* areas, and when Rumasa took control in 1979, it constructed a new vinification plant and bodegas for maturing the wine just outside Jerez. An interesting feature is that most of the wine is fermented in cement *tinajas* like those used in Montilla (see p. 31).

Best-known of the Garvey wines is *fino* 'San Patricio', one of the most reliable pale and delicate *finos*, comparable to (perhaps a shade softer than) 'Tio Pepe'. Other labels are 'La Lidia' *manzanilla*, 'Tio Guillermo' *amontillado*, 'Ochavico' dry *oloroso*, 'Long Life' medium *oloroso* and 'Flor de Jerez' cream.

GONZALEZ BYASS, S.A.

The story of Gonzalez Byass, the largest of the sherry firms in terms of sales and stocks of wine, began in 1783 when the King of Spain appointed Don José Antonio Gonzalez y Rodriguez, a member of the royal bodyguard, administrator of the Royal Salt Marshes at Sanlúcar de Barrameda. His fifth son, Manuel María Gonzalez Angel was a bit of a problem child, but after engaging in various business enterprises in Cádiz and marrying the daughter of the richest man in the place, he moved to Jerez and started a small wine business in 1835. He worked hard, shipping a little sherry to England, then found a rich backer, a Señor Aguera, and with funds provided by him first built a large bodega, La Sacristía. Trade grew on such a scale that Señor Aguera took fright; Manuel bought him out and found a new partner in Juan Dubosc, an energetic Catalan, who travelled Europe selling the wines.

Under the name of Gonzalez & Dubosc – the name still used for the sparkling wine made by Gonzalez Byass in Catalonia – expansion continued apace, and the great new Constancia bodega was finished in 1855. By this time the English trade had become so important that the company's English agent, Robert Blake Byass, became a partner; after Dubosc's death in 1859 the name of the firm was eventually changed to

ABOVE **Palomino grapes, the most important variety used in the making of sherry.**

RIGHT **La Concha bodega at Gonzalez Byass, designed by Gustave Eiffel.**

Gonzalez Byass & Co. It remains a joint Spanish and English concern, all the directors being direct descendants of the founders.

By the name of its biggest-selling wine, 'Tio Pepe', there hangs a tale. Manuel María Gonzalez's maternal uncle, Tio Pepe or 'Uncle Joe' in anglicized form, lived in Sanlúcar de Barrameda and was an enthusiast of the light and dry *manzanilla*, having little taste for the heavier Jerez wines. Manuel María therefore set aside for him two butts of his lightest *fino*; its fame spread and it is now the biggest-selling *fino* in the world.

Manuel María Gonzalez's grandson, Don Manuel M. Gonzalez Gordon, Marqués de Bonanza, was one of Jerez's most outstanding figures in recent times. After the doctors despaired of his life at the age of four months, the tot signalled that he wished to be given a little sherry. It was done; the dose was continued, and Don Manuel survived into his nineties,

becoming a foremost taster and writing his classic book, *Sherry, The Noble Wine*.

Gonzalez Byass owns some two thousand hectares of vineyards, all in Jerez Superior to the north and west of Jerez de la Frontera, and was the first firm to begin picking the grapes into plastic containers. It runs its own Oenological Investigation Centre and has for a number of years been experimenting in its nurseries with the 'cloning' or vegetative reproduction of vines, the object being to produce the very best and healthiest specimens of Palomino, which, when grafted on to resistant North American stocks and planted in sterilized soils, resist insect pests and produce the highest quality of wine.

The old bodegas in the centre of the town are vast in size: the semicircular, cantilevered La Concha, designed by Gustave Eiffel, houses 12,400 butts, and the more modern concrete Tio Pepe bodega another 30,000 on three

floors. Picturesque features of the old bodegas at the centre of the complex are Manuel María Gonzalez's tasting room, exactly as he left it when he died, with bottles wreathed in cobwebs and a wooden *camera* with candle for gauging the brightness of the wines, and the gargantuan butt, 'El Cristo', filled with sherry for Queen Isabella on her visit to the bodega in 1862 and now flanked, as in the Last Supper, by twelve 'apostles' holding samples of the best wines.

Even these massive installations proved incapable of meeting the demand for the firm's sherries, which currently amount to twenty-eight per cent of world markets, and a modern vinification plant, Las Copas, equipped with stainless steel fermentation tanks and with a capacity of 60,000 butts, was constructed outside Jerez on the road to Cádiz.

'Tío Pepe', elegant, dry and fragrant, and eminently consistent in quality, well merits its position as the most popular *fino*, both in Spain and worldwide. Its very popularity often en-

sures its being exceptionally fresh. No *fino* should be kept too long in bottle. The 'Santo Domingo' pale cream and 'Nectar' cream are the biggest-selling sherries of their type in Spain. Other top-flight wines are the dry 'Alfonso' *oloroso* and 'Viña AB' *amontillado*. In limited amounts, Gonzalez Byass also makes some quite exceptional old *olorosos*: these include the dry 'Apostoles Oloroso Muy Viejo' and the dessert 'Matusalem' and 'Solera 1847' *oloroso dulce*. Over long years, most of the sugar has been consumed and they are almost black

OPPOSITE ABOVE **A cask of the dessert sherry 'Matusalem', an** *oloroso muy viejo*, **dedicated to Sir Winston Churchill.**

OPPOSITE BELOW **The modern Las Copas bodega of Gonzalez Byass.**

BELOW **The tasting room of Manuel María Gonzalez, founder of Gonzalez Byass, preserved as he left it.**

in colour, with huge intensity of flavour and dryish bitter-sweet finish.

Gonzalez Byass is a large-scale producer of brandy (see p. 31), *anis* (see p. 72) and 'Milton' gin, and also makes Rioja (see p. 97) and sparkling wines (see p. 146).

JOHN HARVEY & SONS (ESPAÑA) LTD

This famous Bristol firm was founded in 1796, but it was not until 1822 that the first John Harvey decided against going to sea, like his father and grandfather, and joined it. There is a long tradition of shipping and blending sherries in Bristol, and Harvey's had been blending their 'Bristol Milk' and 'Bristol Cream' with wines bought from suppliers in Jerez before buying their own vineyards and bodegas in 1970. First acquiring the bodegas of Mackenzie & Co., the firm next took over those of the Marqués de Misa adjoining; impressive in size, the bodegas stand amidst wide green lawns and trees, and in a corner of the garden you will be surprised to

find a Mississippi alligator basking in its pool. Since 1973 the firm has been developing large vineyards in association with Garvey and Barbadillo. A subsidiary of Allied Breweries, it has more recently acquired the large concerns of de Terry and Palomino & Vergara, formerly within the Rumasa group.

'Bristol Cream' is the biggest-selling sherry in the world, with huge sales in the United Kingdom and United States. It is a good cream, but perhaps not the Rolls-Royce of sherries that one remembers once. Other labels include 'Luncheon Dry' *fino*, the somewhat sweeter 'Bristol Dry' and 'Club Amontillado'. To compete with 'Croft Original', 'Finesse' Pale Cream is a recent addition to the range. Among traditional styles Harvey's 'Palo Cortado' remains reliable and true to type. To compete with vermouth, Harvey's have introduced a slightly herbalized 'Tico', specially blended for drinking with ice and mixers.

LA RIVA, S.A.

Founded in 1776 and bought by Pedro Domecq in the 1970s, La Riva describes itself as an 'artesan bodega' and still operates under family management, producing beautiful wines from some of the best *soleras* in Jerez, albeit in small amounts. *Fino* 'Tres Palmas' is a relatively full-bodied *fino*. Some of the ancient *solera* wines of La Riva ('Oloroso 1830', for example) are so concentrated as to be almost painful to drink. It may seem lacking in respect, but in such a case blending with a less formidable sherry can safely be undertaken at home. The character of the old *solera* will dominate whichever younger wine it is blended with.

OSBORNE Y CÍA, S.A.

The largest of the sherry firms in Puerto de Sta María, Osborne was founded in 1772 by a Devonshireman, Thomas Osborne y Mann. Since then the firm has passed from father to son, and in 1869 Thomas Osborne Böhl de Faber was created Conde de Osborne, becoming the first sherry shipper to be granted an hereditary title. The old bodega, set in spacious gardens, is one of the most beautiful in the Jerez region, and the modern vinification plant, employing horizontal rather than vertical tanks, among the most technically innovative.

Well-known labels from Osborne include 'Fino Quinta', 'Bailén' dry *oloroso*, 'Coquinero' *amontillado* and 'Osborne Cream'.

Osborne is an important producer of brandy (see p. 31) and anís; it also owns bodegas in the Rioja (see p. 105) and has interests in Portugal and Mexico.

PEDRO DOMECQ, S.A.

Domecq and Gonzalez Byass are the two largest sherry firms in the region. The bodega was founded in 1730 by an Irish farmer, Patrick Murphy, who had settled in Jerez. When he died in 1762 he left the business to his partner Juan Haurie, who in turn bequeathed it to his nephew Juan Carlos Haurie. Haurie became the largest shipper in Jerez; but the family was of French extraction and during the Peninsular War he went out of his way to succour the French invaders, providing food and wines to Marshal Soult's armies. For this, he was never forgiven by the Jerezanos, and with the end of the war the business went into rapid decline. Its fortunes were revived by a kinsman, Pedro Domecq Lembeye of an aristocratic family from the Basses-Pyrénées, who had worked as a clerk in the offices of its London agents.

When the quarrelsome Haurie fell out with them, Pedro Domecq joined forces with another clerk – none other than the father of the famous writer John Ruskin – and they were soon shipping some three thousand butts of sherry annually. Even this did not save Haurie from bankruptcy and Domecq moved to Jerez to reorganize operations on the spot. He died in 1839 when he collapsed into a cauldron of boiling water during treatment for his rheumatism, but long before this he had set the firm on its feet and renamed it Pedro Domecq.

The urbane and aristocratic Domecq family, one of the great sherry dynasties, has retained control of the firm, and its senior member, Don José Ignacio Domecq, renowned for the acuteness of his nose, is one of the great sherry authorities of his generation. The splendid Palacio Domecq in the centre of Jerez, no longer lived in by the family, is still used for receptions and banquets remarkable for their elegance and the excellence of the food and wines.

Domecq owns dozens of bodegas and vineyards in and around Jerez, Puerto de Sta María and Sanlúcar de Barrameda. The Macharnudo vineyard, surmounted by the old Castle of Macharnudo depicted on some of the labels, once a summer residence but now used only for entertaining, is one of the best in the region. In the oldest of the bodegas, El Molino, built in 1730, you will be shown butts laid down centuries ago for Pitt, Nelson, Wellington and others; the contents are used in minute quantities for lending character to younger wines.

'La Ina', very slightly sweeter than some, is among the freshest and most fragrant of *finos*; 'Río Viejo' is an outstanding dry *oloroso*; while other Domecq wines include the nutty 'Botaina' *amontillado*, the popular 'Double Century' cream and an older and richer 'Celebration Cream'.

Apart from its bodega in the Rioja (see p. 98), Domecq has extensive interests in Mexico.

SANDEMAN HERMANOS Y CÍA, S.A.

George Sandeman was born in Perth in 1765 and began a wine business in London with a loan of £300 from his father. The firm prospered, and he first entered the port trade and later bought the extensive sherry vineyards and bodega of Julián Pemartín, an exuberant character who had constructed a palace in Jerez in the style of the Paris Opera House and whose bankruptcy coincided with a reception there for the King of Spain. The Sandeman ports and sherries have become household words, not least because of their famous advertising symbol – a figure dressed in a stylized Portuguese student's cape, and sporting a wide-brimmed hat like those still worn by the *caballeros* of Jerez – and acquired for the company with typical Scots acumen for the sum of 50 guineas in 1928.

The firm has been sold to the Seagram group, but is still managed by the Sandeman brothers.

Sandeman makes some very fine sherries, vinifying most of them by traditional means in oak butts, later passed on to the distilleries in Scotland for maturing their whisky. Since the takeover, some of the wines have been restyled. 'Fino Apitiv', always one of the most delicious dry sherries, has been replaced by the rather fuller 'Don Fino'; and 'Armada Cream', again one of the best wines of its type, by 'Oloroso Cream'. The 'Light Oloroso Pale Cream' is a new departure, less sweet than most wines of this type, with a lot of class. Traditional Sandeman wines, such as the 'Imperial Corregidor' *oloroso* and *palo cortado*, are outstanding. 'Imperial Corregidor' falls almost into the same category as a grand old tawny port: a nectar to be sipped on a frosty day or at the close of a dinner with fine wines.

WILLIAMS & HUMBERT LTD

The story of Williams & Humbert is one of sturdy Victorian self-improvement. Alexander Williams, a clerk working for the established firm of Wisdom and Warter, married a young wife and, unable to support her on his low income, suggested that he might be made a partner. Summarily turned down, he was lent £1,000 by his father-in-law on condition that his son, Arthur Humbert, should be taught the business and in due course become a partner in the new firm. The two never looked back, and Williams & Humbert is now one of the most substantial firms in Jerez.

It is an interesting bodega to visit. In the days when there was a British Vice-Consul in Jerez, he worked from an office within the bodega. It has been preserved as the last of its occupants left it. There is also a splendid display of coaches and harnesses.

The first wine to be shipped by Williams & Humbert was its excellent 'Pando' *fino*, but the most popular is the 'Dry Sack' medium *amontillado*; other well-known brands are 'Canasta Cream' and 'Walnut Brown', both sweet, and 'Dos Cortados'.

Sherry Shippers – 1984

(BODEGAS DE CRIANZA Y EXPEDICIÓN)

JEREZ DE LA FRONTERA
Abad, S.A., Tomás
Argüeso, S.A., Manuel de
Blázquez, S.A., Hijos de Agustín
Bodegas Internacionales, S.A.
Bodegas Rayón, S.A.
Bustamente, S.L., José
Croft Jerez, S.A.
Diéz-Mérito, S.A.
Domecq, S.A., Pedro
Estévez, S.A., José
Fernández, S.A., Manuel
García Delgado, S.A., Fernando
Garvey, S.A.
Gil Galán, S.A., M.
Gil Luque, S.A., M.
Gonzalez Byass, S.A.
Gordon, Sucr., Luis G.
Guerrero Ortega, José Maria
Harvey & Sons (Spain) Ltd, John
Hidalgo, S.A., Emilio M.
J.H.E.S.A.
Lagos, S.A., B.M.
Lustau, S.A., Emilio
La Riva, S.A.
Marqués del Real Tesoro, S.A., Herederos
Muñez, Antonio
Paez, S.A., Luis
Palomino y Vergara, S.A.
Pino y Cía, S.L., Cayetano
Sánchez Romate Hermanos, S.A.
Sandeman Hermanos y Cía
Soto, S.A., José de
Valdespino, S.A., A.R.
Vergara, S.A., Juan Vivente
William & Humbert Ltd
Viñas, S.L.
Wisdom & Warter Ltd

PUERTO DE STA MARÍA
Caballero, S.A., Luis
Cuvillo y Cía
Ferris Marhuenda, Jesús
Gómez, S.A., Miguel M.
González y Cía

González Obregón, José Luis
Jiménez, S.A., F. Javier
Osborne y Cía, S.A.
Portalto, S.A.
Terry, S.A., Carlos y Javier de
Terry, S.A., Fernando A. de

SANLÚCAR DE BARRAMEDA
Argüeso, S.A., Herederos de
Argüeso, S.A., Manuel de
Barbadillo, S.A., Antonio
Bodegas Infantes de Orleans-Borbón, S.A.
Bodegas San Cayetano
C.A.Y.D.S.A.
Delgado Zuleta, S.A.
Escobar Suárez, Ana Ma.
Florido Cano, Gaspar
García de Velasco, Francisco
Medina y Cía, S.A., José
Parra Guerrero, A.
Pérez Marin, S.A., Hijos de
Pérez Megía, S.A., Hijos de A.
Reig y Cía, S.A., Rafael
Romero, S.A., Pedro
Sánchez Avala, S.A., Miguel
Vinícola Hidalgo y Cía, S.A.

Jerez brandy

Most of the sherry concerns make brandy, sometimes on a very large scale. It is, in fact, vastly more popular than sherry in Spain itself, and with sherry facing stiff competition in traditional foreign markets from vermouth and from chilled white wine drunk as an aperitif, it has proved the salvation of more than one of the large houses.

Brandy has long been made in Jerez for the fortification and treatment of the wines, but it was not until the 1880s and 1890s that it was first sold as such. At that time it was made in the Charentais-type stills used in Cognac and for that reason was known as *coñac*; much to the chagrin of the French producers and despite the use of the term 'Spanish Brandy' on labels, this is still how Spaniards refer to it.

The great bulk of Jerez brandy is no longer made by the Cognac method (though in Catalonia smaller amounts of superior brandy, in fact approximating more to Armagnac than Cognac, are produced in pot stills by discontinuous distillation). The first step is the production of a grape spirit containing some sixty-five per cent of alcohol in large steam-heated columns resembling those used for making grain whisky. It would be too expensive to manufacture the *holandas*, as the spirit is called, from the scarce Palomino grapes of the sherry region, and most of it is made in areas with large surpluses of grapes such as La Mancha and Extremadura; some of the sherry firms maintain their own distilleries.

The raw *holandas* is then shipped to Jerez and broken down with distilled water to the required strength. The second big difference between Cognac and Jerez brandy is that it is not normally matured in individual oak casks, but aged like sherry in a *solera*, often with as many as fourteen 'scales' (see p. 18). This results in more oxidation of the flavouring ingredients, so giving the Jerez brandy its own individual taste. The Spaniards have a sweet tooth in brandy and like it to be dark in colour, so that inexpensive brands for the mass market are coloured with caramel and somewhat sweetened with syrup.

The biggest-selling Spanish brandy is 'Soberano' from Gonzalez Byass, which, like 'Fundador' from Pedro Domecq, is less sweetened and caramelized than most. Running it a close head in domestic sales is the enormously popular 'Veterano' from Osborne, rather sweeter and darker, like the brandies from de Terry. A feature of the Spanish market in recent years has been the growing demand for rather older and smoother brandies in the medium price range, such as 'Magno' from Osborne and Gonzalez Byass's 'Insuperable'. There are also some really old brandies, intensely fragrant and fine by any standards, among them 'Lepanto' from Gonzalez Byass, 'Marqués de Domecq' and 'Gran Duque de Alba', now marketed by Diéz-Mérito.

There are those who find some brandies indigestible, however fine. No one can prescribe on such an individual matter, but good Spanish brandies can suit those who find that Cognac, for example, gives them sleepless nights.

Montilla-Moriles

Montilla conjures up the shaded alleys of the *Judería*, the old Jewish quarter of Córdoba. Pass through the discreet arched entrance of one of its many *tabernas*, and you will discover a thronged interior with whole families enjoying their pre-meal *copita* in the cool patio. The wines are, in fact, made in the hill town of Montilla and the nearby village of Moriles, some forty-five kilometres across the dry and rolling countryside to the south on the borders of the province of Málaga.

Until the region was demarcated in 1945, much of its sherry-like wine was sold to the bodegas in Jerez for blending. This is now forbidden, so that even abroad one may now enjoy the dry, soft wines in their own right.

The chalky white *albero* soil very much resembles the *albariza* of Jerez, but here the vineyards are variegated with wide olive groves, and the predominant grape is the Pedro Ximenez, sunned and used only for sweet wines in the Jerez region. In Montilla-Moriles the grapes are picked ripe, but not overripe, and fermented without delay and to completion, so that all the sugar is converted to alcohol.

The recorded history of Montilla, the *Munda Betica* of the ancients, goes back to Roman times, and it was here that Julius Caesar defeated Pompey's army under the command of his sons. A legacy of this period are the earthenware *tinajas* in which the wine has traditionally been fermented: directly descended from the Roman amphorae, they are also to be found in the older bodegas of Málaga, Valdepeñas and the Portuguese Alentejo. This is one of the ways in which Montilla differs from sherry, though in the large bodegas steel tanks are now replacing both the oak butts in Jerez and the *tinajas* in Montilla.

As in Jerez, the wines are matured in *soleras* (see p. 18), the older wine being 'refreshed' with younger, so that again there are no vintages. Here, it seems, the ubiquitous stainless steel has no part to play! A Montilla *solera* normally contains five 'scales' for the *finos* and four for the *olorosos*. This is one of the hottest and sunniest parts of Spain; the ripe grapes contain large amounts of sugar and the wines are naturally high in alcohol, so that Montilla is very rarely brandied.

Like sherry, Montilla develops in different styles, officially classified by the Consejo Regulador (or regulatory body) as follows:

Type of wine	% Alcohol by volume	Characteristics
Fino	14-17.5	Pale, straw-coloured, dry, slightly bitter and fragrant on the palate
Amontillado	16-22	A dry wine with pungent, nutty nose, smooth and full on the palate, amber-coloured or old gold
Oloroso	16-18, rising to 20 when very old	A full-bodied wine, velvety, aromatic, lively. Dry or semi-dry and mahogany-coloured
Palo Cortado	16-18	A wine combining the nose of an *amontillado* with the flavour and colour of *oloroso*
Raya		A wine similar to *oloroso*, but with less flavour and bouquet
Pedro Ximénez		An inherently sweet wine, made in part with sunned grapes and containing at least 272 g/litre of sugar; dark ruby colour

These are the names used in Spain, but some time ago the sherry shippers contested in the English courts the use of *amontillado* and *oloroso* as descriptions of Montilla. Montillas are therefore sold in the UK as 'Montilla Dry' or 'Fino', 'Montilla Medium Dry', 'Montilla Pale Cream' and 'Montilla Cream'.

There have been difficulties in selling Montilla abroad in competition with the more widely publicized sherry, and in 1981 the old and respected firm of Cobos, together with its associates, Montialbero and Cruz Conde, closed down, the bodegas being dismantled and the contents sold off. More recently there has been a marked revival in foreign sales of Montilla wines, thanks to their excellent quality and very modest prices.

The largest of the firms is the family concern of ALVEAR, which with seventeen thousand American oak casks in its *soleras* and the very sizeable capacity of five million litres, exports twenty-five per cent of its production, more than sixty per cent of it to Britain. It was founded in 1729 and much expanded by Don Francisco de Alvear y Gómez de Cortina, Conde de la Cortina, during the early 1900s. Its historic old bodega with its wide, palm-fringed avenues is well worth a visit, as is the old family house in the centre of Montilla. Built around a marble-paved, arcaded patio, it now houses a school for girls.

OPPOSITE **The elegant arcaded patio of the house of the Alvear family in Montilla.**

Like the *manzanillas*, which they somewhat resemble (although generally being softer in the mouth, without quite the same 'tang'), the best-known of the Montillas are the *finos*. Alvear makes an excellent 'Fino C.B.', pale, dry, fragrant and slightly bitter. Its 'Fino Festival' is rounder, fuller and slightly sweeter. As well as an *amontillado* and *olorosos*, dry and sweet, there is also a 'Pedro Ximénez 1927' (referring to the laying down of the *solera*, not the vintage), a dark, sweet wine tasting of figs.

Other leading producers and their wines are:

BODEGAS MONTULIA

'Fino Montulia', the fuller and nuttier 'Fino J.R'. and 'Dulce Fabiola', a dark, sweet dessert wine. Montulia also makes a first-rate *palo cortado*.

BODEGAS NAVARRO, S.A.

The company markets a wide range of wines in Spain and also exports. Its dry, light and fresh 'Fino Andalucía' is available in the UK.

CARBONELL Y CIA

Best-known for its excellent olive oil, Carbonell makes its wines in the demarcated area, but matures them in *soleras* in Córdoba. It makes a range of wines, some labelled as 'Moriles', including the dry 'Solera Fina 1ª' *fino*, a nutty 'Flor Montilla' *amontillado* and 'Carbonell Oloroso' cream.

CIA. VINÍCOLA DEL SUR, S.A.

Formerly owned by Rumasa and known as Monte Cristo s.a. The new owners have kept the name 'Montecristo' for the wines, exported in quantity to the UK, where they are sold as 'Dry', 'Medium', 'Pale Cream' and 'Cream'.

GRACIA HERMANOS, S.A.

In Spain you will find the wines made by this excellent family firm labelled as 'María de Valle' *fino*, 'Montearruit' *amontillado* and 'Oloroso Cream'; in the UK they are sold as 'Kiki Pale Dry', 'Montiole Medium Dry' and 'Ben-Hur Rich Cream'.

PÉREZ BARQUERO, S.A.

Another concern formerly owned by Rumasa, for whose wines it built up a sizeable export market. They are sold in the UK as Pérez Barquero 'Dry Montilla', 'Medium Montilla' and 'Cream Montilla'.

Málaga

There are interesting, almost surprising undertones beneath its unctuous richness, like the dark fires in the heart of a jewel. Just as the touch of something very cold leaves you uncertain whether it has frozen or burnt you, so in the taste of great Málagas the sugar is sublimated and becomes almost astringent.

HARRY YOXALL in *Wine & Food*

I think that this description by Harry Yoxall, that grand old man and great gentleman of English wine writers, exactly captures the quality of a fine Málaga. The heyday of Málaga was in late Victorian times, when vast quantities were exported and it was somewhat superciliously known as a 'lady's wine' – one wonders in this day and age, when so many of the best tasters and wine writers are women, whether the phrase might not qualify as sex-discrimination! Today, the vogue is for dry wines, but this again is largely a matter of words and snobbery, since the mass market is for sweeter wines (witness the success of pale cream sherries) and the oldest trick in the trade is to label a sweetish wine 'dry' or 'semi-dry'. With Madeira, perhaps more akin to Málaga than any other wine, now staging a comeback, there seems no reason why Málaga should not do the same.

Together with sherry, Málaga has the longest history of any Spanish wine. It was a prime favourite of the Romans and was surreptitiously swigged by the Moors despite the Koranic ban; in the fourteenth century, Tamerlane, the ill-fated Sultan of Samarkand, sent to Málaga for supplies, and it is said that Catherine the Great of Russia was never without it.

You will occasionally come across old silver

wine labels inscribed 'mountain' (and can obtain elegant modern replicas from the leading British shippers, Laymont & Shaw of Truro), and this refers to the location of the vineyards in the hills above the city. They lie to the north of Málaga in the Antequera plateau on the way to Montilla and Córdoba, and in the Axarquia, a more extensive area bordering the Mediterranean coast to the east. The vines grow in a rich loam on a shaly substratum sometimes intermingled with limestone. Málaga was the first region in Spain to be blighted, in 1876, by the disastrous phylloxera epidemic. Prior to that a great variety of vines was grown, but many disappeared, and the Consejo Regulador now authorizes only two varieties for new plantation : the Pedro Ximénez and Moscatel. Most of the Pedro Ximénez is grown in the hills to the north, while much of the Moscatel from the Axarquia is sold as dessert grapes or used for making raisins.

Because of the steep and difficult terrain, the wine was traditionally vinified in small bodegas in the vineyards or mountain villages, and the large firms still make most of it in the outlying districts. It must, however, be brought into Málaga for maturation to qualify for *Denominación de Origen* (corresponding to the French *Appellation d'Origine*). Because of the explosive building boom in Málaga and the Costa del Sol and the sky-rocketing value of land, the bodegas are in fact moving out of the centre of the city to less picturesque surroundings on its outskirts.

The wines are matured very much as in Jerez by the *solera* system with continuous 'refreshment' of the old wine with younger (see p. 18), the *criadera* normally consisting of six 'scales'. One of the oldest is Scholtz Hermanos's Solera Pedro Ximénez 'Lagrima Bisabuelo' (*bisabuelo* meaning a great-grandfather) originally laid down in 1787. A little of the wine, black and undrinkable as it is when drawn off, is blended with the famous 'Scholtz Solera 1885' to give it character. The sweet Málagas are blended with a dark, treacly *arrope* (syrup) made by evaporating down must in a copper pan with the addition of alcohol to stop it fermenting.

The Consejo Regulador lays down strict regulations for wines sold with *Denominación de Origen* :

1.

(a) According to their sugar content, Málaga wines may be sweet, semi-sweet, semi-dry, *abocado* or dry. Their alcohol content will be between 15° and 23°.

(b) As regards colour, there is a distinction between the white, golden, golden-red, dark and black.

(c) The following distinctions must be made according to the type of must :
Lágrima This is sweet Málaga made without any mechanical pressing of the grapes whatsoever ; only the must which flows from the grapes is used.
Moscatel Sweet Málaga made exclusively from the Moscatel grape.
Pedro Ximénez or *Pedro Ximen* A sweet Málaga obtained exclusively from grapes of this variety.

2.

The names *Crema* and *Pajarete* may be used for the sweet and semi-sweet wines, as also the terms common in the trade, such as 'sweet', 'cream', 'brown', 'dunkel', 'golden' and others descriptive of the characteristics of the product.

3.

The wines should exhibit the accepted organoleptic and oenological characteristics, especially in regard to colour, aroma and flavour. Wines which in the opinion of the Consejo Regulador have not acquired these characteristics will not qualify for the *Denominación de Origen* 'Málaga'.

Among the largest and most prestigious of the Málaga firms is SCHOLTZ HERMANOS with an annual production of two million litres, half of which is exported. It was founded in 1807, but the name dates from 1885 when it passed into

German control; since the end of the Second World War it has again been in Spanish hands. The best-known of its wines is the 'Scholtz Solera 1885', bitter-sweet in flavour with a long dryish finish and with similarities both to *oloroso* sherry and a good tawny port. Other remarkable wines are its 'Seco Añejo, 10 year-old', a dry, nutty and aromatic *amontillado*, the luscious 'Moscatel Pálido' and ten-year-old 'Lágrima', toffee-coloured with a deep *oloroso* nose and long sweet finish.

The biggest exporter of Málaga wines is HIJOS DE ANTONIO BARCELÓ, founded in 1876. Three of its long range of styles are available in the UK, all of them sweet dessert wines: 'Gran Vino Sansón'; 'Málaga Lágrima', made without mechanical pressing of the grapes; and the rich and intense 'Gran Málaga Solera Vieja'.

LARIOS is the household word for gin in Spain; the firm is also well-known for its rum, brandy and fruit liqueurs, and makes good Málagas, especially the fruity and honey-like 'Colmenares Moscatel'.

Huelva

The wines from Lepe in the province of Huelva, to the far south-west across the River Guadalquivir from Seville, were among the first from Spain to be drunk in England; in the *Pardoner's Tale*, Chaucer describes their 'fumositee' and warns his readers about the treacherous after-effects of drinking them. They were probably *generosos* of the sherry type until the demarcation of the region in 1964, the best of the Huelva wines, like those from Montilla, were sent to Jerez for blending.

The wine-growing area centres on the Condado de Niebla, named after the Guzman Counts who were ceded the district after its reconquest from the Moors. The soils, though darker than those of Jerez and Montilla, are of the same general type. Most of the vineyards are planted with the native Zalema grape, but this is being replaced by the Palomino, Pedro Ximénez and other varieties.

Apart from aperitif and dessert wines,

Huelva also makes white beverage wines. Fresh and fruity at their best, they are not much drunk outside the region, though efforts are now being made to export them. Large amounts of the more ordinary wine are distilled as *holandas* (see p. 31) and used for making brandy.

Most of the bodegas and distilleries are in Bolullos del Condado, including the best of the cooperatives, the BODEGA COOPERATIVA DEL CONDADO. Its labels include 'Listán Pálido Mioro', a pale dry *fino*; 'Solera Especial Mioro', an old dessert wine; and a fresh young white table wine, also called 'Mioro'. The small family firm of HIJOS DE FRANCISCO VALLEJO is typical of those making pleasant wines of the sherry type.

The Cuisine

Like so many other facets of life, the Andalucían cuisine was strongly influenced by the Moors. It was they who introduced spices such as saffron, nutmeg and black pepper, and first planted almond groves; sugar was unknown in Western Europe (the common sweetening agent was honey) until they planted sugar cane in the conquered territories along the Mediterranean; bitter oranges, lemons and grapefruit were also cultivated in southern Spain some two centuries before the returning Crusaders brought the first specimens to Sicily and Italy from the Near East. It would therefore seem that we have the Moors to thank for that most English of confections, marmalade – much of the best is, in fact, made in Seville by cooking the flesh and coarsely cut peel of the bitter oranges, the cooked fruit then being despatched to England in barrels for sweetening and maturing.

Another staple of Andalucían (and Spanish) cooking is of even earlier origin. Olives and olive oil were introduced to Spain by the Romans. The province of Jaén in the mountainous north of Andalucía, with sixty-four per cent of cultivated land under olives, is the largest grower in Spain, followed by Córdoba and Seville; and the trees, marching along whole valleys and hillsides, their grey-green foliage contrasting with the red soil, are one of the most beautiful features of the Andalucían landscape.

Meals in Andalucía begin with a *copa* of chilled *fino* sherry, like 'Tio Pepe' or 'La Ina', although in cooler weather some prefer a dry, light-bodied *oloroso*, such as 'Rio Viejo', accompanied by *tapas*.

The word *tapa* originally meant a 'cover' and perhaps dates from the custom of covering the glasses to keep out flies. Today it is used for the multiplicity of small dishes served as aperitifs with the drink. Especially in southern Spain, the custom was to serve a few olives, a wedge of cold *tortilla* (Spanish omelette), or a few prawns or anchovies with the compliments of the house. *Tapas*, except for the simplest, are no longer free; and the more substantial, such as squid, crisp-fried in rings or stuffed and fried in their own ink, stuffed peppers, fresh fried anchovies, mussels in marinade, shellfish like the delicious *percebes* (a form of edible barnacle), or Russian salad, are no longer cheap. Nevertheless, by choosing from the assortment of dishes, both hot and cold, lining the top of any bar, one can make a most appetizing lunch.

Another favourite *tapa* in these parts, also served as a first course, often with melon, is *jamón Jabugo*, an uncooked, highly cured ham from the province of Huelva, cut razor-thin. This is the best of the many varieties of *jamón serrano*, made all over Spain and akin to Parma and Bayonne ham, but even fuller in flavour.

The Cádiz region is celebrated for *tapas* prepared with fish and shellfish from the bay and cooked to perfection in restaurants such as El Faro (see p. 40). They include:

Acedías fritas: fried baby sole.
Barbujitos: small fresh anchovies, fried.
Boquerones de la Isla: fried fresh anchovies, locally caught.
Cañaillas de la Isla: a sea-snail typical of the coast. It is lightly boiled and eaten cold, the sharp tail of one snail being used to extract the meat from the others. This was the fish from which the ancients extracted Tyrian purple.
Cazón: baby shark, marinated with red paprika and vinegar.
Puntillitas: the Andalucían name for minute squid, known in other parts of Spain as *chipirones*. They are dipped in a light batter and fried in olive oil.
Tortillas de camarones: crisp fritters, made with batter and tiny shrimps and fried in oil.

Perhaps the best-known of Andalucía's contributions to cooking, its cold soups or *gazpachos*, so refreshing in summer, are directly attributable to the Moors. They always contain garlic and a little olive oil, but are made with a variety of uncooked vegetables, chopped or puréed. The most popular version contains peppers, tomatoes and cucumbers, with breadcrumbs either incorporated or served on the side. On no account miss the *ajo blanco de Málaga* with its whole fresh grapes or the *sopa de almendras* from Granada, made with a basis of ground almonds. During the winter the Andalucíans also make a hot *gazpacho*. Because they contain vinegar, *gazpachos* are best eaten without wine – but try *fino* sherry if you must,

Lubina rellena, or stuffed sea bass, one of the many excellent fish dishes of the region.

and ask for the *gazpacho* to be made with lemon juice.

The best of the other soups are made with fish : *sopa de pescado gaditana* is a rich stew akin to *bouillabaisse* ; the delicious *sopa al cuarto de hora*, so-called because it is cooked for quarter of an hour, contains *ostiones* (Portuguese oysters), diced ham and hard-boiled eggs – and, of course, sherry ; *sopa A.B.* is named after the *amontillado* sherry from Gonzalez Byass used in it. Favourites with less hearty trenchermen are consommés into which it is customary to pour a small glass of *fino* at the table.

It is said that the Moors' favourite method of cooking, because of a shortage of fuel in their north African homelands, was stewing rather than frying, and the *olla*, a meat and vegetable stew resembling the French *pot au feu* was the

The waters of the Andalucían coast yield a wide range of fish which is supplied fresh to retailers and restaurants.

prototype of the many *pucheros*, *cocidos* and *ranchos* now cooked all over Spain. A favourite ingredient was, and still is, the *garbanzo* or chick-pea, introduced much earlier by the Carthaginians and a source of merriment to Plautus and other writers after him. Alexandre Dumas *fils*, who found so little to please him when he made a gastronomic tour of the country in the nineteenth century, wrote of it that : 'The garbanzo which can be cooked in half-an-hour is without price, but those grown in the barren soil of Spain can be cooked for a year and only become harder – hence the name "musket ball".'

Today, Andalucía is often labelled on gastronomic maps as the *Zona de los fritos* or region of fried food, and high on the list of such dishes must come the fries of mixed fish, often containing *boquerones* (fresh anchovies), *chanquetes* (akin to whitebait) and *calamares* (squid). On the menu of a restaurant these appear under such names as *frito variado de pescado* or *fritura gaditana*, but are often called *parejas* in Cádiz – this being the name of the dish cooked by the fishermen while at sea in their boats. Cádiz is perhaps the original home of the fish and chip shop in the form of its *freidurías*, where fish in wide variety may be bought to take away, of which that famous revivalist of genuine Spanish cookery, Dr Thebussem, wrote a century ago :

> Fish from the *freidor* is unbeatable : it is as different from that prepared by chefs or cooks as the wine of Jerez from other wines, the sword from Toledo from other swords, and the olives from Seville from other olives. Because of the special and secret method of cutting the fish and the temperature of the oil, the aroma rising from the sole, mullet, whiting, sardines and other fish cooking in the steaming olive oil is an invitation to eat ; and few suppers are more agreeable than this fried fish, washed down with half-a-dozen glasses of aromatic *manzanilla*.

Frying, of course, is only one method of cooking the fish available in such splendid variety around the coasts of Cádiz, Málaga and

Murcia – and no self-respecting Andaluz would serve anything that had not been caught the same day. Shellfish such as *gambas* (large prawns), *cigalas* (sea crayfish), *ostiones* (Portuguese oysters), *langostas* (spiny lobsters) and *bogavantes* (lobsters large enough to serve a party of six) are heaped in the local markets, which are always worth a visit. The Atlantic coast is exceptionally rich in fish, particularly tuna, sardines (grilled over charcoal), the gleaming silver *paire* (scabbard fish, cut diagonally into steaks and cooked under the grill), the ugly but delicious *perros* and *gatos* ('dogs' and 'cats', akin to whiting) and the shad, such a favourite of the Moors, which swims up the rivers in spring. Unknown elsewhere is the untranslatable *urta* caught near Rota, which acquires great flavour by feeding on shellfish and is served with a rich sauce of tomatoes and red peppers as *urta a la roteña*.

Not so long ago, some of this fish was caught by allowing it to swim into *caños* or pools, which were then dammed up. During the year the salinity of the water increased because of evaporation, and when the fish had grown and multiplied the pool was emptied and the owner and his friends gathered to scoop them out by hand.

Although Andalucía is best known for its fish dishes, so fertile and extensive a region runs to a great many other regional dishes.

Around Jerez in the rolling hills there is game in plenty, prepared in such novel ways as *perdices a la torera* ('bullfighter's partridge'), which is garnished with bacon, anchovies, green peppers and tomatoes. Jerez, as might be expected of a place with centuries-old ties with England, has its own ways with beef, notably *bistec salteado al Jerez* (steak sautéed with sherry). Another meat dish, now served all over Spain but entirely typical of the region, is *riñones al Jerez*, for which small lambs' kidneys are sliced, sautéed in hot oil and then cooked with a freshly made tomato sauce and dry sherry.

Popular dishes from Seville are the *ensalada sevillana* (a salad made with rice, red peppers, spring onions, tomatoes and olives) and *huevos a la flamenca*, eggs cooked in an earthenware dish with onions, ham and sliced tomatoes, and decorated with prawns, slices of *chorizo* (see p. 195), asparagus tips and red pepper.

Favourite dishes in Córdoba are *salmorejo*, a thick version of *gazpacho* but without peppers or tomatoes; *callos a la andaluza*, tripe stewed with calf's feet and chick-peas; *rabo de toro*, stewed oxtail with vegetables; and *ternera con alcachofas a la cordobesa*, veal served with artichokes and cooked with Montilla and spices.

The gypsy-inspired *tortilla al Sacromonte* from Granada is a substantial variation on the Spanish omelette, and another main dish popular in the area is *menudo gitano*, prepared from chicken giblets and other ingredients.

Spain has never been known for any wide choice of sweets. Perhaps the favourite in Andalucía is *tocino de cielo – not* 'little pigs from heaven', as we have seen it translated, but a confection of eggs and sugar flavoured with a vanilla pod. The usual way of finishing a meal is with fresh fruit; the local strawberries are available earlier than most in Europe, and a small glass of good sweet *oloroso* poured over them is the perfect adjunct.

Andalucía produces one or two worthwhile cheeses. The *queso de Grazalema*, from a town high in the mountains near Ronda celebrated for its fierce resistance during the Peninsular War, is a hard ewe's milk cheese rather similar to the better-known *manchego* (see p. 73). *Queso de los Pedroches* from near Córdoba is made from ewe's milk, but is a soft cheese which will not keep for more than three months, as is also the *queso de cabra de Málaga*, made from goat's milk. A pleasant accompaniment to these cheeses, which are not served with bread in Spain, is *membrillo*, the quince paste from Seville which was such a favourite of Pedro de Luna, the last of the Antipopes; it was by dosing it with arsenic that his enemies in Rome made an unsuccessful attempt to kill him.

Finally, there is the multitude of small cakes and sweetmeats in the Moorish tradition, best bought in the *confiterías* or confectioners. These are often made at the local convents, from almonds and the egg-yolks that remain after the whites have been used to clarify wine in the bodegas. Among the best-known are the *yemas de San Leandro*, reputedly made by dripping strands of egg yolk from a small inverted and perforated cone into hot syrup – but the secret remains with the nuns.

In Andalucía sherry is often drunk with a powdery sweetmeat wrapped in twists of paper, and these *polvorones* are manufactured in Estepa on the main road from Córdoba to Málaga. The whole town is fragrant with the aroma of hot sugar and almonds, and if you stop off at one of the manufactories to sample their wares, they will serve the sherry free.

Apart from the white wines from Huelva and a few fresh young white beverage wines from the sherry region, Andalucía does not produce table wines, and it is the custom, especially with fish, to drink a chilled *fino* sherry or Montilla throughout the meal. The Jerezanos have recently been experimenting with the matching of different types of sherry to dishes other than fish, drinking them throughout a varied menu. To celebrate its fiftieth anniversary in October 1985, the Consejo Regulador in Jerez called a conference of leading Spanish chefs and food writers to assess the possibilities. I was fortunate enough to attend and to take part in a lunch at the Palacio Domecq with a menu specially devised by the master chef Paul Schiff from La Hacienda in Marbella.

It began with a swordfish mousse served with *fino* sherry; followed by sweetcorn blinis with cockles and basil accompanied by *amontillado*; ducks' breasts with figs in a bitter-sweet sherry sauce, accompanied by a dry *oloroso*; and finally ice cream with a *sabayon* and strawberries, served with a dessert *oloroso*. Schiff cooked the meal with all his accustomed delicacy and lightness of touch; the flavours of food and drink were very carefully balanced and it was undoubtedly a *tour de force*, but one was left with the feeling that, basically, the different sherries tasted too alike to be served one after another through the meal.

Restaurants

Arcos de la Frontera

PARADOR NACIONAL CASA DEL CORREGIDOR

Arcos de la Frontera, half-an-hour's drive to the east of Jerez de la Frontera, is a picturesque old Moorish town, its white houses and narrow streets ranged steeply on a hill overlooking the Guadalete River. There are splendid views from the Parador, perched on a cliff above the river, and it is a pleasant place either to stay or to drive to from Jerez for lunch or dinner. It serves *entremeses variados* (mixed hors d'oeuvres platter) in the profusion usual at Paradores, and a range of regional dishes. Ask for the very drinkable house wine with its sherry-like flavour from Chiclana.

Cádiz

EL FARO★★

This is the place to sample the great variety of fish from the Bay of Cádiz. The inventive and gastronomic Gonzalo Córdoba buys from fishermen who use rod and line, so that on the menu there are fish not obtainable in local markets. The best plan is to order an assortment of dishes and share them. *Cazón* (baby shark), *acedías* (baby sole), *puntillitas* (minute squid) and *cañaíllas de la Isla* (sea snails) are all available here. The crisp shrimp fritters melt in the mouth; and a great speciality is the *dorada a la sal*, gilthead baked in a thick paste of sea salt to preserve the juices and flavour, and removed at the table by the waiter. Try also the *urta* (see p. 39) soup or saffron potatoes with fish, and finish (if you have room) with *tocino de cielo* (see p. 39) or the raisin ice cream with *oloroso*.

VENTORRILLO DEL CHATO★

Open uninterruptedly since 1780, but tastefully redecorated, this is a restaurant with great period charm. It serves first-rate *jamón de pata negra* (cured ham from the Extremadura) and well–cooked regional dishes, including fish and seafood from the bay, together with wines from Chiclana, the Rioja and elsewhere.

Córdoba

EL CABALLO ROJO★★★

This famous restaurant is conveniently situated by the side of the Great Mosque. You will be welcomed with a glass of Montilla and large olives, and the menu is the result of lifelong researches by its distinguished proprietor, Pepe García Marín, into the authentic dishes of Andalucía. Start with the *salmorejo* (p. 39), *gazpacho ajo blanco con manzana* (garlic soup with apples) or the wonderfully fresh artichokes with Montilla. You might follow with *rape mudéjar* (monkfish with raisins, pine kernels and Montilla), *cordero mozárabe* (lamb cooked with vinegar and honey) or Pepé's *pièce de resistance*, the oxtail, famous all over Spain. The bread is home-made and, though the restaurant is always crowded, the service deft and smiling.

The Parador de San Francisco, Granada.

EL CHURRASCO★

Since opening his restaurant in 1970, Rafael Carrillo has always believed in buying the best and freshest produce and charging very moderately for his irreproachably cooked dishes. Try the *gazpacho ajo blanco*, *pez espada a la cordobesa* (swordfish) or the meats from the barbecue.

Granada

PARADOR SAN FRANCISCO

To eat typical Granadan dishes at their best you should go to CUNINI★ or SEVILLA★, charmingly situated in the old Jewish quarter opposite the cathedral, but on a day-visit to see the Alhambra, the picturesque surroundings and location of the Parador within the palace precinct probably outweigh strict gastronomic considerations. It offers excellent cured ham from the Alpujarras mountains, *gazpacho al ajo blanco* (see p. 44), *sopa de pescado malagueña* (fish soup Málaga style), *macedonia de legumbres de la vega* (mixed vegetables), *huevos al plato granadina* (eggs with broad beans and ham), *filete de*

ternera andaluza (veal in regional style) and *hojaldres* (Moorish-style puff pastries from the gypsy quarter of Albaicín across the ravine from the Alhambra).

Jerez de la Frontera

HOTEL JEREZ

The Hotel Jerez, with its garden, swimming pool and air-conditioned rooms, is undoubtedly the most comfortable place to stay in Jerez, and its lounge bar is the meeting place for fashionable Jerez society. One would not choose its restaurant for the originality of the cooking, but it is where you may well decide to eat after a hot and tiring day in the bodegas. Best bets for a light meal are the excellent *jamón Jabugo*, *consomé al Jerez*, assorted French omelettes, and fresh melon and asparagus. There is a good wine list, including Riojas and Penedès wines as well as sherry.

GAITAN★★

This is an intimate and friendly restaurant serving a range of Andalucían dishes, as well as others from the Basque region at very moderate prices. Antonio Orihuela varies the menu according to what is available in the market, but you may well find an excellent *berza* (Andalucían stew), *ajo caliente* (hot garlic soup), *calamares rellenos a la abuelita* (stuffed squid), *fritura gaditana* and *pato a la sevillana* (duck with olives). He also makes delicious thick cream soups of peas, artichokes, beetroot or crab.

VENTA LOS NARANJOS★

A roadside restaurant between Jerez and Sanlúcar de Barrameda specializing in fish and seafood from the Bay of Cádiz, and much patronized by the *bodegueros*. The langoustines and lobsters are brought daily from Sanlúcar de Barrameda and expertly cooked by Rosario, the wife of the proprietor, Antonio Archidona. It was here that with a party of six (or was it eight?) I lunched off one of the freshest – and certainly the largest – lobsters I can remember. Do not expect to be served with anything except *fino* sherry or *manzanilla*, of which there is a remarkable choice.

Málaga

ANTONIO MARTÍN★

In the centre of Málaga with a terrace facing the port, this is a restaurant known for its fish and seafood, such as the *fritura de pescados* (see p. 38), *chanquetes* (whitebait) and fresh fried anchovies.

CASA PEDRO★

Casa Pedro is on the shore overlooking the Playa del Palo; it has always been popular with Malagueños for its fries of fish and fresh shellfish, and despite large extensions is always crowded.

Marbella

Marbella and the Costa del Sol have some of the most elegant and sophisticated restaurants in Spain, catering for wealthy visitors from abroad. Standards are up to the best in Europe.

LA FONDA★★★

Installed in a beautiful eighteenth-century Andalucían house with an enchanting terrace garden, this is an outpost of the famous Horcher in Madrid (see p. 76). It is a restaurant with the highest standards, and the classical, sometimes Austrian-inspired dishes from Horcher alternate with the traditional Andalucían, such as *gazpacho*, *riñones al Jerez* (kidneys in sherry) and oxtail.

LA HACIENDA★★★

The Belgian-born Paul Schiff, both proprietor and chef, offers *haute cuisine* in the French style; his great achievement has been to apply the best of the *nouvelle cuisine* to the splendid fish and other fresh ingredients from the region, and to create dishes with inventiveness and lightness of touch. Outstanding are the hot shrimp paté, guinea fowl with raisin sauce, monkfish with leeks and iced soufflé with Málaga. La Hacienda is naturally not inexpensive.

LA MERIDIANA★★★

Opened in 1982 by Paolo Ghirelli, this is the third of the front-runners in Marbella. Try the tartlets of *cigalas* (sea crayfish), the duck with cherries and cinnamon and the *turrón* (nougat) tart.

Sanlúcar de Barrameda

CASA BIGOTE★

A simple restaurant serving magnificently fresh fish and seafood from the Bay of Cádiz; the fishermen who supply it are paid in kind by eating here. It provides, as might be expected, excellent *manzanilla*, and also the fresh white 'Castillo de San Diego' from the local firm of Antonio Barbadillo.

San Roque

LOS REMOS★★★

Close to Gibraltar, this ranks among the best restaurants on the Costa del Sol. It specializes in fish and seafood, like the exotic giant crab from the Strait of Gibraltar with *urta* (see p. 39), and the cold display at the entrance is about as long as the local 18-hole golf course!

Seville

SAN MARCO★★

In palatial surroundings with beautiful flower arrangements, Ansano and Angelo Ramaciotti present a mainly Italian cuisine, with such dishes as spinach pasta with shellfish and escalopes of veal with Roquefort. There are home-made sweets, and you will be pleasantly surprised by the modesty of the bill.

Recipes

Riñones al Jerez/Kidneys with Sherry

Serves 6

METRIC/IMPERIAL

1 kg/2¼ lbs veal or lamb's kidneys

100 ml/4 fl oz olive oil

2 wine glasses (300 ml/10 fl oz) *fino* sherry

25 g/1 oz melted butter

2 teaspoons arrowroot

150 ml/5 fl oz meat stock

Salt and freshly ground white pepper

AMERICAN

2¼ lbs veal or lamb's kidneys

½ cup olive oil

1⅓ cups *fino* sherry

2 tablespoons melted butter

2 teaspoons arrowroot

⅔ cup meat stock

Salt and freshly ground white pepper

Soak the kidneys in cold water and a little vinegar for twenty minutes. Drain, remove fat and membranes, cut up and season with salt and pepper. Sauté them in hot oil for two or three minutes, then drain in a colander and discard the liquid. Take a fresh pan, add the strained kidneys and sherry and cook for two minutes.

Mix the butter, arrowroot and meat stock, then pour over the kidneys and cook together for five to ten minutes, stirring with a wooden spoon. Do not overcook, since they will get tougher rather than tenderer. Serve on a bed of boiled rice, spooning the kidneys on top.

Ajo Blanco/ Cold Garlic Soup with Grapes

Serves 6

METRIC/IMPERIAL

2 cloves garlic, chopped

225 g/8 oz pine kernels

100 g/4 oz fresh breadcrumbs

100 ml/4 fl oz olive oil

3 tablespoons wine vinegar

1½ litres/2½ pints water

Freshly ground salt

250 g/9 oz seedless white grapes, peeled

AMERICAN

2 cloves garlic, chopped

8 oz pine nuts

2 cups fresh breadcrumbs

½ cup olive oil

3 tablespoons wine vinegar

5 cups water

Freshly ground salt

1 cup seedless green grapes, peeled

METHOD WITH A FOOD PROCESSOR

Grind the garlic and pine kernels to a fine consistency in a food processor. Stop the motor, add the breadcrumbs and stir with a spatula. Now add the oil, vinegar, water and salt through the feed tube and process again. Pour the contents into a large bowl, add the grapes, then cover with plastic wrap and cool. This soup can be made the day before. If desired, it may be served with garlic-flavoured crôutons.

Gambas Fritas/Fried Prawns

Starter for 6

METRIC/IMPERIAL

2 tablespoons olive oil

1 kg/2¼ lbs boiled prawns in shell

4 cloves garlic, crushed

2 tablespoons chopped parsley

AMERICAN

2 tablespoons olive oil

2¼ lbs boiled shrimps in shell

4 cloves garlic, crushed

2 tablespoons chopped parsley

Heat the oil in a heavy pan, add the prawns and garlic, stirring with a wooden spoon and making them hot as quickly as possible. Garnish with parsley and serve at once. Provide finger bowls and accompany the prawns with fresh French bread.

METHOD BY HAND

Grind the garlic and pine kernels in a mortar, add the breadcrumbs and olive oil and stir as if making mayonnaise, trickling in the vinegar. Transfer to a large bowl and add the water, salt and grapes. Cool and serve as described in food processor method.

Levante

T HE SPANISH LEVANTE is not of course to be confused with the Levant of the eastern Mediterranean; it comprises the coastal strip stretching along the Mediterranean shore of Spain from the Cabo de Gata, just east of Almería, to the delta of the Ebro in the north. The long coastline takes in scores of holiday resorts and beaches, from Benicarló and Benicasim in the north to Denia, Calpe, Benidorm and Playas de San Juan south of Valencia, and the new marinas and developments around Cartagena in the province of Murcia.

What gives the area geographical unity is the fertile, semi-tropical plain extending back from the sea, sometimes as far as forty kilometres, to the mountains ringing the high interior plateau. It is a region of sweet-smelling orange and lemon groves, sugar cane, ricefields and palms; and not unnaturally its mild climate and rich soil attracted colonists from the ancient world. The Phoenicians, Greeks and Carthaginians were all here in strength; and as Rose Macaulay has so evocatively written: 'This is a haunted shore: ghosts crowd each bay, each little town, each castled rock, whispering in the lap of the waves and in the low rumour of the sea wind in the palms.'

The sacking of Sagunto (the Saguntum of the Romans, where the great theatre and ruined castle still survive just north of Valencia) by Hannibal in 219 BC precipitated the Second Punic War and the occupation of the Peninsula by the Romans. The area subsequently came under the sway of the Umayyad emirs and caliphs of Córdoba and after the collapse of the caliphate broke up into a number of independent Moorish principalities, of which the largest was Valencia. Valencia del Cid, as it is still sometimes called, enshrines the memory of the legendary hero, who, with his friend and enemy Alfonso VI of Castile, was one of the twin architects of the Christian Reconquest during the eleventh century.

After quarrelling with Alfonso, El Cid was banished from Castile and rode out from Burgos with a handful of followers to undertake the conquest of the Levante, culminating in the capture of Valencia. In the wake of a twenty-month siege, which reduced the beleaguered inhabitants to scouring the drains for olive stones and eating the flesh of mules and rats, the city fell to El Cid in June 1094 and remained his headquarters until his death in 1099, after which Alfonso ordered its evacuation in the face of a renewed Berber invasion from north Africa. When the region was finally reoccupied by the Christians it was not at the hand of the Castilians, but of another great soldier, James the Conqueror of Aragón-Catalonia, who re-took Valencia in 1238.

The influence of the Moriscos (Moors who were Christianized, at any rate in name) is still evident today, not least in the blue-tiled domes of the churches, rising above the white houses of the villages and towns, and in the low-arched aqueducts and cisterns for irrigating the fields. The manufacture of ceramics and tiles, of which the most typical are the *azulejos*,

RIGHT **Picturesque old houses in the mountain town of Morella in the Maestrazgo, inland from Castellón de la Plana.**

PREVIOUS PAGE **A farmyard in the hills near Castellón de la Plana.**

with their high glaze and designs in an intense blue on a white ground, was brought to a fine art by the Moriscos, and they are still made by traditional methods.

Valencia possesses the best ceramics museum in Spain, installed in the Baroque palace of the Marqués de dos Aguas ; one of its features is a traditional Valencian kitchen, with tiled walls and fireplace and a complete *batterie de cuisine*. The city, surrounded by its orange and lemon groves, is the queen of the Levante, and despite the devastations of the Napoleonic and Civil Wars, parts of the old walls with their gates and turrets, and narrow streets flanked by balconied houses still remain. The liveliest time for a visit is during the *Fallas* in mid-March, when huge figures are built in the streets and set alight on the last night of the fiesta.

On the coast north of Valencia, near the provincial capital of Castellón de la Plana, the old walled town of Peñíscola, surmounted by a castle of the Knights Templars, rises steeply out of the sea and, like Mont St Michel, is connected to the mainland only by a narrow causeway. It is of interest as being the final refuge of the last of the Antipopes, that indestructible old warrior Pedro de Luna, who held out there until his death in the face of repeated assaults by his Roman adversaries.

Another place off the beaten track but well worth a visit is the medieval town of Morella in the mountainous hinterland of Castellón de la Plana. Apart from its towering castle, approached by a long spiralling ramp and with artillery pieces from the Napoleonic and Carlist Wars still in position, there is a fine thirteenth-century church, and a kilometre or so from the town the mountain road to Alcañiz passes beneath one of the arches of a lofty Moorish aqueduct. Further afield, at Morella la Vella, the rock shelters are decorated with paleolithic and neolithic paintings of hunting and war.

The large cities of Murcia and Alicante lie to the south of Valencia, and both are places of wide modern avenues lined with palm trees, though Murcia, on the fringe of the desolate country used for shooting 'spaghetti westerns', has preserved its many churches with blue-tiled cupolas and some of its tortuous streets and old houses. Alicante is one of the mildest places in Spain during winter, and its serried cafés, which face the wide harbour across a marble-paved promenade lined with palms, are among the pleasantest in the country to relax with a glass of sherry or montilla and the accompanying *tapas*.

A Napoleonic gun guarding the hill fortress of Morella.

The Wines

The four provinces of the Levante, Castellón de la Plana, Valencia, Alicante and Murcia, produce huge amounts of wine, most of it for everyday drinking, and in terms of production rate second only to La Mancha and the districts of central Spain. There are five demarcated regions: Valencia, bordering the coast; Utiel-Requena, on the fringe of the central plateau; Alicante, extending back from the coast; and Yecla and Jumilla, in the hills of Murcia to the west of Alicante.

The wines from Castellón, especially those from Benicarló, are of historical interest, since until the outbreak of the phylloxera epidemic in the late nineteenth century they were very much in demand for blending. English tastes at the time, influenced by the popularity of port, were very much for strong, full-bodied red wine. In deference to this, the well-known London shipper Nathaniel Johnson wrote to his partners in London of the 1803 Bordeaux vintage:

> If the wines have the body and colour which others represent more favourably than you do, I think that they ought to be made up very lightly this year – the first and even good second growths with not more than three to four gallons of Spanish wine and about three gallons of Hermitage and the other wines not to have more than five gallons of Spanish wine.

He also suggests making a French 'port' by 'getting a Tun or two of Roussillon red wine and fretting it with a can of Benicarlo'; but experiments such as these came to an abrupt end – and perhaps as well – when phylloxera broke out in Castellón. Unfortunately the vineyards were replanted not with grafted vines but with American hybrids, producing coarse and inferior wines. Large areas have subsequently been abandoned, and the district now produces little except wines for local consumption.

Valencia

The alluvial soils and semi-tropical climate of the coastal areas of the province are more suited to crops such as oranges, lemons, sugar cane and rice than vines, and the three demarcated sub-regions lie back in the hills inland. The best of the wines are the whites from Alto Turia in the high and cooler north-west of the province; fresh, fruity, with a greenish cast and containing $11.5-13°$ of alcohol, they are made from the Merseguera grape. The largest of the sub-regions, Valentino, also to the north-west of the city of Valencia, incorporates the former *Denominación de Origen* of Cheste. Its best wines are again the whites, heavier and more full-bodied, made with the Merseguera and Pedro Ximénez. It also produces some excellent sweet Moscatel, and red wines from the Garnacha tinta and Tintorera. Clariano in the far south makes red wines from the Monastrel in full-bodied, spicy Mediterranean style.

Valencia is in fact best known as a large-scale exporter of inexpensive beverage wines, and some half of all foreign shipments of Spanish wine go through its port or Grao. It is the headquarters of a number of very large shippers, which not only export demarcated wines from the Levante, but also buy and blend wines from other parts of Spain.

JUAN ANTONIO MOMPÓ, S.A.
Founded in the middle of the nineteenth century, the firm is still in family hands and exports young wines in bulk, principally to Japan and Africa. *See also* VINIVAL and UTIEL-REQUENA.

SCHENK, S.A., BODEGAS
The Swiss firm of Schenk has large interests in Spain and buys wine not only from the Levante, but from other regions such as La Mancha; it is then bottled in its Valencia plant and shipped from its port. There is strict quality control and the firm has done a great deal to improve the quality of local wines, e.g. by supervising their vinification and introducing cultured yeasts

from its Swiss laboratories. Apart from bulk exports, it also bottles some superior wines, such as the red 'Monteros' made with one hundred per cent Monastrel, a light and fruity rosé from Utiel-Requena, and a luscious Moscatel.

VICENTE GANDÍA PLÁ, S.A.

Starting as a family concern in the late nineteenth century, the firm has expanded and is now a sizeable exporter with up-to-date vinification and bottling plants. It sells the pleasant and modestly priced red, white and rosé 'Castillo de Liria' wines, of which the best is the red, cherry-coloured, fragrant and fruity, made from Bobal and Garnacha grapes.

The huge modern winery of Vinival in Valencia.

VINIVAL (EXPORTADORA VINÍCOLA VALENCIANA, S.A.)

This very large enterprise was founded in 1969 by the old-established firms of Garrigos, Mompó, Teschendorff and Steiner to handle the export of their wines. The huge plant with its brick-built domes near the port has a storage capacity of thirty million litres and is equipped with modern bottling lines and refrigeration and filtration machinery. Annual exports worldwide are around one hundred million litres. Its very drinkable young red, white and rosé wines are sold as 'Torres de Serrano'.

Utiel-Requena

The old towns of Utiel and Requena, which have given their names to the region, lie on the

main road from Valencia to Madrid in the hills bordering the province of Cuenca, where there are much greater extremes of climate than in the coastal strip. Their wines, which were favourites of Vicente Blasco Ibáñez, author of *The Four Horsemen of the Apocalypse*, are made with ninety per cent of the black Bobal grape (with small amounts of the Cencibel and Garnacha) in a fashion employed elsewhere only in other parts of the Levante.

The grapes are destalked, lightly crushed and left in a vat for a few hours to extract colour from the skins. Half of the must is then drawn off and pumped into a second vat, where fermentation continues *en virgen* as in making a white wine. The rosés made in this way are among the best from Spain, pale in colour and exceptionally light, fruity and delicate.

Once the *vino de lágrima* for the rosé has been drawn off, the first vat is topped up with another load of grapes and the wine is fermented out. The result is a *vino de doble pasta*, thick, almost black in colour with an intense flavour of blackberries and containing up to 18° (per cent by volume) of alcohol. It is sold not for drinking but for blending with the thinner wines from northern Spain.

Not all of the wine is made in this way, and Utiel-Requena also produces some pleasant reds by the normal method after destalking of the grapes.

Most of the wine is made in cooperatives, some of which are very large.

COOPERATIVA AGRÍCOLA Y CAJA RURAL DE UTIEL

This huge cooperative was formed in 1927 with 128 *socios* (or members), but now numbers some two thousand and operates from a modern bodega with a capacity of thirty-three million litres; it also possesses oak casks for maturing some of the wine. The younger wines, of which the best is the remarkably fresh rosé, are labelled 'Sierra Negrete'; there is also a round and full-bodied red, five-year-old 'Sierra Rampina'.

SOCIEDAD COOPERATIVA REQUENENSE (COVINENSE)

Founded in 1935, this very large cooperative in Requena was modernized in 1976, when a bottling line and modern equipment for filtering, refrigerating and pasteurizing the wine was added. It makes mainly red wines from Bobal, Garnacha and Tempranillo grapes, labelled as 'Monumento' or 'Fortaleza', and a small amount of 'Palacio del Cid', matured in oak and currently of the 1975 vintage.

CASA DE CALDERÓN

This small and picturesque bodega near Requena belonging to the Mompó family (see also Valencia) is a complete contrast to the vast cooperatives. Set among pine trees, with a private chapel, the old winery makes superior red, white and rosé wines, labelled as 'Casa de Calderón' or 'Cap del Paso', by traditional methods, and also a port-like dessert wine.

Alicante

The vineyards of Alicante are in the hills inland from the city, the best of them around Villena and Monóvar. The predominant red wines are made with some ninety per cent Monastrel, and the whites with eighty-five per cent Verdil, together with smaller amounts of Fartó, Merseguera, Pedro Ximénez and Airén. The traditional way of vinifying them is to make a stout *vino de doble pasta* as in Utiel-Requena, with a light rosé as a by-product. In general, the typical red wines are dark in colour and high in extract and alcohol.

H.L. GARCÍA POVEDA, S.A.

These are the Alicante wines which you are most likely to encounter. They are made in Villena, on the road from Alicante to Albacete, the younger ones being labelled as 'Terreta' or 'Costa Blanca'. Also available are 1964, 1970 and 1975 red *reservas* matured in oak; the velvety and full-bodied 1964 has been much praised, but contains a hefty 15° of alcohol. The bodega also makes a range of vermouths, again characterful and full-bodied.

PRIMITIVO QUILES, N.C.R.

The Quiles family has been making wine in the area since 1780, and the bodega is known for its young 'Rosado Virgen' rosé and white 'Blanco Caña', the three-year-old red 'Cono 4' and 'Raspay', and a *solera*-made dessert 'Fondillo' made from Moscatel grapes.

SALVADOR POVEDA, S.A.

This much respected family bodega in Monóvar regularly gains prizes for its wines. They include a red and rosé 'Viña Vermeta' of 13° strength, a red 'Doble Capa' with a formidable 16° of alcohol and a white 'Cantaluz'; but the outstanding wine is the dessert 'Fondillon', orange-coloured, fragrant, a little sweet and the favourite after-dinner drink of the present King of Spain.

Yecla

Continuing into the hills west of Villena, one enters the demarcated region of Yecla. It is a region of strong, full-bodied red wines, some ninety per cent made from Monastrel grapes, often grown ungrafted in the chalky soils, since this was one of the few regions of Spain to be little affected by phylloxera. The wines may approach a block-busting 18°, and Luis Antonio de Vega relates an amusing story about their inky black colour in his *Guía vinícola de España*.

It seems that he sat down in a tavern in these parts, only to observe that the glasses looked dirty. He turned in some surprise to his neighbours at the next table and asked if the glasses were not washed. 'Yes, they wash them,' he was informed, 'but the wine from Yecla clings like a drowning man.'

By far the largest producer in the region is the huge COOPERATIVA LA PURÍSIMA, with its capacity of some fifty-five million litres, in the upland town of Yecla, otherwise given over to the manufacture of furniture. It makes a young rosé 'Vino Calp' and red 'Gran Vino Yecla', and a full-bodied 'Gran Vino Calp Reserve', all containing about 13° of alcohol. It has also been experimenting with lighter wines for export, made from fruit picked earlier. Neither the Spaniard of today nor his export customer shares the tastes of a generation ago. The strength and concentration that was seen as a virtue, especially in wine being exported for blending, is instead a disadvantage in modern eyes. There is no inherent reason why, with the benefit of modern technology, wine from the chalk hills of Yecla should not exhibit the finesse of wines from other famous chalky areas in Spain and elsewhere.

Jumilla

The larger region of Jumilla lies directly to the west and south of Yecla and produces similar dark red wines high in alcohol from the Monastrel grape, which is grown ungrafted, since the region was not affected by phylloxera. Apart from the enormous cooperative, there are a number of private firms making very drinkable wines, mainly red.

COOPERATIVA DE SAN ISIDRO

This modern and well-run cooperative in the town of Jumilla rivals that of La Purísima in Yecla in size (the two are among the largest in Spain). Numbering some 2,500 *socios*, it vinifies the wine in twenty towering concrete fermentation vats, each of half a million litres capacity with provision for cooling; and the equipment for refrigeration, filtering and bottling the wine is of the most up-to-date. It also possesses large numbers of oak casks for maturing the better wines. Mostly sturdy reds, they are marketed as 'Rumor', 'Sabatacha', 'Sambra' and the 'Solera' *reserva*, matured for ten years in oak.

OPPOSITE **Modern fermentation vats containing half a million litres at the Cooperativa de San Isidro in Jumilla.**

BODEGAS ASENSIO CARCELÉN

Carcelén possesses its own vineyards and exports its well-made wines to Germany, Switzerland and the United States, both bottled and in bulk. It is an interesting bodega to visit, with a museum displaying old wine-making equipment and presses dating from the fourteenth, fifteenth and sixteenth centuries. The wines, lighter than most from the region and running to 12.5-13° of alcohol, include the red 'Bullanguero', 'Acorde' and 'Astilla' made from the Monastrel, and the white 'Bullanguero' and 'Astilla', for which a blend of Monastrel and Airén is used.

BODEGAS BLEDA, N.C.R.

This family firm founded in 1917 makes some of the best traditional full-bodied Jumilla and was the first firm in the region to bottle its wines. Its labels include 'Castillo de Jumilla' and 'Oro de Ley', both of about 15° strength. Recent bottlings of 'Castillo de Jumilla' have been well-made and are very good value.

BODEGAS GARCÍA CARRIÓN, S.A.

A family firm founded in 1890 and one of the main exporters of Jumilla wines. It is best-known for its young red, white and rosé 'San Simón' and for the red 'Castillo San Simón' *reservas*, particularly good in 1970, 1976 and 1979.

BODEGAS SEÑORÍO DEL CONDESTABLE

The red 'Condestable' from this branch of Savín S.A., a wine company with bodegas all over Spain, is a very pleasant wine for those who like them fruity and full-bodied. Other labels are the rather lighter red 'Vilamar' and the fresh white 'Emparrado'.

The Cuisine

The Levante in general and Valencia in particular are best known for a great variety of rice dishes, such as *arroz abanda* (rice served with fish and shellfish), *arroz con pescado* and *arroz a la marinera* (both made with rice and fish), as well as the famous *paella*.

The original *paella* contained only eels, snails and shelled green peas in addition to rice and saffron. These eels came from the large salt-water lagoon of the Albufera, south-east of Valencia – from which Marshal Suchet took his title of Duke of Albufera after capturing the city for Napoleon in 1812 – and the rice was provided from the swampy fields on its borders.

Cooking a *paella* out of doors by the traditional method, over a wood fire.

It was traditionally cooked in a large *cazuela*, a round dish made of brown earthenware, glazed on the inside but not underneath, which was set on a wood fire.

Cazuelas in all sizes and depths, from the small, shallow dishes used for cooking individual portions of fried prawns or *huevos a la flamenca* to pots capacious enough to make a stew for a family of twelve, may be bought in shops and markets all over Spain. Inexpensive as they are, it is well worth bringing home a set if you are travelling by car and weight is no problem. Apart from their decorative appearance and heat-retaining properties, they are excellent cooking vessels, since they preserve the flavour of the ingredients better than pots and pans made of metal, and may be heated directly over a gas ring if you are careful. It is, however, easier to cook a *paella* in the two-handled metal *paellera* now generally used for the purpose. It, too, is most decorative and may

be brought to the table, unlike an ordinary frying pan.

Paella is now more or less the national dish, as typical of Spain as roast beef is of England. The ingredients that may be used in it are legion, and Dionisio Pérez writes in his *Guía del buen comer español* that 'failing the classical ingredients, each locality in the Kingdom of Valencia and each village in the neighbouring provinces has put into the *paella* every form of meat, fish, shellfish and fresh vegetable; and the marvellous rice goes well with all of them'. Cut-up pieces of chicken, small sausages and small pieces of cooked meat are all useful ingredients, but perhaps the most satisfactory version is *paella marinera*, made entirely with shellfish (apart, of course, from the usual garnish of olives and strips of red pepper). This is also cooked well along the Basque coast with the superb fish from the Atlantic. But be on your guard: the most expensive restaurants with the best shellfish can make deplorable *paellas*, and unless the rice is properly cooked with exactly the right amount of water (two cupfuls to each cupful of dry rice), the dish is a disaster. The grains, though tender, must remain individual when brought to the table; and for this purpose it is essential to start with the round-grained Spanish or Italian rice – the fluffy white Indian or American varieties make excellent curry, but not *paella*.

A great variety of Mediterranean fish is caught off the coast of the Levante: to see it in all its variety, from heaped piles of prawns, red mullet, sardines and langoustines to squid, octopus or exotics such as *rascasio* – the ugly *rascasse* so essential to *bouillabaisse* – tour the stalls of a big fish market in one of the larger ports like Castellón de la Plana. One variety of shellfish is so unusual as to deserve special mention. You will occasionally see on a menu '*sopa de dátiles*'; this does not, as you might think, mean 'date soup', but refers to a particularly delicious chowder made with a small and rare dark brown mussel (*dátil de mar*) fished off the coast near Peñíscola and Benicarló.

The *huertas* or 'gardens' of Valencia are proverbial for their fertility, and justifiably so, since there are two crops of oranges and vegetables a year. Further south, around Murcia, you will see square miles of polythene-sheeted enclosures for forcing the crops. These methods have changed the life-style of the area; many of the farmers are now plutocrats. The export of spring vegetables is one of the region's most important industries – as becomes only too obvious when one is caught along the main coast road in a convoy of trucks carrying beans, peas or greens to the markets of France.

Unlike those from Seville, the oranges are of the sweet variety and range in size from large navels to tangerines and the seedless *celestinas*, exported in large quantity to Japan for making crystallized fruit. In springtime one can drive for mile upon mile through the dark green citrus groves along roads heavy with the scent of blossom; but oranges and lemons are far from being the only fruit. Figs, both green and black, are so prolific that they are sometimes fed to the pigs; and among the exotics are dates, pomegranates, passionfruit and loquats. The coastal area between Valencia and Alicante is famous for its moscatel grapes; and until the Civil War there was a thriving British community in the small port of Denia, occupied in the export of raisins. Almonds are another favourite crop and form the basis for many of the sweetmeats made in the Levante, as in Andalucía, since the time of the Moors.

The most famous of these is *turrón*, a nougat formerly packed in small wooden boxes, like those used for liqueur chocolates, and eaten at Christmas time. It is now hermetically sealed in plastic and exported all over the world. There is a story that *turrón* takes its name from a Don José Terrón of Alicante, who won a prize in a competition organized by King Ferdinand VII after his return from exile in France during the Peninsular War, with a confection of honey and chopped almonds. However, it seems entirely likely that Señor Terrón was elaborating on an earlier form of Moorish sweetmeat, since there is an old rhyme about *giraboix*, as it is called in Jijona, where most of it is made:

*Si la reina saber
lo que es giraboix
a Xixona vendría
a llepar el boix.*

If the queen knew
Turrón and its taste,
She'd go to Jijona
To eat it in haste.

Jijona, a small mountain town north of Alicante, is completely given over to the confecting of *turrón*; there are some forty small manufactories scattered along its hilly streets and the whole place is redolent with the comforting aroma of toasted almonds and honey. There are two main types. The *turrón de Alicante*, made from almonds, toasted and coarsely chopped, sugar, honey and whites of egg, is brittle and must be broken into lumps. The *turrón de Jijona*, equally delicious and made from ground almonds, ground pine kernels, sugar and egg yolks, is a soft tablet and kinder to the teeth.

There are some pleasant, though mild, local

OPPOSITE An orange grove in the Levante.

BELOW An open market selling an assortment of nuts and spices, dried herbs and vegetables.

cheeses. *Tronchón*, also known as *queso de Aragón*, is mentioned in *Don Quixote*: semi-hard, it is made from ewe's milk mixed with a little goat's milk. *Queso fresco valenciano*, or *puzol*, is a fresh goat's milk cheese for immediate consumption.

Restaurants

Alcoy

VENTA DEL PILAR*

The Venta serves pleasant regional food in the charming surroundings of an old house decorated in regional style. Typical of its repertoire are *pericana* (dried cod, shredded and fried with garlic), *olleta* (white beans, vegetables, bacon and blood sausage with onion), a variety of fresh fish, and boned leg of lamb and pork with apple sauce.

Alicante

DELFIN**

The best restaurant in Alicante, Delfin specializes in the rice dishes so typical of the Levante. Of other dishes, the best is the *lubina con costra* (baked bass), but try the *suprême* of hake with seafood sauce, grilled turbot with hollandaise sauce, pig's trotters with snails, oxtail with cuttle fish, and stewed pigeons. Sweets include ice cream with *turrón de Jijona* (nougat) and a delicious lemon tart.

Benidorm

EL CISNE

Benidorm is better-known for its beaches, fish and chips and *Deutsche Küche* than its cuisine, regional or otherwise; but El Cisne, in its quiet garden, is to be recommended for its *paella*, *arroz abanda* and *arroz marinera* (different ways of cooking rice with fish), and also serves good steaks, bringing the meat from Galicia. Good cellar with vintage Spanish wines.

Calpe

EL GIRASOL★★★
Heinz Orth travelled widely after leaving his native Germany, settling finally in the charming village of Moraira, near Calpe and the great crag of the Peñon de Ifach, and establishing one of the best restaurants in Spain. Specialities include *savarin* of cardoons and scallops with champagne, salmon in pastry with smoked mackerel mousse, cocotte of monkfish with prawns, ribs of lamb house-style, and duck with cassis. Good sweets and cheeses, and a short list of Rioja and Catalan wines.

Cullera

LES MOUETTES★★
Jean and Jaqueline Lagarce offer a sophisticated French cuisine at this restaurant on the coast 40 km south of Valencia, with dishes such as endive salad with salmon, quiche Lorraine, salmon quiche, sole with a cream and rice sauce, entrecôte with plums or fillet steak *au poivre*, and fruit sorbets in season. The select wine list includes Château Lafite, Romanée-Conti and Château d'Yquem, as well as Vega Sicilia and vintage Riojas.

L'Alcudia

GALBIS★★
At his restaurant near Alcira Juan Carlos Galbis has made a name for himself as the initiator of a *nueva cocina valenciana*, lightening the traditional dishes and doing away with excessive spices and fats. Among his dishes are *pastel de anguilas en all i pebre* (elvers in pastry), *suc de llobarro* (fried kid with garlic shoots) and orange flan with cream. Regional wines and vintage Rioja.

Murcia

RINCÓN DE PEPE★★★
In distant Murcia, Raimundo González Frutos has created one of the great Spanish restaurants, drawing on the fish from the nearby Mediterranean and fresh vegetables from his farm, grown without chemical fertilizers. He offers three regional menus, long or short and priced accordingly, including such specialities as fish baked in sea salt, *menestra* (mixed vegetable dish), stuffed artichokes and peppers Murcian-style. To finish with there are sorbets made from prickly pear and other fruits in season.

HISPANO★★
Another good restaurant in Murcia serving regional dishes such as *arroz en caldero* (rice dish), *paella murciana*, langoustine and leek pie, stewed pigeon and lamb chops with *ajo cabañil* (garlic).

Valencia

ELADIO★★
Eladio, which takes its name from its proprietor and *maître de cuisine*, Eladio Rodriguez Blanco, has established a firm reputation for its turbot, hake, monkfish and sea bass. Try too the *suprême* of turbot roes, the seafood vol-au-vents and the entrecôte Rasputin flambéed in vodka.

LAS GRAELLES★
This is the place to go for regional food and rice dishes such as *paella*, *arroz amb fessols naps*, *arroz abanda* and *rosexat*. Other good dishes are *lubina all-i-pebre* (sea bass in piquant sauce), *brandade* of *bacalao* (dried salted cod), boned chops and roast leg of lamb. For dessert there are lemon sorbet, orange and egg tarts, fresh oranges and melon soufflé.

Recipes

Paella

Serves 6 to 8

METRIC/IMPERIAL	AMERICAN
Olive oil for frying	Olive oil for frying
$\frac{1}{2}$ kg/1 lb 2 oz boned chicken breasts, flattened and cut into long strips	1 lb 2 oz boned chicken breasts, flattened and cut into long strips
250 g/9 oz chipolata sausages	9 oz chipolata sausages (or other spicy sausage)
$\frac{1}{2}$ kg/1 lb 2 oz squid, cleaned, body cut into rings	1 lb 2 oz squid, cleaned, body cut into rings
6 teacups rice	$3\frac{3}{4}$ cups rice
Salt and freshly ground pepper	Salt and freshly ground pepper
Few strands saffron	Few strands saffron
2 cloves garlic, finely chopped	2 cloves garlic, finely chopped
16 large boiled prawns in shell (if freshly boiled, reserve liquid)	16 large boiled shrimps in shell (if freshly boiled, reserve liquid)
16 mussels, scrubbed, washed and boiled to open (reserve liquid)	16 mussels, scrubbed, washed and boiled to open (reserve liquid)
100 g/4 oz freshly boiled peas (reserve liquid)	1 cup freshly boiled green peas (reserve liquid)
2 or 3 canned red peppers drained and cut in strips	2 or 3 canned pimientos drained and cut in strips
2 lemons, cut in wedges for garnishing	2 lemons, cut in wedges for garnishing
250 g/9 oz stuffed olives, drained, for garnishing	$1\frac{3}{4}$ cups stuffed olives, drained, for garnishing

Cover the bottom of a *paellera* or large frying pan with a thin layer of oil; when hot, sauté the chicken strips for a few minutes until brown, then take out and reserve on a plate. Do the same with the chipolatas and reserve. Add a little more oil if necessary and sauté the squid for two or three minutes only. Reserve on a plate. Again adding a little more oil if required, fry the rice, stirring all the time with a wooden spoon, until the grains are pale brown and separate, and season with salt and pepper. Pound the saffron strands and garlic in a mortar, dilute with a teaspoonful of hot water and add to the rice. Now add 12 teacups (Metric/Imperial) or $7\frac{1}{2}$ cups (American) of stock from boiling the prawns, mussels and peas, making up the amount with chicken stock from a cube (the amount of liquid must be twice the volume of rice, and you should allow approximately 50 to 75 g/2 to 3 oz of rice per person). Stir together well and bring to the boil, making sure that the contents are cooked right through.

Now add the chicken, chipolata sausages and squid, stirring them well into the rice. Leave to simmer very slowly for eighteen to twenty minutes, no longer stirring but shaking the pan at intervals. Meanwhile, start garnishing the dish, first arranging the prawns and mussels, then putting the peas and red peppers between them, finally scattering with the stuffed olives and lemon wedges. Turn off heat, cover with a clean cloth and rest for ten minutes. Serve from the *paellera* in which it has been cooked.

The variation of ingredients is enormous: lobster, clams, firm white fish, lean pork and other vegetables may all be used.

Naranjas Caramelizadas/Caramelized Oranges

Serves 6

METRIC/IMPERIAL	AMERICAN
8 medium-sized oranges	8 medium-sized oranges
300 ml/10 fl oz water	$1\frac{1}{3}$ cups water
6 tablespoons caster sugar	6 tablespoons fine white sugar
$\frac{1}{2}$ vanilla pod	$\frac{1}{2}$ vanilla pod

Remove the skin of the oranges with a potato peeler, cut into thin strips and put into a saucepan with the water, sugar and vanilla pod. Bring to the boil, then simmer slowly for about one hour, watching carefully until the peel is caramelized. In the meantime, cut the oranges into segments with a sharp kitchen knife, removing the white pith and collecting any juice in a bowl underneath. Arrange the segments in a serving dish, pour the juice over them, cover with the caramelized peel and leave to cool before serving.

New Castile and Madrid

*B*ETWEEN THEM THE TWO CASTILES occupy the great central table-land of Spain. Old Castile, so-called because it was the first part of the area to be reconquered from the Moors, lies north of Madrid. South of the capital, at an average height of three thousand feet, New Castile extends as far as the Sierra Morena and Andalucía. The most southerly part is known as La Mancha. Its empty, rolling plains, bitterly cold in winter and unsheltered from a pitiless sun in summer, are relieved only by the occasional whitewashed village or clustered windmills. This is Don Quixote country, and Cervantes mirrors the tough fibre and frugal character of its inhabitants when he writes of his hero:

> In a place of La Mancha, whose name I do not remember, there lived not long ago one of those gentlemen who boasts a wooden lance and an old buckler, a scraggy horse and a greyhound for coursing. An *olla* stew containing more cow's meat than mutton, scratch fare most nights, grief and bickering on Saturdays, lentils on Fridays and perhaps a pigeon on Sundays consumed three-quarters of his substance . . .

PREVIOUS PAGE **The castle of Alarcón, built by the Moors and now a Parador.**
BELOW **Windmills in La Mancha, Don Quixote country.**
OPPOSITE **A stretch of the dry and stony landscape of New Castile.**

The historical capital of New Castile – and of Spain until 1561 – was Toledo. After its recapture from the Moors in 1085 it was the home of a school of translators of transcendent importance in transmitting the learning of the ancient Greeks and the Arabs to western Europe. With its great five-aisled Gothic cathedral, it remains the see of the Primate of Spain. Toledo later became the adopted home of El Greco, and his house, now a museum containing some of his paintings, still stands. Seeing the city from a distance, silhouetted on its crag against a thundery sky, with the lightning striking down towards the jagged outline of its towers and spires, one might even today be looking at one of his canvases.

Toledo has long since yielded pride of place to Madrid; but this was a place of little importance when recaptured from the Moors in 1083, serving only for occasional meetings of the Cortes (parliament). It was not until 1561 that Philip II, whose austere character matched the bleak expanses of his native Castile, made it the capital of Spain. Parts of Old Madrid survive, notably the colonnaded Plaza Mayor and surrounding streets, but during the Peninsular War, Joseph Bonaparte demolished much of the centre and the larger part of the city is comparatively modern. The world-famous Prado Museum was completed only after the end of the Peninsular War, and the principal thoroughfare, the Avenida José

Toledo, the old capital of Spain, standing high above the Tagus.

Antonio or Gran Vía, with the monumental buildings that flank it, was constructed during the early years of the present century. More recently, Madrid has attracted new inhabitants like a magnet, and wide new boulevards and new residential areas with their shops and restaurants have multiplied in the fashionable district towards the airport.

One or two places within easy reach of Madrid are well worth a visit. Some fifty kilometres away in the hills to the north stands the massive El Escorial, half palace, half monastery, where from his simple room looking on to the altar of the church, Philip II conducted the affairs of half the world and received news of the defeat of the Armada. This is a pleasant excursion in late spring or summer when the restaurants set out inviting tables in the open air.

About the same distance to the south in Aranjuez is the altogether less sombre summer palace of the Kings of Spain. Elegant, beautifully furnished, with a wealth of fine paintings, it is set amongst gardens and fountains. Here, on a hot summer's day, one may repair to one of the restaurants overlooking the Manzanares River and enjoy the best fresh asparagus and strawberries in the country.

The Cortes, Spain's Parliament building, in the centre of Madrid.

The magnificent summer palace of the Kings of Spain in Aranjuez, south of Madrid.

The Wines

New Castile, with vineyards stretching to the horizon, is much the biggest producer of wine in Spain. In hard figures there are some half million hectares of land under vines, mostly farmed by small proprietors who take their grapes to be vinified in one or other of its hundreds of cooperative wineries. The bulk of its wine is made for everyday consumption, but is by no means to be despised. As Richard Ford once said of it: 'The thirsty traveller, after a long day's ride under a burning sun, when seated quietly down to a smoking peppery dish, is enchanted with the cool draught of these *vins du pays* . . . and wonders that "the trade" should have overlooked such delicious wine.' The trouble, of course, was that it was not made to keep and, even if not tapped and watered by the muleteers, arrived flat and stale at its destination. A hundred and fifty years later, 'the trade' *is* now shipping pleasant Mancha wines made with the benefits of modern technology.

There are four large demarcated regions: Almansa, Mancha, Méntrida and Valdepeñas; the Tierra de Madrid, just south of the capital, also makes some worthwhile wine.

Valdepeñas

Valdepeñas, bordering Andalucía and the most southerly of the regions, has been famous for centuries for its red *aloques*, made with a blend of red and white grapes. During the sixteenth century the Emperor Charles V had them sent across Europe on muleback to inspirit his soldiers in the Low Countries. Light and fresh in taste, they are today the staple house wines of the bistros and bodegas of Madrid. Writing in his *Handbook for Travellers to Spain* in 1845, Richard Ford had this to say of them:

Hence to Valdepeñas, a straggling place of 10,000 souls, and a decent inn. The red blood of the grape issues from this valley of stones.

This delicious wine is the produce of the Burgundy vine, transplanted into Spain. The liquor is kept in huge *tinajas* or jars; when removed it is put into pig skins, *cueros*, such as Don Quixote attacked. These are pitched inside; hence the peculiar *Borracha*, or resiny flavour, which is agreeable to Spaniards and to no-one else . . .

Valdepeñas wine, to be really enjoyed, must be drunk on the spot; the true vinologist should go down into one of the *cuevas* or cellars, and have a goblet of the ruby fluid drawn from the big-bellied *Tinaja* . . .

What Ford wrote remains largely true of the old traditional bodegas – except, of course, that the wine is no longer kept in the pig-skin *cueros*, although its baby brother, the leather drinking bottle or *bota*, is still popular in country districts. You will see them hanging in rows in souvenir shops, and in case you are tempted to buy one, Ford's advice is very much to the point:

The way to use it is thus – grasp the neck with the left hand and bring the rim of the cup to the mouth, then gradually raise the bag with the other hand till the wine, in obediance with hydrostatic laws, rises to its level, and keeps always full in the cup without trouble to the mouth. The gravity with which this is done, the long, slow, sustained, Sancho-like devotion of the thirsty Spaniards when offered a drink out of another man's *bota*, is very edifying . . . No drop of the divine contents is wasted, except by some newly-arrived bungler, who, by lifting up the bottom first, inundates his chin . . .

The Burgundy vine referred to by Ford is probably the red Cencibel (or Tempranillo of the Rioja), sometimes thought to be descended from the Pinot Noir brought to Spain by Cluniac monks and early French merchants. It is still the preferred variety in Valdepeñas, but much larger amounts of the white Airén, a thick-skinned grape highly resistant to the summer heat of La Mancha, are grown.

Although the best and most typical of the Valdepeñas wines are light reds, they are usually made from a blend of Airén with not less than twenty per cent of Cencibel.

The vines are grown in a soil compounded of gravel, chalk and clay, and it was this same clay, dug at Villarrobledo, the scene of Don Quixote's first adventure, that was used for making the huge, pear-shaped *tinajas* in which the wine is still fermented in the older bodegas. In larger wineries they have been replaced by concrete vats (coated with vitrified epoxy resin in the most modern ones) or by temperature-controlled stainless steel tanks.

The wine has traditionally been sold as a fresh young two-year-old from the *tinaja* in which it is made, but is now increasingly being bottled on the spot, and some of the better, containing a large proportion of the red Cencibel, is aged in oak casks. This is a new departure and not typical of the region – as some writers who habitually associate wine-

Tinajas, traditionally used for fermenting wine in Valdepeñas and La Mancha.

making with casks would have one think. To quote again from the informative Richard Ford :

> ...next to glass bottles, wooden barrels are here wanting... The native simply takes the *raw* materials which nature lavishes gratis, but leaves to others to *labour* them into manufactures. He imports bottles from England, while from the scarcity of barrels vast quantities of *old* wine are thrown away in good years of vintage, in order not to waste the *new* wine, which is placed in the then emptied casks. From the want of fuel in these treeless plains, the prunings of the vines often become a more valuable produce than their grapes...

Although Valdepeñas no longer boasts an inn where one may either dine or breakfast (stay at the comfortable Motel Meliá El Hidalgo, seven kilometres to the north), it is worth a visit as it contains more bodegas than any other town of its size in Spain (in the past almost every house ran to an underground cellar). The old bodegas with their serried *tinajas* are most picturesque : facing the narrow streets are high, blank walls, with great double doors opening on to a wide courtyard and at the rear a lofty building, its red-tiled roof supported by shrunken timbers, which contains the fermentation vessels.

BODEGA LOS LLANOS

Founded in 1875 as Bodegas Cervantes, the first of the bodegas in Valdepeñas to mature its wines in oak, the firm was taken over in 1972. Its present owners, Cosecheros Abastecedores were the first to bottle their wines, and have constructed large new premises outside Valdepeñas equipped with stainless steel tanks and ten thousand American oak *barricas* for maturing them.

The fresh and fruity two-year-old red, white and rosé are sold as 'Don Opas'. Los Llanos also makes red *reservas* and *gran reservas* aged in oak and labelled 'Señorío de Los Llanos'. The 1978 *reserva* is a bright ruby colour, light, clean and fresh, but somewhat short in finish. The 1975 *gran reserva* is a darker wine with more body and a raisiny flavour and longer oaky finish. At a tasting in London in 1986 the '75 had become velvety in texture and showed the lingering sweetness of a fine wine in full maturity – certainly of a standard that surprised those who had never tasted well-selected Valdepeñas given the opportunity to age. The wines are exported to the United Kingdom, United States, Germany, Belgium and other countries.

BODEGAS MORENITO
This sizeable family firm, which has recently changed hands, was founded in 1896 and is one of the best-known abroad, since it exports to some thirty-five different countries. It bottles its wines and ages the best of them in oak. Its labels include 'Morenito', 'Fino Tres Pistolas', 'Fino Morenito' and 'Copa de Oro'.

LUIS MEGÍA, S.A.
This largest of the wine concerns in Valdepeñas was founded in 1947 and now belongs to a subsidiary of the Banco Español de Crédito. Here there are no *tinajas* and the installations are the last word in modernity. The grapes are vinified in continuous fermentation tanks of French design and the must is then pumped into huge open-air concrete *depósitos* of $1\frac{1}{2}$ million litres capacity, capped with nitrogen gas and linked to a heat exchanger.

The two-year-old wines are labelled 'Luis Megía', and the firm also makes vintage wines sold as 'Luis Megía' or 'Islero'.

RAFAEL LÓPEZ TELLO, S.A.
An old-established family firm, now a public company, making traditional Valdepeñas in earthenware *tinajas* in a bodega with great character and atmosphere. The young red and white are sold as 'Rafael López Tello' and the eight-year-old *reserva* as 'Mohino'.

Nitrogen-capped *depósitos* of one and a half million litres at the winery of Luis Megía in Valdepeñas.

Other Demarcated Regions of the Centre

By far the largest of the three other demarcated regions is La Mancha, which in fact produces some thirty-five per cent of all Spanish wine, for either direct consumption, blending or distillation. The typical grape is the thick-skinned white Airén, which is both resistant to disease and able to flourish in near drought conditions; the bulk of the wine is therefore white.

The lion's share of this wine is made in the cooperatives, of which there are hundreds in the region. As in Italy and Portugal, the *socios* or members of such a cooperative deliver their grapes to a central winery, managed and operated by an executive committee of the local growers under a president who is usually a prominent local figure chosen from among them. The farmers are paid for their grapes on the basis of weight, sugar content and quality,

and later share in the proceeds from the sale of the wine. In the past, the quality of the wine from the smaller cooperatives was very variable, but in the large modern cooperatives, equipped with concrete vats lined with vitrified epoxy resin or with stainless steel tanks, there is much stricter quality control and scientific supervision by trained oenologists.

There is a saying in Spain that when the harvest in La Mancha is bad, the price of all Spanish wine goes up. This is because an average Manchegan white, sound, but somewhat neutral in flavour and without pronounced nose, low in acid but containing a healthy 13° or 14° of alcohol, has proved ideal for blending with scarcer, more acidic and characterful wines from the north. Though anathema to the purist, the result is an acceptable wine sold at a more competitive price.

The present thrust in La Mancha, however, strongly supported by the Ministry of Agriculture with an eye to foreign sales, is to improve quality and produce lighter, fresher and more fragrant wines. This can be done by earlier picking of the grapes, so leaving more acid in the fruit, and fermentation at low temperatures in stainless steel vats which conserves all the fruity flavour and aroma of the grapes. An outstanding example of a much improved wine is the big-selling white 'Don Cortez' so popular in the United Kingdom. When the English shippers Grants of St James's called for a lighter and more refreshing wine, the producers, RODRIGUEZ Y BERGER, re-equipped their bodegas with stainless steel fermentation tanks, and the new-style 'Don Cortez' bears little relation to its earthier and heavier predecessor. Another large private firm making much improved wines in this fashion is the VINÍCOLA DE CASTILLA S.A., whose labels include 'Gran Verdad', 'Viña Bonita', 'Castillo de Manza' and the exceptionally fruity young 'Señorío de Guadianeja'.

Among the growing number of cooperatives producing fresh young wines by modern methods is the COOPERATIVA DEL CAMPO 'NUESTRA SEÑORA DE MANJAVACAS' in the province of Cuenca. Founded in 1948 with only twenty-eight *socios*, it now counts some thousand and is able to deal with thirty million kilograms of grapes. Its wines, white, red and rosé, are labelled as 'Zagarón' and are available in the United States.

The best conducted of cooperatives will never make wine of the same individuality as a small private bodega with its own vineyards – the reason being, of course, that, though the best cooperatives are choosy about the quality of their fruit, it is necessarily somewhat of a *mélange*.

At the other end of the scale, the adventurous Marqués de Griñón, with advice from the well-known French *vigneron* Alexis Lichine and the celebrated Professor Peynaud of Bordeaux University, has planted Cabernet Sauvignon on his estate at Malpica de Tajo near Toledo and is making a superior red wine, aged in oak casks. There is little question here that a classic is in the making – and a maverick one comparable to some of Italy's best *vini da tavola*, made by men of conviction quite happy to be technical outlaws, to follow their own stars. The Marqués de Griñón is officially discouraged from growing Cabernet in Castile. He is prepared to pay fines if necessary to grow the grapes he wants. Results so far have amply justified his confidence. With a Bordeaux-style blend of Cabernet and Merlot, and using Bordeaux *barriques*, he has made wines that already stand comparison with very good Bordeaux – or perhaps more precisely with very good Cabernets from Italy, California and Australia.

Almansa, a small demarcated region to the east of La Mancha, makes mainly red wines from the Monastrel and Garnacha. Most of them are sold for blending, and only three of the bodegas bottle their wines. BODEGAS PIQUERAS, in the town of Almansa itself, dominated by a fairy-tale castle, nevertheless won a place for its fruity red 1981 'Castillo de Almansa' in the hundred best Spanish wines chosen by *Club de Gourmets* magazine for 1985. HIJOS DE MIGUEL CARRIÓN, in nearby Alpera, also make worthwhile red wines aged in wood and sold as 'Cueva de la Vieja', 'Abuela' and 'Viña Pandoble'.

Méntrida, to the south-west of Madrid in the province of Toledo, makes robust red wines, mainly from the red Garnacha, with a high alcohol content of 14-15°. They are largely used for blending or drunk young since they do not age well either in barrel or bottle. BODEGAS LA CERCA and BODEGAS VALDEORO make pleasant young red wines, and there is a vogue in Madrid for serving the rich 'Abuelo' from Bodegas La Cerca with that popular aperitif *gambas a la plancha* (grilled prawns in shell).

Tierra de Madrid

This small wine-growing area in the immediate vicinity of Madrid, comprising the sub-districts of San Martín de Valdeiglesias, Navalcarnero and Arganda-Colmenar de Oreja, is as yet undemarcated, but will probably be covered by a *Denominación específica* in the near future.

Its wines were more reputed in the past than they are today, especially after the court abandoned Valladolid for Madrid in 1607. It is on record that there were vineyards at El Escorial; Fuencarral, now a suburb of Madrid, made delicate and aromatic white wines; Barajas, now the site of Madrid airport, possessed flourishing vineyards; while Carabanchel was then more famous for its luscious Moscatels than its prison.

The best of the wines are from Arganda-Colmenar de Oreja, south-east of the capital. Smooth and light, they are made from a mixture of the red Tempranillo and Tinto Madrid and the white Malvar and Jaén. There are also pleasantly fruity, straw-coloured whites.

Much the best-known of the bodegas is that of HIJOS DE JESÚS DÍAZ in Colmenar de Oreja. When chosen by a Spanish wine club in 1980 its red wine, sold as 'Colmenar', caused something of a sensation, and there was general surprise that it had not originated in the Rioja or Catalonia. The 1981 vintage has once again won

A wide expanse of the wine-growing country in the province of Toledo.

the top award in the fifth *Semana del Vino de Madrid* celebrated in 1985.

Central Spain, it seems, has been waiting for modern techniques of vinification to add its name to the list of internationally known wine regions.

Spirits

Apart from producing vast amounts of grape spirit in the form of *holandas* for making brandy (see p. 31), La Mancha is also well known for its *anís* from the small town of Chinchón fifty kilometres to the south-east of Madrid. This picturesque little place has given its name to quinine, since the wife of a seventeenth-century Governor of Peru, the Marqués de Chinchón, discovered the medicinal properties of the drug; and the cinchona tree, from whose bark it is extracted, was named after her.

Chinchón has been distilling wines for centuries, and in the early years of the present century most of the distillers banded together to form a cooperative, later to become the ALCOHOLERA DE CHINCHÓN S.A., bought by the sherry firm of González Byass in 1969. Since then it has built a large modern distillery producing *anís*, 'Milton' and 'Butler's' gin, 'Koltoff' vodka, and 'Old Sailor' and 'White Sails' schnapps.

The *anís*, comparable in quality with the best French anisette, is made by distilling aniseed in a mixture of alcohol and water, and is sold as 'Anís Chinchon', Dulce (sweet), Seco (dry) and Seco Especial (special dry). It may be drunk straight, on the rocks or chilled, or as a long drink.

The Cuisine

In the country districts and small towns of New Castile the fare is as simple as it was in the days of Don Quixote. It is based on the fruits of a barren land given over mainly to wheat and vines, or on the proceeds of Sunday expeditions when the silence of the rolling sierra is punc-

Harvesting the garlic crop in La Mancha.

tuated by the crack of guns, and little groups of hunters return with their pouches full of rabbit, partridge and quail.

On his gastronomic tour of Spain, Alexandre Dumas *fils* noted down a recipe for *sopa de ajo*, a garlic soup containing bread, paprika and beaten eggs. This is still popular, as is the cold *gazpacho manchego* in summer. Two vegetable dishes, *pisto* and *mojete*, very much resemble the French *ratatouille* and are sometimes served with eggs scrambled into them. Eggs, of course, are a standby in a region with limited culinary resources, and *tortilla a la española* figures on every menu. This thick, round omelette (recipe p. 77) always contains potatoes and sometimes onion, which makes it juicier; between wedges of crusty bread in the form of a *bocadillo* it is the staple midday meal of the shepherds and agricultural workers. Another omelette, *tortilla a la magra*, is made with strips of cooked fillet of pork. The favourite method of cooking partridge is by stewing it as *perdíz estofada*, with white wine, chopped ham and spices; rabbit is stewed with garlic as *atascaburras*.

Potaje de garbanzos a la madrileña – chick-pea stew Madrid-style.

As in Don Quixote's time, the *pièce de résistance* of Manchegan cooking is the famous *cocido castellano*, a substantial dish like *pot au feu*, in which vegetables and a variety of meat are stewed together and then eaten separately. First to be served is the broth; then the vegetables, which always include *garbanzos* (chick-peas) and generally potato and cabbage; and finally the assorted meat, chicken and spiced sausage. According to the variety of ingredients it is a dish which may be simple or complicated, like the *olla en grande*, of which Don Quixote remarked that it was eaten only by canons and presidents of colleges.

There are one or two typical sweets, like *miel con hojuelas* (pancakes with honey) or *bizcochos borrachos* (sponge cake in rings, soaked with wine or liqueurs), but you will do better to finish with fresh fruit in season or cheese. There are splendid melons in September, and Manchego is the best-known of Spanish cheeses. Made from ewe's milk in large rounds and sold all over the country, it is a hard cheese with full flavour, intensified when it is matured in jars of olive oil. Like Cheddar or Parmesan it is often used in cooking, and is sometimes dredged in egg and breadcrumbs, then fried and served as *queso frito*. *Queso de Oropesa*, made in Toledo, is similar in type, but rather darker in colour with a harder, thicker rind.

Toledo is almost as famous for its Moorish sweetmeats as for its tempered sword blades, and is especially noteworthy for marzipan, traditionally made at Christmas and fashioned into small figures. It is a confection for which credit has been claimed by the French. The fact that the name is derived from the Arabic *mawthapan* would seem to discredit this theory; and there is a well-founded tradition that it was first made in the eleventh century during the siege of Toledo by Alfonso VI, when the Moors were left with few provisions except bread, almonds and sugar. Egg white was a later addition.

Madrid is the capital of Spain in gastronomic matters as well as others, and has for long typified two styles of cooking: the native, in effect that of New Castile; and that of the aristocracy and monied classes. This is reflected in its restaurants, which have more recently been swollen by a third category catering to the tastes of the army of newcomers from the other regions of Spain.

A thoroughgoing feeling of inferiority about the national cuisine appears to have spread downwards from the aristocratic court circle of the first of the Spanish Bourbons, Philip V, who left France in 1700 to be crowned King of Spain. Ordinary Spaniards were far from accepting such strictures, hence in Madrid two styles of cookery prevailed: the would-be French of the court and better-to-do, and the traditional of the rest of the populace. There are echoes of this controversy in Richard Ford's description in *Gatherings from Spain* of how 'a clever French *artiste* converts an old shoe into an *épigramme d'agneau*...' Ford himself was critical enough about much that he ate and

drank in Spain, but he knew and loved the country and was never as scathing as Alexandre Dumas *fils*, who could issue an invitation in the following terms:

> So, Madame, our luncheon arrangements are settled. As for dinner, M. Monnier recommends us to try a restaurant owned by an Italian, Lardi by name, where we should be able to obtain a reasonably good meal. In Italy, where one has poor meals, the good innkeepers are French; in Spain, where one finds no meals at all, the best innkeepers are Italian...

Today there is no dearth of restaurants serving the most sophisticated food, some of it much influenced by the *nouvelle cuisine*; one need mention only such famous establishments as Zalacaín, Jockey or Horcher; the Ritz, one of the most perfect hotels in Europe; Bajamar, whose seafood is flown in daily from the north coast; or Valentín, more specifically Spanish in style and the rendezvous now, as in the past, of bullfighters, actors and writers.

Without leaving Madrid you may well sample Basque dishes at their best at Alkalde, Guria or Jai-Alai; Galician at La Toja, Casa d'a Troya or O'Pazo; Asturian at Horno de Sta Teresa; Murcian at La Panocha; or Andalucían at Las Cumbres – the list is endless.

The regional food of New Castile is to be found in smaller and often quite humble restaurants, fittingly enough located in Old Madrid, in the area of the Puerta del Sol and the magnificent Plaza Mayor with its Baroque arches. Some of these places, such as Botín or the Mesón de San Javier, famous for its roast lamb, are household names; alternatively, a most enjoyable way of sampling the authentic cooking of New Castile is to make for the Calle Ventura de la Vega or the parallel Echegaray, narrow, old-fashioned streets off the main artery of Alcalá and within easy walking distance of the Prado. Here the tiled bodegas (which serve excellent *tapas* and first-rate Valdepeñas) and unpretentious eating places stand cheek by jowl, and you may take your pick.

Two phrases recur on their menus. *A la manchega* means simply that the recipe originated in La Mancha; *a la madrileña* was first used during the nineteenth century, and was originally descriptive of dishes prepared quickly and simply to satisfy the impatience of customers frequenting the numerous restaurants which sprang up at the time. In a city where so much of the cooking is eclectic, it is also used of a few dishes specific to Madrid, such as *callos a la madrileña*, squares of highly spiced tripe, worlds – or a country – apart from the bland English tripe and onions.

People in big cities are always in a hurry, and the tradition of quick service survives in the crowded and popular *cafeterías*. Their staples are substantial toasted sandwiches and *platos combinados*, in which a combination of fried meats, sausage, eggs and fried potatoes, of cheese or egg salads, or of fish with various accompaniments, constitutes a complete meal.

Restaurants

Cuenca

FIGÓN DE PEDRO*

On the eastern boundary of New Castile, towards Valencia, the historic old town of Cuenca is well worth a visit, if only to see the *Casas Colgadas* ('hanging houses') perched over the defile of the River Huécar. This atmospheric restaurant serves well-cooked regional food, including *gazpachos* and *galianos* (cold summer soups), hot *morteruelo* (a highly spiced liver pâté), partridge, roast ribs of pork, *lomo de orza* (loin of pork), *pestiños* (sweet fritters) and *alajú* (a Moorish sweetmeat with honey and figs).

El Escorial

FONDA GENERA

The restaurant is housed in the old Royal Theatre, dating from 1733 and decorated with engravings and other souvenirs of the artists who once performed there. The cooking is simple but good, and the house wine is from Cebreros.

Madrid

ZALACAÍN★★★★

Generally rated the top restaurant in Spain, Zalacaín opened in 1973 when Jesús Oyarbide migrated to Madrid from the Basque country. Both he and his *maître de cuisine*, Benjamín Urdiaín, have won many awards for the superb quality of the cooking. The traditional is represented by scallops in Albariño wine, hake in green sauce with clams and *cocochas* (strips from the 'cheek' of the hake), sea bream soup, steak *au poivre* and cardoons, to choose at random.

Other dishes are strongly influenced by the *nouvelle cuisine* and are remarkable for their delicate combination of flavours and subtly aromatic dressings. Examples are the escalope of salmon *au poivre*, creamed hake with basil, puff pastry with truffles and artichoke mousse with clams, among many others.

Prices are commensurate with the quality of the cuisine and the impeccable service.

JOCKEY★★★

Jockey has the highest international standards, and is best-known for its French cuisine, but has displayed great initiative in adapting the *nouvelle cuisine* to the preparation of native ingredients; it also offers a different regional dish each day. Typical of its menu are poached eggs with smoked salmon, braised duck with fresh figs, langoustines in Champagne, bass pie, pheasants with grapes, and stewed partridge. The desserts, especially the iced soufflés, are excellent, and there is a splendid selection of Spanish cheeses.

EL AMPARO★★★

The rise to fame of El Amparo has been rapid since it was opened in 1979 by Ramón Roteta (who has since departed, leaving it in the expert hands of Ramón Ramírez), and it is currently one of the most fashionable restaurants in Madrid. A typically sophisticated and well-prepared menu might consist of snail pâtés with sauce bourgignonne, fillets of sole stuffed with lobster mousse, and stuffed rabbit with fresh vegetables, followed by a dessert or a selection of Spanish cheeses.

HORCHER★★★

Founded by the Austrian Otto Horcher, this is the oldest of the top-flight restaurants in Madrid, and over the years has offered the very best of central European cooking. It is especially famous for game, represented by such dishes as *ragoût* of deer, *civet* of hare and pressed partridge or pheasant. As might be expected from its Austrian origins, sweets from the trolley, such as Apfelstrudel, Baumküchen and crêpes, are delicious.

HORNO DE SANTA TERESA★★★

Among the leading Madrid restaurants this is the best-known for traditional regional food. It was founded by the Iglesias family from Asturias, and many of the best dishes, such as the *fabada* (broad bean stew) and the salmon and trout from the *ríos* of the north, are Asturian. However, the menu also embraces such dishes from other regions as stuffed turkey, ham with plum sauce and duck with Rioja.

LUARQUES★★

This simple and very moderately priced bistro is included because of its excellent home cooking and continuing popularity with the Madrileños. Try the first-rate *fabada* (broad bean stew), John Dory *a la romana*, *morcillo de ternera* (stewed veal) or *codillo de cerdo* (knuckle of pork). There is a good four-year-old Rioja house wine. Tables cannot be reserved and you may have to wait your turn.

LHARDY★★

Founded in 1839 in the heart of Old Madrid, this was one of the very few restaurants to meet with the approval of Alexandre Dumas *fils* and the first to offer *haute cuisine* in Madrid. In ambience perhaps the most colourful of all the capital's restaurants, it continues to offer well-cooked food to its guests, including *cocidos* (stews), stewed partridge, stuffed capon, good fish and home made patisseries. Good Rioja house wine and rare old vintages.

Oropesa

PARADOR NACIONAL VIRREY DE TOLEDO

In an area where hotels and restaurants are few and far between, the Parador, housed in the magnificent castle of the Counts of Oropesa with views towards the distant Sierra de Gredos, is a pleasant stopping place on the high road from Madrid to Portugal. It serves a variety of game and fish, and the partridge and freshly made *natillas* (custard) are particularly to be recommended.

Puerto Lápice

VENTA DEL QUIJOTE

One of the few ports of call on the main road south from Madrid to Córdoba, this roadside inn is straight from the pages of Don Quixote. The cooking is hardly up to the ambience, but it serves excellent Manchego cheese and good Valdepeñas wine.

Toledo

HOSTAL DEL CARDENAL★★

Beautifully set in an eighteenth-century baronial house, this is a sister ship of the famous Botín in Madrid and serves some of the same specialities, such as the sucking pig and lamb roasted in wood-fired ovens. The *perdiz toledana* (stewed partridge) in season is first-rate, as are the asparagus and strawberries from Aranjuez in spring and summer.

Recipes

Tortilla a la Española/Spanish Omelette

Serves 4 to 6

Unlike a French omelette, the Spanish *tortilla* is a large, round cake about an inch thick.

METRIC/IMPERIAL	AMERICAN
Olive oil for frying	Olive oil for frying
1 kg/2¼ lbs potatoes, peeled and cut into thin slices	2¼ lbs potatoes, peeled and cut into thin slices
2 large onions, peeled and sliced	2 large onions, peeled and sliced
Salt	Salt
6 large eggs, beaten	6 large eggs, beaten

Heat some olive oil in a large non-stick frying pan and fry the potatoes and onions slowly for about twenty-five to thirty minutes, with the lid on. The potatoes should be cooked and soft, but not crisp and brown.

Mix the cooked potatoes and onions in a bowl with the beaten eggs and season with salt. Empty most of the olive oil from the pan into a clean jar for further use, leaving only a little in the pan. Heat it until it begins to smoke, then empty the contents of the bowl into the pan, shake gently and cook for a few minutes. Now put a large plate on top of the frying pan and turn the half-cooked omelette on to it. Slide the uncooked side into the pan, shake again and cook until done. The finished omelette should be crisp on the outside and a little runny in the middle. Cut into wedges and serve with a salad, including cooked green pepper cut into strips if available.

Carne de Membrillo/Quince Sweetmeat

Choose quinces with nice yellow skins and put them to boil in a large pan with plenty of water. When the skins begin to crack, take out the fruit, peel it, cut it into chunks and pass it through a sieve or blend in a food processor. Weigh the purée and add the same amount of sugar.

Transfer to a pan and boil for about twenty-five to thirty minutes, with frequent stirring so that the mixture does not stick to the bottom. Smooth into a mould (I like moulds 10 × 18 cm/4 × 7 in and 1.25 cm/½ in deep) and chill in the refrigerator, covered by plastic wrap. You will be able to make two or three moulds according to the amount of fruit. *Membrillo* is excellent with cheese.

Pepitoria de Gallina/Chicken with Almonds

Serves 6

METRIC/IMPERIAL	AMERICAN
Olive oil for frying	Olive oil for frying
2 $1\frac{1}{2}$-kg/$3\frac{1}{2}$-lb chickens cut into small pieces, seasoned and dusted with flour	2 $3\frac{1}{2}$-lb chickens cut into small pieces, seasoned and dusted with flour
1 large onion, finely chopped	1 large onion, finely chopped
50 ml/2 fl oz *oloroso* sherry	$\frac{1}{4}$ cup *oloroso* sherry
225 ml/8 fl oz chicken stock	1 cup chicken stock
12 roasted almonds, peeled and ground	12 roasted almonds, peeled and ground
6 large walnuts, shelled and ground	6 large walnuts, shelled and ground
2 hard-boiled egg yolks	2 hard-boiled egg yolks
Freshly chopped parsley for garnish	Freshly chopped parsley for garnish
Salt and pepper	Salt and pepper

Heat some oil in a large pan and fry the pieces of chicken until brown, then transfer them to a clean pan. In the same oil, sauté the onion until soft, but not brown, and add to the pan with the chicken. Now add the sherry, chicken stock, salt and pepper, and simmer for about thirty minutes until tender – but check by tasting. Ten minutes before serving, mix the ground walnuts, ground almonds and egg yolks in a bowl with a little of the liquid from the pan and add to the chicken. Correct the seasoning and garnish with the parsley. This is excellent accompanied by saffron rice.

Pepitoria de Gallina – chicken with almonds.

Old Castile and Rioja

OLD CASTILE, the heartland of Spain, extends northwards of Madrid across the Guadarrama mountains and as far as Santander on the Atlantic coast. Much of it is barren upland plateau, and that great Spanish philosopher Miguel Unamuno equates the character of its people with the climate when he writes of the Castilians as 'a race of abstemious men, the product of slow selection by the frosts of the bleakest winters and long periods of destitution, accustomed to a hostile sky and a life of poverty'. The grip of the Moors on the region was never secure; another writer, Pérez Galdós, described their opponents as 'dried beef wrapped in tinder', and it was from Burgos in the north that El Cid began his one-man campaign against the emirates in the Levante.

Castile did not in fact emerge as a state in her own right until about the time of the Count Garci Fernández (970-95), and the reoccupation of al-Andalus was achieved with help from the other most powerful kingdom in the Peninsula, Aragón-Catalonia; but when Castile and Aragón were united in 1479 under the Catholic Monarchs, Ferdinand and Isabella, the balance of power tilted irrevocably towards Castile. The conquered territories in America owed their allegiance not to Spain but to its Castilian rulers; and although they were titled 'King of the Spains' and not 'King of Spain', their policies were habitually directed towards the greater glory of Castile.

The great and lovely cities which one thinks of as typically Castilian emerged from the repopulation of the area south of the River Duero after Alfonso VI had driven back the Moors at the end of the eleventh century.

Seen from a distance, Avila, north-west of Madrid, with its encircling wall looks more like the dream of a medieval city than actual stones and mortar. It will always remain the city of Santa Teresa, the remarkable woman born in 1515 who inspired the leaders of the Counter-Reformation in Europe and whose work was largely responsible for preventing the spread of Protestantism in Spain. The massive fortified cathedral, part Roman, part Gothic, stands 3,400 ft above sea level – higher than any other in Europe. Avila is full of churches and convents, many related to Santa Teresa, like the Convent of La Encarnación, where she lived for twenty years and which preserves some of her manuscripts.

Further to the west, Salamanca with its university founded in 1218, where Columbus sought advice before sailing for the New World, is both the Oxford and Cambridge of Spain. The great stone-paved Plaza Mayor is one of the most beautiful squares in the country, and the Casa de las Conchas is so-called because its façade is completely covered with the sculptured scallop shells worn by the pilgrims bound for Santiago de Compostela and the shrine of St James.

The most impressive monument in Segovia, due north of Madrid, is the lofty Roman aqueduct in the heart of the town. The sixteenth-century cathedral incorporates beautiful

PAGE 79 The fortress of Monzón de Castilla, now a Parador, in the rugged country of Palencia.

OVERLEAF The impressively fortified walls of Avila, city of Santa Teresa.

OPPOSITE The great Roman aqueduct that spans the city of Segovia.

Gothic cloisters surviving from an earlier foundation; and the Alcázar, with its towers and pinnacles, dramatically poised on a jagged crag, is everyone's idea of a fairy-tale castle. Valladolid, further north, was the seat of the Kings of Castile and the capital of Spain until Philip II moved his court to Madrid in 1560; it, too, possesses a famous university.

It was in Burgos in the north of Castile that Mío Cid Ruy Díaz El Campeador received the news from the innkeeper's daughter, 'a little girl of nine', of his banishment by Alfonso VI and rode out to begin his campaign against the Moors. Its cathedral, begun in 1221 and three hundred years in building, is one of the most remarkable Gothic churches in Spain.

There is another fine Gothic cathedral in León, once the capital of an independent kingdom until its amalgamation with Castile. It is particularly noteworthy for its flying buttresses and splendid medieval glass. The Hotel San Marcos, housed in a great sixteenth-century monastery of the same name, is built around a colonnaded patio and incorporates the old chapter house with its beautiful *artesonado*-work ceiling of carved sandalwood; it is as much a museum of antiquities and period furniture as a hotel.

Formerly on the borderland between the Christian north and the Moorish-occupied south, the Rioja with its warlike and turbulent past has a great deal beyond its wines to interest visitors. The walled townships crowning its hills – Laguardia, Briones, San Vicente and the rest – were once bastions in the fight of Christian against Moor, and in more than one of them a mosque now masquerades as a church. The great monasteries lying in the green folds of the Sierra de la Demanda to its south saw the rebirth of wine-making after the expulsion of the Moors. One of them, San Millán de Yuso, whose sacristy with its gilt plasterwork is among the most beautiful in Spain, has the distinction of being the home of Gonzálo de Berceo, who in the early thirteenth century wrote the first poems in Castilian rather than in Latin.

The old pilgrim route to Santiago de Compostela lay through the heart of the Rioja; parts of the *calzada* or cobbled track still survive, as do staging posts on the route, notably Nájera, where the church of the monastery of Santa María contains the tombs of many of the monarchs of Navarra, León and Castile. At Santo Domingo de la Calzada, near Haro, the wine capital of the region, one of the old pilgrim hostels survives in the form of a Parador.

In the cathedral, where Santo Domingo is buried, a cage containing a live cock and hen commemorates a strange legend of pilgrim times. A young man on his way to Santiago spent the night at a local inn and refused the advances of its hostess. She spitefully hid some valuables among his belongings; they were discovered and he was hanged. His agonized parents sought out the *corregidor*, whom they found at dinner, but were told that their son was as dead as the fowl on the table in front of him. At this the bird sprang up and began crowing, and hastening to the gibbet they found the young man miraculously alive.

OPPOSITE RIGHT **The cloister of the seventeenth-century monastery of San Millán de Yuso.**

OPPOSITE FAR RIGHT **The entrance to the Parador of Santo Domingo de la Calzada, once a hostel for medieval pilgrims.**

The Wines

Apart from Rioja and the other demarcated regions of Rueda, west of Valladolid, and Ribera del Duero, lying along the Duero valley to its east, Old Castile produces a variety of wines, ranging from the sturdy growths of Cebreros, between Madrid and Avila, to the light red wines from Cigales, just north of Valladolid, and El Bierzo in the northerly province of León.

The Rioja

The Rioja produces many of the best and, apart from sherry, certainly the best-known wines from Spain; there are still people abroad who take the name to apply to Spanish table wines generally, and I have indeed come across this confusion in the catalogues of wine merchants who should know better. This is because Rioja was the first of the Spanish table wines to be exported on any scale: thanks to consistent good quality and reasonable prices, foreign sales have soared over the last decade, and Rioja has become as much a household name as Bordeaux or Burgundy.

Although it is only within recent history that Rioja has been 'discovered' abroad, the region was making wine long before the Roman occupation of Spain. It was, however, the Romans who, as in other parts of the country, put the industry on a sound footing. At Funes, just across the River Ebro in Navarra and near San Adrián, there are the remains of a large Roman winery dating from the first century AD, which to judge from the size of the fermentation chambers and storage vessels, produced a good seventy-five thousand litres annually. The Romans made wine both to ship to Italy and to supply the needs of their legions in Spain, two of which were stationed in the area; the wine-making town of Cenicero takes its name from *cenicero*, meaning an ashtray, and was so-named because the legionaries cremated and buried their dead on the site.

As in other regions, wine-making declined during the Moorish occupation, and the revival began at the monasteries of San Millán de Suso, San Millán de Yuso and Valvanera in the hills south of Nájera and Santo Domingo de la Calzada. The vines were high-growing, like those of the Portuguese Minho today, but as time went on low-growing vines were planted in the valleys of the Ebro and its tributaries. It is of interest that during the medieval period, and as late as the early seventeenth century, the Rioja produced a great deal more white wine than the red for which it is better known today.

One of the uses of the wine made by the Benedictine monks from Cluny, who pioneered the *calzada* or pilgrim way to Santiago de Compostela, was to slake the thirst of the pilgrims staying in their hospices along the route. Some of the French merchants who mingled with them settled in the region – a few of the old houses in the *barrio de francos* (French quarter) in Logroño still survive – and it has been suggested that the most characteristic of Riojan grapes, the Tempranillo, is derived from the Pinot Noir, introduced from Burgundy at the time.

Until well into the eighteenth century the quality of the wine was very variable, and it was rated much below that of the sturdy reds from Toro, near Zamora to the west, the favourites of the schoolmen of the University of Salamanca. One of the first steps towards improving them was taken by Manuel Quintano of Labastida in what is now known as the Rioja Alavesa. Impressed by reports of new methods used by the châteaux of the Bordeaux, he experimented with considerable success in ageing the wines in oak casks, describing them as *finos* because they were fined (or clarified) with egg-whites. His success in stabilizing and exporting them to the West Indies provoked the jealousy of the other producers; he was forbidden by the authorities to charge as much for them as for the short-lived wines made by his competitors, and his premature attempts to improve quality and standards came to an end with the outbreak of the Peninsular War in 1808.

It was another French 'invasion' that was to result in the production of superior Rioja wines as we know them today. With the outbreak of oidium, or powdery mildew, in the Bordeaux vineyards in 1852 and of that even more catastrophic pest of the vine, phylloxera, in 1867, French wine merchants began turning to the Rioja to replenish their supplies. Some were simply interested in shipping wine, but others settled in the Rioja, setting up wineries and introducing modern French methods for making the wines.

Until this period the wine had been made by lightly treading the grapes, stalks and all, in an open *lago* or cistern made of stone or plaster-lined brickwork. The process then took place in stages, with most of the wine resulting from the fermentation of more or less whole grapes without access to air. The method therefore resembled what is now known as *macération carbonique*, and small bodegas continue to make fresh young wines in this way (on a larger scale 'new wine' is also being made in some of the commercial bodegas).

The first wine-maker to introduce up-to-date Bordeaux methods to the Rioja was Don Luciano de Murrieta (later created Marques de Murrieta in recognition of his services) at the bodegas of the Duque de Victoria in Logroño. However, the first bodega to be purpose-built for making wine in Bordeaux fashion was that of Don Camilo Hurtado de Amézaga, Marqués de Riscal, in 1860.

Enlisting the help of a French *vigneron*, Jean Pineau, who, at the instigation of the Provincial Legislature of Alava, had unsuccessfully been preaching the new gospel to the small producers, Don Camilo modelled his winery on the best French examples of the time. The fermentation vats and all the other receptacles were made of oak. The grapes were destalked and crushed, and after tumultuous fermentation the wine was run into large *tinas* on concrete legs to settle and rest. The *marc* or solid matter remaining in the fermentation vats was pressed in a hydraulic press with slatted wooden sides (some such are still in operation), some of the dark, tannic press wine being blended with the rest. The wine was next transferred to 225-litre *barricas* (also called *bordelesas* because of their origin) and clarified by periodic racking, i.e. decanting the wine off the lees into a fresh cask. The final stage was to fine the wine with beaten egg-whites. Although a little was bottled at the bodega, the normal practice was to ship it in cask, a technician from the bodega sometimes travelling with the consignment and bottling it in the cellars of the purchaser.

Although it later became the norm to bottle fine wines at the bodega, this in essence remained the way that Rioja was made until the technological revolution of the 1970s. When the châteaux in Bordeaux began reducing the time in cask to some eighteen months, the *bodegueros* in the Rioja continued to age their wines, both red and white, for long years in wood, so giving them the oaky, vanilla-like nose which has become their hallmark.

Racking red Rioja at CVNE.

As the phylloxera epidemic in France worsened and the French government reduced the duties on foreign wines, dozens of French firms established themselves around the station in Haro to take advantage of the newly opened railway line to Bilbao. When the crisis receded and their owners returned to France, their premises were taken over by newly formed Spanish firms, and many of the best-known Rioja houses, such as R. López de Heredia, CVNE, La Rioja Alta and Bodegas Franco Españolas, date from the late 1880s or turn of the century.

The Rioja itself was invaded by phylloxera in 1901-5, when half of the vineyards in the province of Logroño were wiped out. Although the situation was slowly restored by grafting the native vines on to resistant American stocks, the industry did not reap much benefit from the shortage of French wines during the 1914-18 war because of dependence on casks and bottles from France; the Spanish Civil War of 1936-9 resulted in the uprooting of vineyards for the planting of food crops and the temporary closing of some of the bodegas.

The present great revival dates from the 1970s, with a greatly increased demand for bottled wine and massive investment in the Rioja by the sherry firms, the Spanish banks and foreign wine and spirit concerns such as Seagrams, Pepsi-Cola and the British International Distillers & Vintners. New bodegas were built and equipped with the latest in stainless steel tanks, refrigeration and filtration machinery and modern bottling lines, while at the same time older bodegas were refurbished and modernized. Another development has been the emergence of new medium-sized bodegas, such as Muga, Beronia and Remelluri, dedicated to making wine by largely traditional methods with an emphasis on quality. The industry has also taken a hard look at the image of Rioja as an old-fashioned, excessively oaky wine – hence the new trend to mature the red wines for less time in oak and more in bottle, and the production of fresh young cold-fermented white wines without ageing in cask.

REGULATION AND LABELLING

Regulation of the wine trade in the Rioja dates from the thirteenth and fourteenth centuries, when royal decrees forbade injurious additives and the blending of wines, especially with those from the neighbouring Navarra. In 1653 the Mayor of Longroño banned horse- and mule-drawn carts in the streets near the bodegas, 'for fear that the vibrations of these vehicles in our streets might affect the musts and thus influence the maturing of our precious wines'.

In 1926 a Consejo Regulador was set up to define the limits of the region, to issue seals of origin to the producers and generally to protect the good name of Rioja. It has since been given much wider powers; and in 1972 the present Consejo, made up of representatives from the Ministries of Agriculture and Commerce, the growers, the cooperatives, and the bodegas and shippers, came under the overall control of the Instituto Nacional de Denominaciones de Origen (INDO), formed by the Ministry of Agriculture.

As early as 1892 a government wine laboratory, the Estación de Viticultura y Enología had been founded in Haro to help the producers improve the quality of their wines, and it now works hand in hand with the Consejo Regulador. The regulations of the Consejo Regulador, enforced by a team of inspectors in the field, are embodied in a lengthy printed *Reglamento* covering such matters as permitted vine varieties, methods of cultivation, density of plantation and yield per hectare of vines, wine-making procedures and the chemical composition of the wines. The Consejo also maintains registers of the vineyards, wine-makers and shippers, limiting the export of wine to establishments with large enough capacity and stocks to maintain consistent quality.

Perhaps of most interest to the consumer are the regulations relating to labelling. Apart from the main label carrying a seal of origin in the form of a facsimile stamp, a small 'back label' specifies the type of wine. The different categories are:

Sin crianza : Without age in cask.

Con crianza : Wine aged for not less than two calendar years, of which one at least must be in oak casks of 225 litres.

Reserva : Wine of good quality aged in the case of reds, for at least one year in oak cask and two in bottle ; they may not leave the bodega until the fourth year after the vintage. White and rosé (*rosado*) *reservas* must be aged for at least two years between oak cask and bottle, with a minimum of six months in oak.

Gran reserva : Wine of good quality aged, in the case of reds, for at least two years in oak cask, followed by a minimum of three in bottle ; they may not leave the bodega until the sixth year after the vintage. White and rosé *gran reservas* must be aged for a minimum period of four years, with at least six months in oak.

It should be noted that the requirements of the Reglamento are for *minimum* periods of maturation, and the traditional bodegas regularly age their wines in oak for much longer.

In the past it has been the custom in Spain to label wines not with a vintage year but with a description, such as 3° *año*, meaning that the wine was bottled during the third calendar year after the harvest (e.g. a 3° *año* wine harvested in October 1982 would be bottled during 1985 and is therefore nearer two than three years old). This is still common practice in Spain, but in accordance with EEC regulations wines are increasingly being labelled with the year of vintage, and this is mandatory for wines exported to Common Market countries. It was again common practice in the bodegas to blend wines from poor years with those from better and more prolific years in the interests of maintaining a consistent standard, so that the year on the label sometimes indicated only that a preponderance of the wine was of the stated vintage. The Consejo now insists that the bottle must contain not less than eighty-five per cent of the stated vintage, and that the only wine that may be blended with it is that of a younger year. Its inspectors regularly check the records and

stocks of the bodegas – but, as always, the best guarantee of the authenticity of a wine is the reputation of its maker.

VINEYARDS AND VINES

The demarcated area of 37,500 hectares extends from the rocky gorge of the Conchas de Haro in the west to the flatter country around Alfaro, some 120 km to the east. It lies along the valleys of the River Ebro and its tributaries, from one of which, the Río Oja, the region took its name. The vineyards are planted on both sides of the Ebro, and in the hilly western area are bounded by the abrupt heights of the Sierra Cantábrica to the north and the rolling hills and wooded valleys of the Sierra de la Demanda to the south. There are three sub-regions: the cooler and hillier Rioja Alta and Rioja Alavesa to the west, and the sunnier and lower-lying Rioja Baja to the east. From west to east the altitude drops from 1,400 ft at Haro to 900 at Alfaro, and the rainfall from 18 in to 10 in.

The Atlantic climate of the Rioja Alta and Rioja Alavesa, with fairly mild winters, wet and windy springs, short hot summers and long warm winters, is better suited to making delicate wines than the hot and more Mediterranean weather of the Rioja Baja. The best of the soils are also to be found in the two westerly regions: in the Rioja Alavesa they are almost entirely of calcareous clay particularly suitable for the Tempranillo grape; in the Rioja Alta there are areas of calcareous clay, orange-red ferruginous clay and alluvial silt. In the Rioja Baja there is a preponderance of alluvial silt with smaller areas of ferruginous clay, and the typical grape is the red Garnacha tinta.

Although many of the large bodegas possess sizeable vineyards, making as much as forty per cent of their wine from the grapes, the Rioja Alta and Rioja Alavesa are a patchwork of small privately owned vineyards, interspersed with fields of potatoes, vegetables and wheat. Because of the splitting up of family properties

OVERLEAF **Labels from Rioja and other Spanish table wines.**

on the death of the father, the average size is only 4.4 hectares. In the undulating expanses of the Rioja Baja, with its wide fields of peppers and asparagus, the vineyards are larger: Bodegas Berberana has an unbroken tract of some thousand hectares under development.

Some of the large concerns, like Pedro Domecq, are experimenting with vines grown in Bordeaux fashion along wires supported by stakes, but in the typical Riojan vineyard they are grown low and unsupported, *a la castellana*, and pruned *en vaso* ('goblet-shaped'). This leaves the vines with three main stems, each bearing two grafted shoots producing two bunches of grapes, or twelve bunches in all.

Grape picking starts officially on 10 October, and the harvest is celebrated in the towns and villages with processions and the carrying of a statue of their patron saint through the streets. The patroness of the Rioja as a whole is the Virgin of Valvanera, whose eleventh-century effigy is preserved in the monastery of Valvanera, high in the wooded gorge of the Najerilla River in the Sierra de la Demanda:

> *María de Valvanera,*
> *Presta calor a las vines*
> *Y nunca jamás me olvides*
> *Ni aun después de que me muera.*

> María de Valvanera,
> Lend warmth to the vines
> And never forget me
> Even after I die.

Logroño, the capital of the recently re-named province of La Rioja and its largest town, celebrates its fiesta of San Mateo late in September, before the serious business of harvesting begins. The city is crowded with workers from the surrounding vineyards and bodegas, joined by whole families arriving from the other rural districts of northern Spain to help with the picking of the grapes. Uniformed bands parade the streets; the restaurants lay trestle tables in the narrow streets leading down

Harvesting the grapes near Rueda.

to the Ebro, and late at night the wide Plaza del Espolón resounds to the noise of fireworks bursting into the mild, still air.

Of upwards of a dozen different vine varieties formerly grown in the Rioja, the Consejo Regulador now authorizes seven for new plantations. The proportions in which they are grown are:

Black grapes

Tempranillo	30.4%
Garnacha tinta	39.5%
Mazuelo	0.7%
Graciano	0.2%

White grapes

Viura	13.6%
Malvasía	0.6%
Garnacha blanca	small amounts

Tempranillo

This is the black grape *par excellence* of the Rioja; it is also grown in Catalonia, as the Ull de Llebre; in Valdepeñas, as the Cencibel; in the Ribera del Duero, as the Tinto fino; and in Arganda, as the Tinto Madrid. It is generally thought to be a native of the region, but there has been speculation that it is descended from the Pinot Noir or Cabernet Franc brought to the Rioja by the Cluniac monks at the time of their pilgrimages to Santiago de Compostela.

Robust and resistant to diseases, it grows best

in the calcareous clay soils of the cooler and more humid Rioja Alavesa and Rioja Alta. The thick-skinned and intensely black grapes make fragrant and fruity wines with good acid balance, which because of their resistance to oxidation repay long ageing.

Garnacha tinta

High-cropping and easy to grow, the Garnacha thrives in the stony soils and hot, dry climate of the Rioja Baja. Its musts are fruity when young, though somewhat hard, and high in alcohol. In poor years they are therefore blended with those of the other grapes to lend body and strength. Pure Garnacha wines oxidize easily, the colour soon changing from dark plum to brick red, and are not suitable for prolonged ageing. Picked young in parts of the Rioja Alta while there is more acid in the fruit, they make delicate and refreshing rosés.

Mazuelo

Found in the oldest vineyards of the region, the Mazuelo is thought to be a native, but has certain similarities to the Crujillon or Carignan of the French Hérault. Because of its susceptibility to oidium its cultivation is on the decline, but its musts, astringent and without much aroma, make a useful addition to wines destined for long ageing, because of their high tannin content and resistance to oxidation.

Graciano

Like the Mazuelo, the Graciano is a traditional grape increasingly rarely cultivated, in this case because of low fertility. Its leaves are the first to change colour in autumn, first to yellow and then through shades of russet and red, and the last to fall. The small, intensely black, thin-skinned grapes contribute great freshness, fragrance and fruitiness to the wines, though because of their low alcohol content (10-12°) and the expense of growing them, it is not feasible to make straight Graciano wines.

Graciano grapes in the vineyards of the Marqués de Riscal.

Viura

The Viura, grown in Catalonia as the Macabeo and in other parts of Spain as the Alcañon or Alcañol, is the preferred white variety of the Rioja. It does best in calcareous clays, producing fragrant and very fruity white wines with good acid balance and resistance to oxidation. It is particularly suitable for the new-style cold-fermented white wines, and in the Rioja Alavesa some 10% is sometimes added to Tempranillo musts to make light red wines, formerly *claretes*.

Malvasía

First introduced to Catalonia from Asia Minor by Greek settlers, the Malvasía is more widely grown in the Canaries (see p. 204) and in Madeira, where it is often known as the Malmsey. It grows best on high ground and in a dry environment, and its bitter-sweet, golden yellow musts are used in conjunction with the Viura to make the traditional luscious white Riojas, though they are easily oxidizable and prone to early maderization.

Garnacha blanca

Though prolific and easily cultivated, the Garnacha blanca is not used a great deal. It makes fresh wines, high in alcohol but low in acid.

The proportions of the varieties of grape used in making the wines differ a great deal from bodega to bodega; a traditional blend for a red Rioja Alta might be sixty per cent Tempranillo, twenty-five per cent Garnacha and fifteen per cent Graciano and Mazuelo. In the Rioja Alavesa, on the other hand, it is customary to use up to ninety per cent or even one hundred per cent Tempranillo. This leads to differences in the style of the wines. As the broadest of generalizations, those from the Rioja Alta are brisker and harder when young, benefiting from longer maturation. The Tempranillo from the Rioja Alavesa, grown with a southern exposure, produces softer, faster-maturing wines with a very pronounced Tempranillo nose (which has been compared with that of both the Cabernet Sauvignon and the Pinot Noir).

Again, the style of the wine depends very much on the time that it has spent in oak. Newer bodegas, like the Marqués de Cáceres, have cut down the period in cask so as to produce something more claret-like in character. Traditional concerns, such as López de Heredia, Marqués de Murrieta and La Rioja Alta, believe in maturing the wine for much longer periods in cask – but here, too, there is a great difference between the slow ageing of a wine in older casks and the use of brand new wood in a modern bodega, which can give the wine an aggressively oaky quality. What matters is that there should be plenty of fruit behind the oak.

Autumn vineyards near Villabuena.

The predominantly Garnacha wines from the Rioja Baja are not as delicate as those from the more westerly sub-regions and are usually sold for early consumption or for blending.

Not so long ago, all the better white Rioja was matured in cask, and well-made whites of this type, like those from López de Heredia and Murrieta, dry, luscious and round, and fresh for all their oaky nose, are wines for the connoisseur. Dry white Riojas of this type are now the exception rather than the rule, and to meet the taste for light, fresh and fruity young wines the

bodegas make most of the white wine by slow fermentation in stainless steel tanks, at temperatures between 14°C and 18°C, for periods ranging from a month to six weeks and without ageing them in oak. The best of them have an immediate appeal and a delicate fruity fragrance like those from the Alsace and Loire.

A third type of white wine, rounder and more intense in flavour, is made by piling up the grapes and leaving them in the vat for the juice to drain off under the weight of the load. The virgin must from the part of the grape nearest the skin is then transferred to a second vat for fermentation.

The light, new-style whites should be chilled and drunk as young as possible. Red Rioja benefits from being opened about an hour beforehand (though one should be careful about old *reservas*, which may need less airing); they should, of course, be drunk at room temperature and rarely need decanting, since they have thrown most of their deposit in cask.

VINTAGE TABLE FOR RIOJA

1950	Very good	1968	Excellent
1951	Good	1969	Average
1952	Excellent	1970	Excellent
1953	Average	1971	Average
1954	Average	1972	Poor
1955	Very good	1973	Very good
1956	Good	1974	Average
1957	Average	1975	Good
1958	Good	1976	Good
1959	Very good	1977	Very poor
1960	Good	1978	Very good
1961	Average	1979	Average
1962	Very good	1980	Good
1963	Very good	1981	Good
1964	Excellent	1982	Excellent
1965	Good	1983	Good
1966	Average	1984	Average
1967	Average		

Naturally the quality of the vintage varies from bodega to bodega, and tasting notes will be found under the descriptions of individual producers (pp. 96–107).

The bodegas and their wines

It is not possible in a book of this nature to detail every bodega in the Rioja. The complete list of the major concerns is:

RIOJA ALTA

A.G.E., Bodegas Unidas	Fuenmayor
Bodegas Berberana	Cenicero
Bodegas Beronia	Ollauri
Bodegas Campo Viejo (Savín)	Logroño
Bodegas Carlos Serres, Hijo	Haro
Bodegas Cooperativas Sta María la Real	Nájera
Bodegas Corral	Navarrete
Bodegas Delicia	Ollauri
Bodegas Federico Paternina	Haro
Bodegas Francisco Viguera	Haro
Bodegas Franco Españolas	Logroño
Bodegas Gómez Cruzado	Haro
Bodegas José Palacio	Logroño
Bodegas La Rioja Alta	Haro
Bodegas Lafuente	Fuenmayor
Bodegas Lagunilla (IDV)	Cenicero
Bodegas Lan	Fuenmayor
Bodegas López Agos	Logroño
Bodegas Marqués de Cáceres	Cenicero
Bodegas Marqués de Murrieta	Ygay
Bodegas Martínez Bujanda	Logroño
Bodegas Martínez Lacuesta	Haro
Bodegas Montecillo (Osborne)	Navarrete
Bodegas Muga	Haro
Bodegas Olarra	Logroño
Bodegas R. López de Heredia, Viña Tondonia	Haro
Bodegas Ramón Bilbao	Haro
Bodegas Real Divisa	Abalos
Bodegas Rioja Santiago (Pepsi-Cola)	Haro
Bodegas Riojanas	Cenicero
Bodegas Velazquez	Cenicero
Bodegas Vista Alegre	Haro
Bodegas y Viñedos	Ollauri
Castillo de Cuzcurrita	Río Tirón
Compañía Vinícola del Norte de España (CVNE)	Haro
Cooperativa Vinícola de Santa Daría	Cenicero

RIOJA ALAVESA

Bodegas Alavesas	Laguardia
Bodegas Campillo	Oyón
Bodega Cooperativa Vinícola de Labastida	Labastida
Bodegas El Coto	Oyón
Bodegas Faustino Martínez	Oyón
Bodegas Murua	Villabuena
Bodegas Palacio (Seagram)	Laguradia
Bodegas Viña Salceda	Elciego
Bodegas S.M.S.	Villabuena
La Granja Remelluri	Labastida
Pedro Domecq, S.A.	Elciego
Vinos de los Herederos del Marqués de Riscal	Elciego

RIOJA BAJA

Bodegas Gurpegui	San Adrián
Bodegas Latorre y Lapuerta	Alfaro
Bodegas Muerza	San Adrián
Bodegas Palacios	Alfaro
Bodegas Rivero	Arnedo
Savín, S.A.	Aldeanueva del Ebro

A.G.E. BODEGAS UNIDAS, S.A.

Formed in 1967 by a merger of Bodegas Azpilicueta, Cruz García and Entrena, A.G.E., jointly controlled by a Spanish bank and the American Schenley, is now one of the largest concerns in the Rioja Alta and a major exporter. The wine for which it is best known abroad is the red 'Siglo Saco', so-called because it is sold in a distinctive burlap sack.

BODEGAS ALAVESAS, S.A.

On the outskirts of the picturesque old walled town of Laguardia in the Rioja Alavesa, the bodega was founded in 1972 by a group of local producers. Most typical of its wines are the light reds, almost rosés, made with ninety per cent Tempranillo and ten per cent white Viura. Named 'Solar de Samaniego' in honour of an eighteenth-century local poet, copious author of the feeblest fables, they in contrast are delicate and refreshing with pronounced Tempranillo nose, and surprisingly long-lived in view of their light weight. The 1973 was outstanding. This bodega's wines are almost a caricature of the Alavesa regional style, being deceptive in colour and apparent lightness while still having enough concentration to mature for as long as many much more obviously beefy reds. They bear some resemblance to the reds of Riscal (q.v.). Whether they will live as long as the old classics of that bodega remains to be seen.

BODEGAS BERBERANA

Founded in 1877 by the Berberana family, the firm was bought in 1967 by Melquiades Entrena, who embarked on the construction of a new bodega in Cenicero. With its temperature-controlled fermentation vats and huge ageing floor accommodating 40,000 oak *barricas*, it is one of the largest in the Rioja. With 130 hectares of vineyards in the Rioja Alta and a further 900 in the Rioja Baja, Berberana, now under new management, grows most of the fruit for its wines.

The characteristic Berberana style has more 'vinosity', more striking full-fruit character, than most Riojas. The top Berberana reds are fermented in new oak to catch the vanilla flavour, then bottled as soon as the rules allow to maintain fruitiness. They appear to mature relatively rapidly: the 1978 seemed fully mature in 1986.

The 2° *año* red 'Preferido' is one of the biggest-selling wines in Spain. The 3° *año* 'Carta de Plata' and more mature 'Carta de Oro', made from eighty per cent Tempranillo, ten per cent Graciano and five per cent Mazuelo, are pleasant fruity red wines, and there are also good *reservas*, especially the 1970, 1973, 1975, 1976 and 1978. The white 'Carta de Plata' is a young new-style wine un-aged in oak.

BODEGAS BERONIA, S.A.

This is one of the new generation of medium-sized bodegas dedicated to making Rioja in the traditional style but with the advantages of modern equipment and technology. Founded by Don Javier Bilbao Iturbe in 1970, it owns ten hectares of vineyards and is equipped with stainless steel tanks for temperature-controlled fermentation of the wines, so as to conserve the full flavour of the fruit. The emphasis on hygiene is typified by the coating of the walls with an anti-cryptogrammic paint obtained from England. The bodega is currently being enlarged since the acquisition of a controlling interest by the sherry firm of Gonzalez Byass.

The red wines, made with eighty-five per cent Tempranillo and fifteen per cent of Garnacha, Mazuelo and white Virua, are matured for a minimum of two years in *barrica* and two in bottle, and are fined with egg-white. Light, brisk and fruity with good balance, they are sold as the young, cherry-red 'Beron' and the darker and more mature 'Beronia' *reservas*, such as the 1973 and 1978. 'Beron' should be drunk as young as possible to catch its vivid but fleeting fruitiness. The *reservas* are soft and intensely fragrant with oak.

BODEGAS BILBAÍNAS, S.A.

The wines from this old-established Haro firm were among the first Riojas to be sold on any scale in the UK, and for many years it maintained a depot under the railway arches at Charing Cross. 'Ederra' is the cheapest and lightest of the Bilbaínas wines, but nevertheless maintains a reliable standard and lively style. 'Viña Zaco' tastes relatively fragile but matures surprisingly well. 'Viña Pomal', while being the most solid product of the house, has a tendency to remain apparently in a time-warp. Twenty years on it is still solid. Bilbaínas also makes a sparkling *cava* wine (see p. 147).

BODEGAS CAMPO VIEJO, S.A.

With its annual output of some 24 million bottles, Campo Viejo in Logroño, owned by the wine combine of Savín S.A., is probably the largest producer in the region, and its very drinkable 2° *año* 'San Asensio' the biggest-selling red Rioja. The forthright style of this bodega is understandably popular and an ideal starting point for learning the appeal of Rioja, whether in the vigour of the second-year wine or the reasonance of the *reservas*. At fifteen years old the 1970 was still rich, even fleshy, with complex spicy flavours that dominated a tasting of its contemporaries. Other outstanding vintages were those of 1964, 1968, 1970, 1973 and 1978, all of consistently high standard.

BODEGAS DOMECQ, S.A.

The Riojan outpost of the great sherry firm owns a large modern bodega in Elciego in the Rioja Alavesa and 571 hectares of vineyards in the surrounding area, planted mainly with Tempranillo and Viura; by a dispensation of the Consejo Regulador, the vines are staked and wired rather than being grown low in traditional fashion. The pleasant, well-balanced red wines, made mainly with Tempranillo, are sold as 'Privilegio del Rey Sancho' in Spain and 'Domecq Domain' abroad. The 1976, with its intense Tempranillo nose, a little reminiscent of Pinot Noir, and deep raspberry flavour is outstanding. The bodega also makes a cold-fermented white from one hundred per cent Viura.

BODEGAS FAUSTINO MARTÍNEZ, S.A.

Situated in Oyón, just to the north of Logroño in the Rioja Alavesa, Faustino Martínez, founded in 1860, is one of the few Rioja firms to remain in family hands. It possesses a sizeable 350 hectares of vineyards, planted with eighty per cent Tempranillo, and a modern bodega for making the wines by temperature-controlled fermentation. It makes excellent 'Faustino V' and 'Faustino I' red *reservas* and *gran reservas*; a fresh young white 'Faustino V', one of the best of the new-style wines; and also a pleasant young red 'Vino de Cosechero', made by fermenting whole grapes in a *lagar* (see p. 87) in the manner of Beaujolais Nouveau.

There was some difference of opinion at a tasting at the bodega in 1984 as to the degree of flavour desirable in white Rioja. 'Faustino V', the 'freshest' in style, tended to lack fruit, while a fruitier one, 'Faustino VII' (including pressed juice) was found to be slightly coarse in comparison. In the days of barrel-ageing whites maximum flavour was needed. Today the un-aged style must be made whiter than white, even at the risk of losing flavour. No such problem is encountered with the red *reservas*, which seem to stay on a plateau of sweetly oaky fragrance for a decade after bottling.

BODEGAS FEDERICO PATERNINA, S.A.

Now one of the largest firms in the Rioja, the company was founded by Federico de Paternina y Josué, a son of the Marqués de Terán, one of the aristocrats who set about the improvement of the wines in the late nineteenth century. In 1898 Federico Paternina started his own business in the village of Ollauri near Haro. It grew rapidly in size, and the wines acquired a great reputation for their quality. Since then the firm has several times changed hands and moved, first to the larger premises of the Cooperativa Católica on the outskirts of Haro, and more recently to the huge modern plant adjoining.

With its 53,000 oak casks and storage capacity of 27 million litres of wine in bulk and 28 million in bottle, it does not vinify the wine, which is bought from cooperatives and independents for blending and maturation. The best-known and biggest-selling is the 3° *año* red 'Banda Azul'; 'Viña Vial', matured for two years in *barrica* and two in bottle, is a consistently fruity and satisfying wine. Of the red *reservas*, the most select are labelled as 'Conde de los Andes'. Like many of the other bodegas, Paternina makes a fresh new-style white, sold in Spain as 'Rinsol' and abroad as 'Banda Dorada'.

Apart from Riscal, Paternina maintains the most remarkable collection of old vintage wines in the Rioja. They are kept deep below ground in the cellars of the original bodega in Ollauri. If

OPPOSITE **Casks of vintage Rioja in the old cellars of Federico Paternina in Ollauri.**

you are lucky enough to be given an invitation, it is more than worthwhile to inspect the casks, ranged against rock walls brilliant with a red iron deposit, and the old bottles behind their iron grills. Many of the wines are in splendid condition, deep in colour, fragrant, fruity, and some still with their quota of tannin. Perhaps the most memorable of a noble range of these old wines tasted in 1978 were the red 1964 (a great vintage throughout Rioja), a 1920 of haunting sweetness, delicacy and length of flavour, and, more surprisingly, a 1923 sweet white wine in a half-bottle which mingled satin and smoke in an unforgettable combination. There are very few sweet white Riojas: the 'noble rot' that resulted in this was a freak. Paternina's cellar conditions are also exceptional.

BODEGAS GURPEGUI

This large family concern with bodegas in San Adrián is the best-known of the firms in the Rioja Baja. Apart from selling large amounts of young *sin crianza* wine (without ageing in oak), it produces full-bodied 'Berceo' *reservas* and *gran reservas*, made from a blend of Tempranillo and Garnacha and named after the famous monk from San Millán de Yuso, the first poet to write in Castilian. One of the most attractive of its wines is a fresh one hundred per cent Garnacha rosé made without mechanical pressing of the grapes.

BODEGAS HEREDEROS DEL MARQUÉS DE RISCAL, S.A.

The bodega was founded at a time when various of the noble families of the Rioja were interesting themselves in improving the wines by Don Camilo Hurtado de Amézaga, Marqués de Riscal. The original buildings (described on p. 87), planned by the French viticulturalist Jean Pineau and constructed by the engineer Ricardo Bellsola, were completed in 1860. They lie on both sides of the road from Cenicero into Elciego and were extended in 1896 and on later occasions, as the demand for the wines increased, both in Spain and abroad, where they won many premier awards in international exhibitions. The old part of the bodega is honeycombed with arched cellars housing the oak *barricas* for maturing the wines. At the heart of the underground complex is the famous 'Catedral', whose thousands of bottles of wine representing every vintage since 1860 are binned away behind locked wrought-iron grills. It is much more than a museum, since the wines are recorked every fifteen years or so and served to honoured guests. I have myself drunk vintages as far back as 1917, still in amazing condition.

The 'Catedral', in fact, forms an epitome of wine-making at Riscal. Pineau not only designed the bodega, but also planted Cabernet Sauvignon from Bordeaux, of which the old vintages, like the 1917, contain some ninety per cent. Riscal still grows Cabernet Sauvignon in limited amounts; of its three hundred hectares of vineyards around Elciego, twenty are planted with Cabernet, half new and half old, and the rest with the native Tempranillo, Graciano and Viura. The red wines are now made from a blend of eighty-five per cent Tempranillo, five per cent Graciano, five per cent Cabernet Sauvignon and five per cent of the white Viura. Apart from the fruit from its own vineyards, Riscal also buys grapes from growers in the immediate district.

Over the years, the bodega has been thoroughly modernized, and the wine (all of it red, apart from a little rosé) is vinified in

Chai de conservation   Chai de vinification

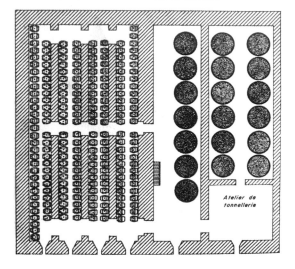

Atelier de tonnellerie

ABOVE LEFT **Ground plan of the original bodega of the Marqués de Riscal.**

ABOVE **The old bodega of the Marqués de Riscal in Elciego.**

LEFT **The 'Catedral' at the Marqués de Riscal bodega.**

RIGHT **The grape harvest in the vineyards of the Marqués de Riscal.**

concrete vats lined with vitrified epoxy resin. The youngest wine is sold at four years old (rather than as a 3° *año*, as with most of the bodegas), small amounts being matured as special *reservas*.

Although Riscal is now a public company, it remains very much a family concern. Don Francisco Amézaga, a direct descendant of the founder, is in charge of operations in Rueda, where the company makes its white wines; the

bodegas in Elciego have for many years been run by Don Francisco Salamero, with the help of his sons Fernando and Javier, one an oenologist and the other an agricultural engineer in charge of the vineyards.

The red Riscal is lighter and more claret-like than most Riojas, and good recent vintages have been the 1971, 1973, 1976, 1978 and 1981, while the 1982 promises to be exceptional. The old *reservas*, up to the standards of *premiers crus* from Bordeaux, are magnificent wines. Don Francisco considers the best to be: 1910, 1920, 1922, 1925, 1938, 1942, 1943, 1947, 1950, 1964, 1965, 1968 and 1970.

Tasting Notes

1917 (90% Cabernet Sauvignon, 10% Tempranillo)

Hugh Johnson: One of the biggest of the wines; very dark in colour and still almost juicy in character. After a while in the glass it seemed to become even darker. Marvellous developing flavour, growing slightly cheesy after a while but immensely long with a lovely, softly yielding finish. Quite outstanding.

1922

Jan Read: Very deep blackberry colour with orange rim. Intense blackberry flavour. Good body and long finish – it resembled one of the best of the St Emilions. Magnificent.

1941 (50% Cabernet, 40% Tempranillo, 10% Graciano)

H.J.: After a rather hard, forbidding first impression the 1941 developed a lovely fragrance. It remained firm, light but very long, ending with fine clean acidity. Excellent.

1950

J.R.: Ripe, fruity nose, extremely soft, lacking a little in body, but still beautiful.

Unloading grapes (OPPOSITE) and hand-bottling an old *reserva* (RIGHT) at the bodega of the Marqués de Riscal.

1952

H.J.: Notably paler than the 1947 tasted earlier (which was sixty per cent of Cabernet). An open wine without great concentration, a harmonious marriage of old Tempranillo and oak, finally sweetish and lacking the astringency to give it a perfectly clean finish.

1964

J.R.: Dark ruby with orange rim. Deep, full nose. Lots of body and fruit. Long finish. Perfect.

BODEGAS LA RIOJA ALTA, S.A.

The firm was founded in 1890 and took over the premises of the French *négociant* Alphonse Viguier in the Barrio de la Estación in Haro. Its best-known wine, 'Viña Ardanza', is named after one of the original shareholders, Alfredo Ardanza y Sánchez. Much of the fruit comes from its 250 hectares of vineyards, and the firm continues to make some of the best red Rioja by traditional methods.

The 3° *año* red 'Viña Alberdi' is one of the soundest young Riojas, and has long been available at Sainsbury's. 'Viña Ardanza' is aged for three-and-a-half years in cask and two in bottle: round, smooth and fruity, it is one of the most popular of mature Riojas. 'Viña Arana' is lighter in style; and the 'Reserva 890' and 'Reserva 904', named after the classic vintages of 1890 and 1904, are splendid old oaky wines, deep in nose and intense in flavour, matured for even longer in cask and bottle.

The bodega's wines are held in very high esteem in America, where the old numbered *reservas* fetch substantial prices. '904' was until recently a selection of the 1970 vintage, excellently poised between vigour and finesse. The 1973 which has succeeded it lacks some of this high quality but is still subtle, smooth and fine.

'890' was for a number of years the 1964 vintage, a wine of dramatic, balsamic aromas which by now, alas, has begun to tail off into a dry finish. In its place the 1970 is astonishingly cockle-warming. The Rioja tradition of releasing *reservas* after long ageing still has its champions.

BODEGAS LAN, S.A.

This large new bodega in Fuenmayor began operations in 1974, and the good quality of its wines have owed much to the skill of its oenologist, José María Aizpura. The younger wines, red, white and rosé, are sold as 'Lan', and the excellent red *reservas* as 'Viña Lanciano' or, abroad, as 'Lancorta'.

BODEGAS MARQUÉS DE CÁCERES

Don Enrique Forner has done more than most to introduce modern wine-making techniques to the Rioja. Exiled to France during the Franco period, he became proprietor of Château Carmensac and Château Trintaudon in Bordeaux, and later turned to the renowned Professor Peynaud of Bordeaux University for advice in setting up his bodega in Cenicero. The operation is organized as a 'Unión Vitivinícola', the carefully selected red wine being bought from the adjoining Cooperativa de Santa Daría and other partners in the enterprise. The wines bear all the marks of Señor Forner's French grounding and knowledge of foreign tastes; and the bodega is in fact one of the few to sell more wine abroad, especially in the UK and US, than at home. Fruity and claret-like, the wines spend less time in cask and more in bottle than the traditional Riojas, and the long corks and elegant maroon labels are in the French style.

Enrique Forner pioneered the new-style, cold-fermented white wines in the Rioja. The white 'Marqués de Cáceres', made from one hundred per cent Viura, remains perhaps the best of its type, astonishingly fragrant and fruity, light and fresh, losing nothing in the glass.

BODEGAS MARQUÉS DE MURRIETA

Don Luciano de Murrieta learned to appreciate fine French wines while a refugee in London after the collapse of the first Carlist rebellion. After studying French methods in Bordeaux, he returned to Logroño in 1850, where he began making wines in Bordeaux fashion for the Duque de la Victoria; they soon began winning medals in international exhibitions. In 1872 he set up his own bodega at Ygay, just outside Logroño, where the old cellars and some of the old presses and oak vats still survive.

Some forty per cent of the wine, red, white and rosé, is made from grapes grown in the bodega's 160 hectares of vineyards, planted with sixty per cent Tempranillo, ten per cent Garnacha and five per cent Mazuelo, Graciano and Malvasía. The balance is supplied by independent growers on whom Murrieta has first call.

Under the regime of Don Pedro-Jesús Marrodán, the great Riojan oenologist who retired some years ago, the bodega was one of the most conservative of Riojan concerns. The grapes, it is true, were vinified in concrete vats lined with vitrified epoxy resin, but the wine then lay in oak vats or *barricas* until it was bottled shortly before despatch. It is now matured in oak for not more than four years and aged in bottle before release.

The Riscal and Murrieta wines have always been regarded as aristocrats, and not simply because of their titled founders. As at Riscal, the youngest red Murrieta is the four-year-old. In style the Murrieta wines are quite distinct from those of Riscal, richer and more intensely flavoured from the start, with more apparent fruit and acidity. In maturity they tend towards velvet, where Riscal's great old *reservas* are more satiny in texture. Whatever may be said for or against long maturation in oak, the old Murrietas, such as the glorious 1960 *reserva*, intensely deep and fruity in nose and flavour and long in finish, are classics of their kind. Apart from the *reservas*, in very special years and at rare intervals Murrieta makes a superb 'Castillo Ygay', of which the best vintages have been 1917, 1925, 1934, 1942 and 1962.

The white Murrieta, traditionally matured in oak along similar lines to the 4° *año* red, is a wine that makes one regret the wholesale abandonment of this style in favour of new-style cold-fermented whites. A deep straw yellow, dry, round and fresh, with a nice blend of fruit and oak, it is a wine of great character and one that goes ideally with full-flavoured dishes. The bodega is now making a rather lighter wine, with less time in cask, containing ninety per cent Viura, eight per cent Malvasía and two per cent Garnacha blanca.

BODEGAS MONTECILLO, S.A.
Established in the late eighteenth century by the Navajas family of Fuenmayor, the firm was bought in 1973 by the sherry firm of Osborne, which constructed a large modern bodega on the outskirts of Navarrete to the south of Logroño. The fruity 3° *año* red 'Cumbrero' has always been excellent value. There are good 'Viña Monty' red *reservas*, and the white 'Cumbrero', fresh, delicate, light and fruity, is one of the better of the new-style wines. At nine years old the '75 'Viña Monty Reserva' was still sound and fresh, fairly fruity and vigorous, showing no signs of drying up.

BODEGAS MUGA, S.A.
If ever there was a family firm with respect for Riojan tradition, it is Bodegas Muga. The firm moved from an old bodega in the centre of Haro to new premises in the Barrio de la Estación in 1971, but all the receptacles for making the wine, including the fermentation vats, are of oak, while the wines are fined with egg-white and the *reservas* encapsulated in wax. The brothers Muga, Isac and Manolo, are in direct charge of all operations, from pressing and vinification to bottling.

Of the two red wines, both well-balanced and very fruity, the 'Muga', exceptional in 1968, 1973 and 1976, is the lighter; 'Prado Enea' is fuller-bodied and deeper in flavour – the 1970 was one of the most complete Riojas that I can remember. Muga epitomizes a contradiction which lies at the heart of many of the very best wines of Rioja. When young and while maturing they are wines that feel too insubstantial to last. Yet their inherent balance keeps them safe and stable long enough for wonderful tapestries of flavour and aroma to emerge. The richer 'Prado Enea' is more obviously complete, yet the very transparency of what would formerly have been called the *clarete* of Muga allows you to perceive how subtle and lovely this wine is.

Muga also makes an attractive *cava*, the 'Conde de Haro', by the champagne method (see p. 147).

BODEGAS OLARRA, S.A.
The last of the great modern bodegas to be constructed during the boom of the seventies, Olarra occupies premises on the outskirts of

Logroño, bold in conception and in the form of a 'Y' to symbolize the three sub-regions of the Rioja. For all the computerized controls and battery of epoxy-lined steel fermentation tanks, the wines, once vinified, are matured in the traditional 225-litre oak *barricas*, and are of consistently high quality. Best are the red 'Cerro Añon' *reservas*, made with seventy per cent Tempranillo: full-bodied, fruity wines with good nose and finish. The fresh young cold-fermented white 'Blanco Reciente' is made with one hundred per cent Viura. In the first excitement of the great new bodega it seemed that Olarra wines might become some of Rioja's greatest. They have settled down to being merely very good.

BODEGAS R. LÓPEZ DE HEREDIA, VIÑA TONDONIA, S.A.

The brick-built headquarters of López de Heredia, with its steep tiled roofs, carved wooden facings and windows like a signal box, dominates the historic area of the old railway station in Haro. It dates from 1881, when the founder of the firm, Rafael López de Heredia, acquired the premises of the French *négociant* Armande Heff, and is strictly in keeping with the staunchly traditional nature of this firm, still in family hands.

Below the stone-built bodega, the network of cellars accommodates 14,000 oak *barricas*; the largest, El Calado, 17 m below ground level, tunnels into the sandstone for 200 m, and the temperature of 12°C and relative humidity of 80° remain the same all year. All the wine-making receptacles, including the fermentation vats, are of oak, and the wines are matured in oak for up to eight years, in the case of the *reservas*, and fined with egg-white.

The firm's four vineyards – Viña Tondonia, Viña Bosconia, Viña Cubillo and Viña Zaconia, totalling in all 170 hectares and planted with fifty per cent Tempranillo, thirty per cent Garnacha, ten per cent Graciano and ten per cent Mazuelo – have given their names to the wines.

These include a 3° *año* red 'Cubillo' which

opens out with age, while the 'Bosconia' and 'Tondonia' *reservas* are among the best reds from the Rioja. López de Heredia is one of the few bodegas which continues to mature its white wines in oak; the 1964 'Tondonia', aged for a surprising six years in cask and twelve in bottle, is still wonderfully fresh and round.

If there is one single bodega to visit to breathe the spirit of the region this is surely it. Traditionalism here is not only theatrical; it justifies itself in wines of startling and haunting character. 'López de Heredia' is the touchstone: love it and you love Rioja.

BODEGAS RIOJANAS

Dating from 1890, the old bodegas in Cenicero with their castellated keep were built with advice from Bordeaux. However, Riojanas has never made its wine entirely by Bordeaux methods, and part of it is still vinified in open *lagares* (see p. 87) by the traditional Rioja method approximating to *macération carbonique*.

Some fifty per cent of the wine is produced from the ten hectares of vineyards belonging to the firm and from another two hundred owned by shareholders. The young 2° *año* is labelled as 'Canchales' and the more mature red wines and *reservas* as 'Viña Albina' and 'Monte Real'. The 'Albina' is a good Rioja Alta wine, light, brisk and more acidic than the softer and faster-maturing 'Monte Real', made with eighty per cent Tempranillo from the Rioja Alavesa. Classic vintages were 1890, 1904, 1915, 1922, 1934, 1942, 1956, 1964, 1966, 1968 and 1970.

COMPAÑÍA VINÍCOLA DEL NORTE DE ESPAÑA (CVNE)

Eusebio Real de Asua y Ibarreta suffered from bronchitis and left the damp clime of his native Bilbao to set up the firm in Haro in 1879. Its first sales director, Luis Perré, had connections with the Cognac and Champagne industries in France, and in its early days CVNE made both brandy and sparkling wine, even setting up for a time in Reims itself. Meanwhile its still wines began winning gold medals and diplomas in the international exhibitions of the late nineteenth century: CVNE has always been a leading exporter.

Some sixty-five per cent of the wine is made from grapes grown in the firm's own 480 hectares of vineyards. Apart from its holdings in the Rioja Alta, CVNE also owns vineyards and a bodega near Elciego in the Rioja Alavesa and another estate of forty hectares at La Serna, bordering the Ebro west of Oyón. The grapes from here are used for a superior 'Contino' single vineyard wine, made with a blend of seventy per cent Tempranillo, seven per cent Garnacha and thirteen per cent Viura.

The other red wines are the $3°$ año 'Cune', good even in the disappointing year of 1977 and even better in later vintages, in particular the very fruity and full-bodied 1982; the well-balanced 'Imperial' *reservas*, especially those of 1966, 1973, 1975, 1976 and 1978, and the glorious 1968 and 1970; and the softer, more feminine 'Viña Real' from Elciego. The white, cold-fermented 'Monopole' strikes a happy mean between the traditional oaky white and the new-style wines without maturation in cask,

and is perhaps the model of what white Rioja should be if it wants to preserve its traditional identity. Balance and a certain firmness in the mouth are CVNE hallmarks. Bordeaux-drinkers find 'Imperial' a most satisfying and reliable point of entry into the exotic experiences of Rioja.

Ribera del Duero

The Ribera del Duero, as the name implies, lies along the valley of the River Duero (the Portuguese Douro), extending some 110 km from Tudela de Duero near Valladolid to El Burgo de Osmo in the east, with Aranda de Duero at its centre. It is a producer of red and rosé wines, some of the best coming from the chalky, pine-fringed slopes bordering the river. The predominant grapes are the Garnacha tinta and Tinto fino, akin to the Tempranillo of the Rioja. The Garnacha makes fresh young rosés,

The chimneys of small underground bodegas at Peñafiel, with the Moorish castle in the background.

but the red wines oxidize too readily to stand long maturation; the Tinto fino, on the other hand, produces wines particularly suited to long maturation in cask and bottle. Fruity, well-balanced and with fine aroma, they are among the most attractive red wines from Spain when well-made.

This is, in fact, one of the lesser-known regions of the country, with the greatest possibilities. The quality of the fruit is superb, though in the past it has often not been vinified with sufficient expertise. With improved methods in the cooperatives, of which the Cooperativa de Ribera del Duero in Peñafiel is in the forefront, and with the emergence of smaller private wineries like that of Peñalba López near Aranda de Duero, the wines are now coming into their own. The legendary Vega Sicilia at Valbuena, which uses a blend of native and French grapes, is, of course, in a class of its own and has long made some of the best and most prestigious wines from Spain.

VEGA SICILIA

The stories about this wine and its scarcity value are legion. At a banquet at the Spanish Embassy in London, Sir Winston Churchill once remarked: 'My vote goes to this unknown claret', and there is a joke in Spain that the Queen approached the bodega about supplying wine for Prince Charles's wedding, only to receive this reply from its illustrious *bodeguero*, Don Jesús Anadón: 'I can let you have two cases.'

The estate of nine hundred hectares lies on the south bank of the River Duero, extending back into the chalky hills with their clumps of pines. The first of the French grapes were acquired from nurseries in Bordeaux in 1864, and the vineyards are now planted with Cabernet Sauvignon, Merlot and Malbec, and with the native Tinto fino, Garnacha tinta and white Albillo. After the lightest of crushings they are vinified slowly for fifteen days, after which the must obtained without pressing is left in large oak vats for a year, and thereafter matured for long years in 225-litre oak *barricas*

and given a further two years in bottle. None of the 'Vega Sicilia' is sold less than ten years old, though a younger third or fifth year wine is available as 'Valbuena'. Although Valbuena is in every sense the junior of the two wines it is actually preferred by some drinkers, who find the sheer concentration and strength of 'Vega Sicilia' overwhelming. Certainly Valbuena makes the ideal 'stepping stone' wine for reaching the heroic heights of its elder brother.

The wines, all red, are deep in colour and intensely fruity with an unmistakable cedar-wood nose. I can only compare them to the old 'Barca Velha' table wine from the port house of Ferreira. They have been described as being old-fashioned with a degree of volatile acidity, but are of such quality as to weather such criticism from Masters of Wine and all comers.

Currently available vintages of 'Vega Sicilia' (you will be lucky to be allocated more than a bottle or two) are 1960, 1965, 1973 and the *Reserva Especial*; and the 'Valbuena' is of the 1978 and 1980 vintages.

COOPERATIVA DE RIBERA DEL DUERO

Founded in 1927, the cooperative is in Peñafiel, a few miles upstream of Vega Sicilia, a pleasant old up-and-downhill town dominated by a massive Moorish castle, beneath which the cooperative has extensive cellars for maturing its wines. It makes a fresh young rosé, a two-year-old 'Tinto fino' with an intense blackberry flavour, the much-admired five-year-old red 'Protos', and *reservas* with a long age in cask and bottle. The comparison between 'Protos' and the wines of 'Vega Sicilia' is that between a delicious but simplistic drink and a wine which is the result of most sophisticated craftsmanship.

BODEGAS PEÑALBA LÓPEZ

The bodegas and vineyards of this small family firm are just outside Aranda de Duero. With advice from Don Manuel Ruiz of the Estación de Viticultura y Enología in Haro, it has in recent years been making some of the best of the wine from Ribera del Duero. The fruity and well-balanced reds, such as those of 1976, 1979, 1981 and 1983, are made with one hundred per cent Tinto fino grown in the bodega's own vineyards, and are matured in cask and bottle. The fresh young 'Clarete', made from Tinto fino, Garnacha and Albillo, is in fact so light as to be a rosé.

Rueda

Rueda has been known for its white wines since the eleventh century, when the area was reconquered from the Moors and vineyards reestablished. Demarcated in 1980, this small region centres on the 'Tierra de Medina' and the villages of Rueda, Serrada, La Seca and Nava del Rey, just to the south-west of Valladolid.

High, windswept, bitterly cold in winter and with an annual rainfall of only fourteen inches, it produces wine of good quality but low in yield. The native grape is the white Verdejo, but there are even larger plantations of the Palomino (known locally as the 'Jerez'), and it was perhaps this which led to the making of maderized white wines, growing a *flor* (see p. 16) and reminiscent of a rough sherry. Wines of this sort are still made in some of the cooperatives, where they are matured either in *soleras* or out-of-doors in loosely stoppered glass carboys (or *bombonas*).

After a careful evaluation of the calcareous soils, the large Rioja firm of the Marqués de Riscal came to the conclusion that the area was better suited to the production of white wines than the Rioja itself, and has since planted Viura and Sauvignon Blanc in addition to Verdejo, vinifying the wines by modern techniques in temperature-controlled stainless steel tanks. Other producers have followed their example and this has led to something of a revolution; Rueda is now producing sizeable amounts of pale, fresh and fruity young white wine very much to the modern taste.

AGRÍCOLA CASTELLANA SOCIEDAD COOPERATIVA

With its storage capacity of eight million litres, this cooperative in La Seca is the largest winery in the region. Its 'Campo Grande fino' and 'Dorado 61' are traditional *flor*-growing wines with a sherry-like flavour, the best made in *solera* and others matured in loosely stoppered glass carboys in the open. Best of its new-type young wines is the 'Verdejo Palido', dry, fruity and fragrant with a greenish cast.

BODEGAS DE CRIANZA CASTILLA LA VIEJA

The firm was founded in 1974 by a group of local growers, and the bodega is equipped with stainless steel tanks, refrigeration machinery and oak casks for maturing the wines. Of these, the best-known is the fresh young white 'Marqués de Griñón', made from one hundred per cent Verdejo and not aged in oak. The wine has the virtues of freshness without a particularly memorable flavour. Certainly the Cabernet red grown by the same nobleman near Toledo is in a higher class in every way.

VINOS BLANCOS DE CASTILLA, S.A.

The Marqués de Riscal did not market a white wine until in 1972 it acquired vineyards around Rueda and with advice from Professor Peynaud of Bordeaux University constructed a large modern winery on the outskirts of the town. It is equipped with horizontal presses, batteries of stainless steel fermentation tanks and refrigeration machinery. The fresh and fruity young white 'Marqués de Riscal' is made with ninety per cent Verdejo and ten per cent Viura and is not aged in oak. The rather rounder and fuller 'Reserva Limousin' spends a few months in *barricas* of Limousin oak, and the bodega has recently begun making an attractive wine with one hundred per cent Sauvignon Blanc.

VINOS SANZ

Apart from the dry young 'Viña Cimbron', this old-established and sizeable family firm makes a range of wines, including a red aged in oak and an attractive dry rosé.

Undemarcated Wines

The best undemarcated wines from Old Castile are from the far north-west of the region.

Cigales, just north of Valladolid, has been famous for its light red wines since medieval times. They are properly made from a blend of black grapes (Garnacha, Tinto de País and Tinto Madrid) and white (Palomino, Verdejo and Albillo), destalked and fermented without skins or pips – but what passes for Cigales in the bars of Valladolid may as often as not be a blend of sturdy Zamora red, made in the area around Toro, and white wine from La Mancha. Production of genuine Cigales is dominated by two firms: HIJOS DE FRUTOS VILLAR and PABLO BARRIGÓN TOVAR.

El Bierzo, in the north-west of the province of León, makes fresh red, white and rosé wines, mainly from the black Mencía and Alicante and the white Palomino. The reds, containing not more than 12° of alcohol, are smooth and velvety, and the whites flowery and less acidic than those from neighbouring Galicia. Leading producers are BODEGAS VALDEOBISPO; LOS ARCOS, which makes a 'Santos Rosado' rosé with a refreshing touch of acidity; and the prestigious PALACIO DE ARGANZA, whose best-known wines are the fresh 'Vega Burbia' and red 'Almena del Bierzo' reserva. On the evidence of these two, particularly the latter, the region has scarcely realized potential for reds of medium weight and refreshing 'cut' – not entirely unlike some of the delicious reds of north-central Portugal.

To the south-east of the city of León, the districts of Los Oteros, La Bañeza and Valdevimbre grow a black grape with a white pulp, the Prieto Picudo, which produces more than drinkable red and rosé wines. In the past they were made in tiny peasant bodegas, constructed by digging deep into the ground, positioning a ponderous beam press, then roofing over the chamber and leaving a chimney for the escape of the carbon dioxide produced during ferment-

Peasant bodegas tunnelled in the ground, near León.

ation of the wine. Dug side by side, they resemble nothing so much as giant ant-heaps.

More recently a consortium of local growers has constructed a large and modern winery, PLANTA DE ELABORACIÓN Y EMBOTELLADO DE VINOS (VILE) on the outskirts of the city of León. Its well-made wines, red, white and rosé, are sold as the 2° *año* 'Viña Coyanza' and more mature 'Catedral de León' and 'Palacio de los Guzmanes'. The red 'Don Suero' *reserva*, with its nice balance of fruit and oak and long finish, is a most satisfying wine. This is, however, a region where the best is still the only wine to choose. A careless order for a carafe of wine will bring a dark rosé of sinister strength.

At the other extreme of Old Castile, between Madrid and Avila, Cebreros has long been known for sturdy red wines, often sold in litre bottles in Madrid, and of a strength that left one reeling. In line with modern tastes, they are now being lightened.

The Cuisine

In gastronomic terms it is sometimes difficult to draw distinctions between Old and New Castile. They share many of the basic ingredients: lamb from the rolling plains, partridge from the mountains, trout from the cold streams (almost every region of Spain claims that *its* trout is the best, and a good Castilian version is *truchas a la montañesa*, cooked with white wine, bay leaves and onions), and the ubiquitous chick-pea and other vegetables in plenty. The *cocido*, a substantial stew of meat and vegetables, is popular in both areas. If one had to name a single type of dish most typical of Old Castile, it would be the roasts of lamb, sucking pig and kid; and for this reason the area is known as the *Zona de los Asados*.

Both Avila and Segovia are renowned for their *cochinillo* (roast sucking pig), prepared from milk-fed piglets, smaller than those usually available abroad, cooked in a baker's oven.

At the famous Mesón de Cándido in Segovia, it is so tender and succulent that the waiters habitually cut the portions with the edge of a plate. *Lechazo*, or roast milk-fed lamb, is perhaps at its best in the north of the region around Valladolid, where it is also cooked in a baker's oven. Another speciality of Avila is the *yemas de Santa Teresa*, a Moorish-inspired sweetmeat made with egg-yolks and sugar and flavoured with cinnamon and lemon peel.

As befits the high tables of its ancient university, Salamanca has a long history of culinary splendour, vividly described by Julián Manuel de Sabando:

> The table is set for, say, eighteen persons, with the finest white porcelain. Each setting is of four plates one above another, a fork, two knives, one large and two small glasses, and a cruet, in addition to polished silver trays and candelabra. In front of each diner is a round wooden box and a large porcelain basin with a lid: the first contains sweetmeats and the second *manjar blanco*, a confection made of rice flour, milk and sugar, sometimes with the addition of minced chicken breasts or ground almonds. The professors and

The flamboyant proprietor of the Mesón de Cándido in Segovia, where *cochinillo* (roast sucking pig) is so tender that it is traditionally cut with the side of a plate.

graduates sit at table and are served by six students chosen for the task. After the preliminaries each diner is served with a roast bird, often turkey . . .

This was a liberal interpretation of the

Harvesting lentils in Old Castile, a region noted for its vegetables and particularly for its many varieties of beans.

university's statutes, which required that every student offering himself for examination should give to each of his examiners, and also to the doctors and masters of the faculty, a variety of fare, including meats, confectionery and three brace of fowl; he was also obliged to entertain them to supper for the whole period of the exams. It is to be hoped that these were not prolonged!

Richard Ford, writing in the 1840s, fills out

this description when he describes the dons as:

> siestose men of protruding and pendulous abdomens... Even up to 1747 it was considered a heresy to assert that the sun did not revolve around the earth; so that the capon revolved around the spit, what cared the senior fellows and drony Doctors, contented when not sleeping to suck in the milk of Alma Mater...?

Riojan cooking is typical of that of Old Castile as a whole. In Spain the region is almost as well known for its vegetables, grown by the smallholders in plots among their vineyards, as for its wines. Potatoes and beans are grown everywhere, and the Rioja Baja in the warm south-east of the area is particularly noted for its red peppers, peaches and asparagus, often served as a starter with mayonnaise. A favourite dish is the *menestra riojana*, made with fresh broad beans, peas, *acelgas* (a type of spinach) and *cardo* (cardoon) or whatever is in season, cooked in olive oil and wine with onions, tomatoes, bacon or ham, and sometimes hard-boiled eggs. *Patatas riojanas*, potatoes in an orange-coloured sauce made from the spicy *chorizo* sausage, are an institution and were much commended by Paul Bocuse when he was engaged by the Compañía Vinícola del Norte de España to cook its centenary banquet. *Chorizo* is also roasted whole *a la brasa* or ground as *picada* before being cooked, both piquant dishes calling for a cold glass of one of the new-style white Riojas. In yet another guise it appears in *pochas riojanas*, another warming dish for cold weather, made with a local variety of haricot bean, allowed to fatten in the pod, but not dried. The red or green peppers may be grilled and served on the side or made into *pimientos rellenos a la riojana*, the local variant of stuffed peppers, filled with a mixture of ground pork, beaten egg, garlic, parsley and spices, fried in hot olive oil and accompanied by a piquant sauce.

Especially in the Rioja Baja, you will see wandering flocks of sheep throwing up clouds of dust from the parched pasturage, accompanied by a shepherd with his trusty leather *bota* and watchful dog. The favourite forms of meat are the *cordero lechal asado* (milk-fed lamb), at its best from the baker's oven of Terete's restaurant in Haro, and *chuletas de cordero*. These lamb chops are often served at lunches in the bodegas, and are cooked by making a roaring blaze of dry vine shoots, raking it out and grilling the chops on a large metal grid placed over the glowing embers. The delicious *cabrito asado* (roast kid) is cooked like the *cordero lechal*.

There is no great variety of sweets, but try the *torrijas*, served with warm honey and ground almonds and made by soaking slices of bread in sherry, sugar and cinnamon, dredging them in beaten egg and frying them crisp in olive oil; or *leche frita*, fried strips or squares of béchamel, sweetened with sugar and flavoured with cinnamon. Perhaps the best way of finishing a meal is with fresh fruit in season or with the *melocotones en almíbar*, the luscious, locally grown peaches preserved in syrup. There is a fresh local goat's cheese, *queso fresco de montaña* (also known as *Camerano*, from the Sierra de Cameros near Logroño, where it is made) ripened for only twenty-four hours; the excellent Roncal (see p. 127) from neighbouring Navarra is also widely available.

Restaurants

Aranda de Duero

MESÓN DE LA VILLA★★
This stronghold of regional cooking organizes an annual *Semana del Cordero* ('Lamb Week'), during which lamb is served as *cordero asado* (roast lamb), *chuletitas* (cutlets), *manitas* (lamb's feet), *mollejas* (sweetbreads), *riñones* (kidneys) and *sesos* (brains). Other specialities are the local *morcilla* (black pudding), *cangrejos de río* (river crayfish), *alubias estofadas* (haricot bean stew) and, in winter, the unusual *ardilla*

con piñones (squirrel with pine kernels). Good Torremilanos wines from the neighbouring bodega.

Burgos

LANDA PALACE★★

This meticulously run hotel, atmospherically housed in an old castle, has an excellent restaurant. Regional dishes include *morcilla de Burgos* (the local black pudding), roast lamb and *chuletitas* (lamb cutlets) and *olla podrida* (meat and vegetable stew), as well as fifteen different types of bread. There are also French-inspired dishes such as the *lubina al hojaldre* (bass with puff pastry), *brocheta de vieiras en camisa* (brochette of scallops with fluffy mayonnaise) and profiteroles.

León

NOVELTY★★

A sophisticated restaurant which makes good use of the excellent locally grown vegetables and offers well-cooked meat and a range of *charcuterie* from the region. Some of its specialities are *zancarrondé de ternera* (veal), *pescados al horno* (baked fish), salmon and *cola de vaca* (oxtail). To finish, there is a choice of fresh fruit salad, nougat and coffee ice cream or *queso añejo* (matured cheese). Local wines from León and also from the Rioja and Ribera del Duero.

REY DON SANCHO★

It is worth eating here, since one should not visit León without at least looking around the magnificent Hotel San Marcos, of which this is the restaurant. The service is attentive and the ambience charming, and there are a number of regional dishes, such as the trout soup, *pimientos del Bierzo con jamón* (peppers with ham) and first-rate lamb chops. Good local wines from El Bierzo.

Salamanca

CHEZ VICTOR★★

Victor trained in France and his wife is French; this shows in the sophistication of the food. Good dishes are the leek and aubergine mousse, *crêpes de changurro* (spider crab crêpes), *vieiras al noilly con pasta fresca* (sea scallops in vermouth with fresh pasta), *rape estofado con verduras* (stewed monkfish with vegetables) and *magret* of duck.

Santander

EL MOLINO★★★

Victor Merino was the founder of the 'New Cantabrian Cooking', aimed at reducing fats, lightening the dishes and using fruit and vegetable juices for the salads. Among a wide variety of innovative dishes at this restaurant in Puente Arce, some 15 km from Santander, are salads of bass or monkfish dressed with lemon juice and clams, fresh anchovy omelette, peppers stuffed with fish, escalopes of veal with *níscalos* (edible fungi) and anchovy sauce, and fillet steak with Cabrales cheese. Good local cheeses, sorbets and tarts, of which the best is the fig.

BAR DEL PUERTO★★

The great seaport with its holiday beaches on the fringe of the Basque country is full of bars and restaurants serving the wonderful local seafood, of which one of the best is the Bar del Puerto. Ask for the *percebes* (edible barnacles) in season, clams, spider crab, lobster salad, *calamares a la romana* (fried squid in rings) or *ventreska de bonito* (fresh tuna).

Segovia

MESÓN DE CÁNDIDO★★

This venerable establishment in the shadow of the great Roman aqueduct was founded at the time of Henry IV (1454-74), when a certain Pedro de Cuéllar, a servant of the king's paymaster, lost a leg in his master's service, was pensioned off and opened a hostelry in Segovia, where he was helped by his wife and daughters. In about 1860 the *taberna*, as it now was, was in the hands of the Duque family, who began to specialize in preparing good food, and on the death of Dionisio Duque in 1931 it was taken over by his brother-in-law, Cándido López, whose son has consolidated its reputation. It is known far and wide for its *tostones*, or roast sucking pigs.

Valladolid

MESÓN PANERO★★

Panero offers a wide range of roast meats and classical dishes of Castile, as well as fish from the Bay of Biscay and specialities of its own, such as venison with cherries, woodcock stuffed with chestnuts, lamb's livers with apple purée, *revuelto de ajos tiernos y setas* (eggs scrambled with garlic shoots and mushrooms) and *cocido maragato* (chick-pea stew). There is a very extensive list of wines from Rueda and the Ribera del Duero, including Vega Sicilia.

La Rioja

Arnedo

SOPITAS★

The restaurant tunnels into the red sandstone cliffs overhanging the picturesque little town in the Rioja Baja, and is divided into small alcoves with swing doors giving off the main chamber. The cooking is homely but good, and its repertoire of regional dishes includes *menestra* (mixed vegetable dish), *revuelto de ajo* (scrambled egg with garlic shoots), roast baby kid, *malvices* (fried redwing), roast partridge and *melocotones en almíbar* (local peaches in syrup).

Haro

TERETE★

One passes the baker's oven in which the meat is roasted on the stairs to the upper floor restaurant. The spartan surroundings and scrubbed wooden tables belie the excellence of dishes like the *lechazo* (roast milk-fed lamb) and *pimientos rellenos a la riojana*; and Terete, a favourite haunt of the *bodegueros* in Haro, is always crowded to the doors.

BEETHOVEN II ★

Quaintly named because of the deafness of the proprietor, one may here, in more sophisticated surroundings, also eat first-rate *lechazo* and other regional dishes. There is an extensive list of Rioja wines.

Logroño

LA MERCED★★★

Housed in an old palace and magnificently decorated, this is far and away the most luxurious restaurant in the Rioja. It offers regional dishes such as *menestra* (mixed fresh vegetable dish) and *lechazo* (roast baby lamb) in their most sophisticated form, and its chef has a light touch with puff pastry in such specialities as *hojaldre con setas*, a starter in which the pastry is filled with mushrooms, or the *hojaldre de almendras*, a delicious almond sweet. As might be expected, there is a long list of vintage Riojas.

Santo Domingo de la Calzada

PARADOR NACIONAL DE SANTO DOMINGO DE LA CALZADA

The Parador, housed in a medieval hospice for pilgrims and centred on a hall with Gothic arches, is a pleasant place to stay when visiting the Rioja. The dining room serves a number of regional dishes, and there is a good list of Rioja wines.

Recipes

Pollo Salteado a la Riojana/Sautéed Chicken Rioja Style

Serves 4

METRIC/IMPERIAL	AMERICAN
Olive oil for frying	Olive oil for frying
$1\frac{1}{2}$ kg/$3\frac{1}{4}$ lbs chicken (a mixture of breasts and drumsticks, the breasts cut into strips), floured	$3\frac{1}{4}$ lbs chicken (a mixture of breasts and drumsticks, the breasts cut into strips), floured
2 large onions, peeled and finely chopped	2 large onions, peeled and finely chopped
2 cloves garlic, chopped	2 cloves garlic, chopped
4 large red peppers, grilled, skinned and cut into strips, or 450 g/16 oz canned red peppers cut into strips (reserve the liquid)	4 large red peppers, grilled, skinned and cut into strips, or 16 oz canned pimientos cut into strips (reserve the liquid)
Salt and pepper	Salt and pepper
225 ml/8 fl oz chicken stock and liquid from canned red peppers	1 cup chicken stock and liquid from canned pimientos

Garnish

$\frac{1}{2}$ kg/1 lb 2 oz freshly boiled asparagus or equivalent of asparagus tips from a can (reserve liquid)	1 lb 2 oz freshly boiled asparagus or equivalent of asparagus tips from a can (reserve liquid)
150 g/5 oz *chorizo*, thinly sliced (if available)	5 oz *chorizo*, thinly sliced (if available)

Heat some olive oil in a heavy pan and fry the chicken. Remove with a slotted spoon and reserve on a plate. In the remaining oil, sauté the onions for about ten minutes until soft but not brown, and add the garlic. Drain off any oil and keep in a clean jar for further use. Now add the peppers and salt and pepper; return the chicken to the pan, add stock, and cook slowly on a low heat, shaking the pan from time to time until done. This will take about thirty minutes, but taste to make sure that the meat is tender and give it a little longer if necessary. Garnish with the asparagus and *chorizo* before serving.

Cordero Asado a la Riojana/Roast Lamb Rioja Style

Serves 4

METRIC/IMPERIAL	AMERICAN
2 onions, peeled and cut into rings	2 onions, peeled and cut into rings
4 bay leaves	4 bay leaves
6 peppercorns	6 peppercorns
2 kg/4½ lbs leg of lamb, boned	4½ lbs leg of lamb, boned
Salt	Salt
2 tablespoons olive oil	2 tablespoons olive oil
2 glasses (300 ml/10 fl oz) dry white Rioja wine	1⅓ cups dry white Rioja wine
2 tablespoons chopped parsley	2 tablespoons chopped parsley
3 cloves garlic, chopped	3 cloves garlic, chopped
1 tablespoon wine vinegar	1 tablespoon wine vinegar

Make a bed of onions, bay leaves and peppercorns in a roasting pan. Put the lamb on top, sprinkle with salt, pour on the olive oil and one glass of wine, and roast for twenty-five minutes per pound at 350°F/180°C/Gas Mark 4, basting from time to time. When the meat is done, let it rest for about ten minutes before carving.

Meanwhile pour the juices into a frying pan and cook the parsley and garlic, adding the vinegar before the garlic changes colour. Add the second glass of wine, cook and reduce for a few minutes further and pour on top of the lamb.

Serve with a salad and boiled new potatoes.

Leche Frita/'Fried Milk'

Serves 4

A popular sweet

METRIC/IMPERIAL	AMERICAN
4 eggs, beaten	4 eggs, beaten
4 tablespoons flour	4 tablespoons flour
4 tablespoons caster sugar	4 tablespoons fine white sugar
300 ml/½ pint milk	1 cup milk
1 stick cinnamon	1 stick cinnamon
25 g/1 oz butter	2 tablespoons butter
Flour for coating	Flour for coating
Olive oil for frying	Olive oil for frying

Pour two of the beaten eggs into a saucepan and add the flour, sugar, milk, cinnamon stick and butter. Stir well together, then simmer over a low heat, continuing to stir until the mixture thickens. Butter a large dish, spread out the dough and allow it to cool.

Now cut it into strips or other shapes, coat them with the other two beaten eggs and dredge with flour, then fry in smoking hot olive oil until browned. They may be fried either in deep or shallow oil; if using shallow oil, turn them over once. Powder with extra sugar, arrange on a serving dish and serve without delay.

Aragón and Navarra

THE MEDIEVAL KINGDOMS of Aragón and Navarra in northern Spain both played a part in the Reconquest of the country from the Moors. The fortunes of Aragón reached a zenith under Alfonso *El Batallador* ('The Battler'), who reoccupied most of the Ebro basin and struck deep into al-Andalus, though he was unable to achieve his objective of recapturing Granada from the Moors. In the words of the chronicler Ibn al-Athir, 'No Christian prince was more valorous than he or possessed such ardour for fighting the Muslims or such powers of resistance ... With his death Allah allowed the faithful to breathe again, free from his hammer blows.' Shortly after this, the shrewd Ramón Berenguer IV of Barcelona succeeded in uniting Aragón and Catalonia by marrying Alfonso's granddaughter in 1137; thereafter the two states were linked under the Crown of Aragón, controlled by the Counts of Barcelona, and during the next three centuries Aragón became one of the most powerful maritime and trading nations of the Mediterranean.

Centring on Pamplona, Navarra at one time extended across the Pyrenees into France; hence the alternative spelling of 'Navarre' and its many links with Béarn. The small half-Basque state, hemmed in as it was by more powerful neighbours, was unable to expand at the expense of the Moors and became fair game for the territorial ambitions of Castile, the Crown of Aragón and France. Successive rulers prolonged its existence by exploiting the differences between the bordering states, but in 1512 it fell to Ferdinand the Catholic and it was then incorporated in Castile, the area across the Pyrenees going to France.

RIGHT **The famous Basílica of Nuestra Señora del Pilar reflected in the River Ebro. This enormous church was built in the seventeenth and eighteenth centuries.**

PREVIOUS PAGE **The vineyards of the Señorío de Sarría, with the Sierra del Perdón beyond.**

BELOW **The Moorish castle which towers above Molina de Aragón.**

The most interesting place in Aragón is Zaragoza (Saragossa), dominated by the great Basílica del Pilar, a domed Renaissance building at the end of the long stone bridge across the River Ebro. It was built to house a small chapel founded by St James in commemoration of a miraculous apparition of the Virgin Mary in AD 40; and the Festival of El Pilar on 12 October, celebrated with services, processions and bull-fights, is the most important in Spain's religious calendar. There is also a fine Gothic cathedral, the so-called Seo, while historical remains dating from Roman times include the Moorish Aljafería with figured plasterwork and beautiful, raftered *artesonado* ceilings.

The capital of Navarra is Pamplona, famous for the bull-running through its streets during the Festival of San Fermín in early July, so evocatively described by Ernest Hemingway in *The Sun Also Rises*. It is an elegant city with an imposing medieval cathedral and a vast arcaded square at the centre, with seas of tables from the adjoining cafés and restaurants spilling over into it. Less than an hour's drive from Pamplona, high in the wooded Pyrenees near the French border, is the Pass of Roncesvalles, where Charlemagne's rearguard was ambushed by the Basques and Roland was killed. The medieval monastery nearby, built as a staging post for pilgrims to Santiago de Compostela, is well worth a visit; and the village of Burguete, a few more kilometres into Spain, is popular with sportsmen, who come from both sides of the frontier to fish and shoot pigeon. It was here that Hemingway stayed to catch trout in the mountain streams. In these Pyrenean valleys,

A shepherd and his flock in the valley of the River Ebro, where wheat, soft fruits – particularly peaches – and olives are grown.

especially on the French side, the pigeons are also netted by driving them up the steep defiles, one party of beaters advancing from the bottom and the others, stationed along the heights on either side, launching wooden batons shaped like hawks so as to keep the flock of pigeons low and direct it into a large net stretched across the top.

Another evocative place is the town of Olite, in less hilly country to the south of Pamplona and more or less in the centre of the wine-growing area. Its fortified palace, begun by Charles the Noble in 1403 and for long a favourite residence of the Kings of Navarra, was one of the largest and most elaborate in Spain, and it is said that it possessed one room for every day in the year. The castle subsequently fell into disuse and only three of the original fifteen towers survive, but it has since been carefully restored and opened as a Parador. Some of the bedrooms have been equipped with four-posters; and as always in such establishments, one must be prepared for the knight in armour or chainmail in an angle of the stairs.

The little town of Puente la Reina, half-way between Pamplona and Olite and on the threshold of the famous vineyards of the Señorío de Sarría, was on the path trodden by the pilgrims from France to the shrine of St James in Santiago de Compostela, and its great stone bridge over the River Arga, with a medieval tower and arch at one end, marked the junction of the routes through the Pyrenees by Roncesvalles and Somport. It is a half-forgotten place, full of mellow, sun-baked Romanesque churches decorated with the scallop shells worn as a badge by the faithful.

A little to the west, Estella, also on the pilgrim route, was another stronghold of the Kings of Navarra. With its old houses rising above the River Ega and its medieval churches with their wealth of sculpture and paintings, it has been called the Toledo of the north.

These are little-known places off the tourist circuit, but well worth exploring.

The bridge over the River Arga at Puente la Reina, which marks the junction of the pilgrim routes to Santiago from France, via Roncesvalles and Somport.

The Wines

Aragón

There is a long tradition of wine-making in Aragón. The best-known of its regions, Cariñena, takes its name from the Roman town of Carae; and it is on record that its inhabitants drank wine mixed with honey in the third century BC. The process of demarcation began as long ago as 1694 when the growers were forbidden to plant new vineyards without a licence. Today there are three demarcated regions: Cariñena, to the south of Zaragoza; Borja, to its east; and the newly demarcated Somontano in the foothills of the Pyrenees to the north.

In the harsh climatic conditions of freezing winters, hot summers and strong winds, the vine that does best is the sturdy black Garnacha, although smaller amounts of other black grapes are grown and also a little of the white Garnacha blanca and Viura. Oddly enough, the black Cariñena is much more widely grown in Catalonia (also in France as the Carignan).

The traditional wines from Aragón are dark red in colour, high in extract and sometimes contain as much as 17–18° (per cent by volume) of alcohol. For this reason, they have been much in demand for blending, and at the height of the phylloxera epidemic the Bordeaux firm of Violet maintained a large establishment in Cariñena for shipping them to France. Most of the cooperative-made wine is marketed in litre bottles, and a great deal of it is sold up and down Spain. However, wine of a block-busting 17° is clearly unsuitable for foreign markets, and forward-looking establishments are beginning to lighten their wines both by earlier picking of the grapes and by installing temperature-controlled fermentation vats. This is making it possible to mature them in oak casks, with a further period of ageing in bottle to allow for development of bouquet and flavour.

The traditional Cariñena is a purplish-ruby colour with a bouquet of violets, 13–17° in strength, full-bodied and deep in flavour and becoming smoother and silkier when aged in oak. Although a very good old Cariñena is rarely seen it is possible to imagine the region producing very fine wine as modern techniques come into wider use.

The strongest wines are from the Campo de Borja, from which the Borgia family took its name – the ancestral castle still survives in the town of Borja.

The Somontano wines, made from a variety of grape varieties in addition to the black Garnacha, are lower in alcohol (12–13°), perfumed, lighter on the palate and slightly acidic. At the turn of the century they were popular in France.

BODEGA COOPERATIVA SAN VALERO

The largest and best-known of the wineries in Cariñena, San Valero now makes some of its wines in temperature-controlled stainless steel tanks and ages the best of the reds in oak casks. The traditional wines, both red and white, are labelled as 'Villalta', 'Monte Ducay' and 'Don Mendo'. The new-style 'Perçebal Rosado' is a vin gris containing only 11° of alcohol, fresh, a trifle sweet with slight pétillance, very clean, but without marked fruit or character.

BODEGA COOPERATIVA COMARCAL DEL SOMONTANO

Founded twenty years ago for making and marketing wine in bulk, this large cooperative changed course in 1980, installing temperature-controlled vats for making the whites and rosés, and oak casks for maturing the reds. It now makes and bottles superior Somontano wines labelled as 'Selección Montesierra Rosado', 'Selección Montesierra Tinto' and 'Selección Montesierra Tinto Monasterio'.

BODEGA ENRIQUE LÓPEZ PELAYO

The much-respected Don Enrique López Pelayo makes good quality red Cariñena available only locally and in Zaragoza. The old 'Cueva de Algairén' reservas are robust wines of great character.

BODEGAS HERMANOS BORDEJÉ MOGÜERZA
(CAMPO DE BORJA)

Though the bodega is tiny, Don Miguel Angel Bordejé makes wines of such character (and not unduly strong for Borja) that they are known nationally. The reds are labelled as 'Don Pablo' and 'Abuelo Nicolás', and the white, from the name of the grape, as 'Macabeo'.

BODEGAS LALANE
(SOMONTANO)

Of French origin, this old-established bodega makes some of the best Somontano wine, labelled as 'Lalane, tinto 3° año', 'Viña San Marcos, rosado, 3° año' and an older 'Lalane tinto', round and well-balanced.

VICENTE SUSO Y PÉREZ, S.A.

One of the best-known private bodegas in Cariñena, making wines of moderate strength and ageing them in oak. Its labels are 'Don Ramón' red and rosé; 'Comendador' *reservas*; and 'Duque de Sevilla', 'Mosen Cleto' and 'Viña Tito' reds.

Navarra

There is a tendency for the wines from Navarra to be overshadowed by those of the neighbouring and more famous Rioja; in fact, some thirteen per cent of the Rioja lies within the province of Navarra, and but for a historic feud between the two regions, much larger areas of Navarra might logically have been included in the *Denominación de Origen* Rioja when it was first codified in 1926, since the large Rioja firms had for long been buying wine from as far afield as Olite and Tudela.

Navarra has been known for its red wines and for rosés among the best in Spain since Roman times and has been exporting them for centuries (they were favourites of Catherine the Great of Russia in the eighteenth century). It was one of the first regions in Spain to organize cooperative wineries, of which it now has seventy-four, accounting for eighty per cent of production.

Energetic efforts are currently being made to modernize equipment and to introduce new methods of vinification, and this is bearing fruit in a general improvement in the quality of the wines and increased sales abroad.

The geography, soils and climate are very varied, the land falling away from the Pyrenees in the north to the much drier and more Mediterranean-like Ebro basin in the south. The predominant grapes are the black varieties grown in the Rioja: the Garnacha (used for the famous rosés), Tempranillo, Graciano and Mazuelo; smaller amounts of the white Viura and Malvasía are also cultivated, and Corella just south of the River Ebro makes a small amount of sweet Moscatel.

When Navarra was demarcated in 1958, five sub-zones were designated. All are south of Pamplona, and from north to south they are:

Valdizarbe

With its chalky soils and temperate climate, this area produces red and rosé wines like those from the Señorío de Sarría and Vinícola Navarra, considered to be among the best from Navarra. The predominant grape is the black Tempranillo.

Tierra de Estella

Lying to the west of Valdizarbe and bordering the Rioja, the sub-zone has much in common with Valdizarbe and makes excellent table wines particularly suitable for maturing in oak.

Baja Montaña

To the east of the province, this is the wettest of the wine-growing areas and marks the northern limit of cultivation. It produces red wines of intense ruby colour, and its fragrant rosés are perhaps the best from Navarra.

La Ribera Alta

This large sub-zone produces some thirty per cent of the wine from the demarcated region. Olite, in the centre of Navarra's wine-growing area, is best known for its fragrant and fruity rosés, but also produces red wine and a little white. Lerín, to the west, makes sturdy reds; and Marcilla, further south, produces fruity enough white, red and rosé wines, which tend to oxidize if aged.

La Ribera Baja

The climate of this most southerly of the *comarcas* is much drier and hotter than that of the other areas. It lies both sides of the River Ebro and the soils contain a great deal of alluvial silt. The wine-making centres of Cintruénigo and Cascante make large amounts of strong, full-bodied red wine.

Only a limited number of the wineries mature their wines in oak and bottle them, but thanks to the energetic efforts of the well-equipped oenological station at Olite, the situation is rapidly changing.

BODEGAS CARRICAS, S.A.

The bodegas are picturesquely located in the subterranean passages of the fifteenth-century castle of Olite. They are of interest for making a red 'Mont-Plané' from whole grapes by *macération carbonique*, a light and fruity young wine entirely different in style to the traditional red Navarra. The innovative Carricas brothers also make a sparkling wine by the *cuve close* process.

BODEGAS IRACHE, S.L.

The bodega is next door to the beautiful monastery of Irache, near Estella and on the old pilgrim route to Santiago. Built to harmonize with the old monastic buildings, it contains some two thousand *barricas* of American oak for maturing the older red wines. Labelled as 'Gran Reserva Irache', 'Castillo Irache', 'Viña Ordoy' and 'Gran Irache', these are obtainable only in Spain. The plum-coloured and full-bodied two-year-old 'Irache' shipped to the UK makes pleasant enough everyday drinking.

BODEGAS JULIAN CHIVITE

This family firm with headquarters in Cintruénigo near Tudela in the Ribera Baja has further vineyards and bodegas in other parts of Navarra and the provinces of Logroño and Aragón. With a total capacity of some nineteen million litres, it is by far the largest private wine concern in Navarra. The most mature of its fruity and full-bodied red wines is the 'Cirbonero', a wine with oaky nose and long finish. The younger wines, red, white and rosé, are labelled as 'Castillo de Mélida' and 'Gran Feudo'; a more recent introduction is a very pale, fresh and fragrant white 'Baronesa' cold-fermented in stainless steel. 'Gran Fuedo' red is a good example of what Navarra can achieve today: clean, balanced and satisfying up to a point, without the real character to make it memorable.

BODEGAS OCHOA

This small firm has been in family hands since 1845, and its oenologist, Don Javier Ochoa, is one of the most expert in the region. It owns twelve hectares of vineyards near Olite in the Ribera Alta and also buys grapes and wine from within the demarcated region. All of its wines are well-made by modern methods. The more mature reds, sold as 'Tinto Ochoa', are deep ruby in colour, harmonious and intense in flavour. The rosé 'Ochoa' and 'Chapitel' are clean and extremely fruity, and the white 'Ochoa', which should be drunk young, is an excellent example of a fruity Viura wine.

BODEGAS SEÑORÍO DE SARRÍA

The Señorío has been making some of the best Navarra wines since the thirteenth century, but in their present form the vineyards and bodega date from 1952, when Don Félix Huarte, of the large Spanish construction firm, bought the abandoned 1,200-hectare estate, planting orchards and cereals, creating a large stock-raising establishment, replanting the vineyards, transferring the bodegas from Puente la Reina to a new model winery and building a palatial mansion in the style of a French château. It is a little kingdom of its own, with a church, school, general store, pelota court, swimming pool and some forty miles of cypress-lined roads.

With the departure of the Huarte family in

1981, the property was bought by a local bank, the Caja de Ahorros de Navarra, but the wines continue to be made by the expert Don Francisco Moriones, who built up their reputation both in Spain and abroad. The vineyards are planted on the rolling slopes of the Sierra del Perdón, with the black Tempranillo (sixty per cent), Garnacha (twenty per cent), Graciano (ten per cent), Mazuelo (ten per cent), together with smaller amounts of Cabernet Sauvignon and the white Malvasía, Viura and Garnacha blanca. With a very sizeable production of one and a half million litres, the bodega possesses some six thousand *barricas* of American, Limousin and Yugoslav oak, made in its own cooper's yard, for maturing the red wines.

The younger wines are sold as the red and rosé 'Vina Ecoyen' and the dry and semi-dry 'Blanco Señorío de Sarría', of which the rosé is particularly fresh and fruity. Both of the mature reds, the 'Viña del Perdon' and 'Gran Vino del Señorío de Sarría', are mellow and fruity with long finish and more than a hint of oak in the nose in the style of good Riojas. Mouth-filling without being heavy, perhaps slightly cloyingly fragrant, they are certainly very good value for money.

VINÍCOLA NAVARRA, S.A.

Located in the village of Las Campanas in Valdizarbe, the firm was founded in 1880 and its bodegas are built against the wall of an old abbey on the pilgrim route. It still uses large oak vats inherited from an earlier French concern to begin maturation of the wines, which are then further aged in 225-litre *barricas*. Its younger wines, red, white and rosé, are labelled as 'Bandeo', 'Alaiz' and 'Las Campanas' (sold in some markets as 'Castillo de Olite'). The best of its wines is the fruity and full-bodied five-year-old 'Castillo de Tiebas' (also available in older vintages) which has slowly evolved into a reliable representative of the native style of Navarra. In the modern market it tends to be overtaken by newer concerns such as Cenalsa.

The Cuisine

Zaragoza has always been renowned for its cuisine, which includes such delicacies as the *sopas de ajo* (garlic soups with lemon and seasoning), *angulas con judías* (freshwater eels with chick-peas), *bacalao a la zaragozana* (made from dried and salted cod) and *lomo de cerdo a la zaragozana* (loin of pork in its special sauce). Aragón is often labelled the *Zona de los Chilindrones*, in recognition of the famous *chilindrón* sauce, made from onions, tomatoes, peppers and garlic, which may accompany either lamb (*cordero en chilindrón*) or chicken (*pollo en chilindrón*).

Migas or savoury fried breadcrumbs are popular all over Spain, and are sometimes said to predate the invasions of classical times and to be an Iberian survival. Particularly associated with Aragón, they are humble enough peasant fare, but are reputed to have been a favourite not only of El Cid, but also of James the Conqueror of Catalonia and the ill-starred Lovers of Teruel.

If you drive south from Zaragoza to Teruel, you will pass mile upon mile of gardens and orchards which produce some of the most luscious fruit in Spain, including peaches, plums, apricots, apples, cherries and strawberries.

The vegetables are no less excellent ; and one salad, prescribed by his doctor for the ailing Martin the Humane, has found its way into the pages of Spanish (not to say medical) history. It was prepared very simply, by making four criss-cross cuts in a raw white Aragonese cabbage and inserting the cut leaves of the curly cardoon (a species of edible thistle). Conrado Solsona, who unearthed the story, goes on to explain :

> The good king of Aragón ate the salad every night, but as the years passed and his lymph accumulated, the royal doctor ordered a modified diet to alleviate his complaint. All dishes containing gelatin, fats and syrups were eliminated and replaced by those rich in protein and roughage.

Even the salad came under review, and while the cabbage and cardoon were retained, they were augmented with lettuce leaves, reputedly rich in protein. It is for this reason the saying goes that lettuce 'makes blood'...

There is a refrain current in Aragón which almost certainly echoes the words of Don Martín's doctor: 'Between cabbage and cabbage ... lettuce.'

The mountains of both Aragón and Navarra are famous for their lamb. In Aragón it may be roasted or served as the picturesquely named *esparragos montañeses* ('mountain asparagus') – in fact, the lambs' tails, stewed and served in a sauce of tomatoes and peppers. Equally well-known in Navarra is the *cochifrito*, made by cooking the particularly tender milk-fed lamb, known as *Tres Madres* ('Three Mothers'), with onion, garlic, pepper, parsley and lemon juice. *Chuletas de cordero a la Navarra* (lamb chops Navarra style) are served with a sauce prepared by frying onion and tomato with ham and garnished with *chorizo* (see p. 195).

Vegetable dishes from Navarra include *menestra de habas de Tudela* (fresh broad beans cooked with garlic, mint, saffron, almonds, artichoke hearts, boiled eggs, white wine, thyme and seasoning) and *garbure*. This substantial vegetable soup is equally renowned in Béarn, the other side of the Pyrenees. It is made from potatoes, cabbage, green peas, belly of pork, loin of pork, sausages and ham bones. The Spanish version differs from the French in that the meat is served together with the other ingredients. Tudela, on the Ebro at the southern tip of Navarra, is famous for its fat and luscious asparagus, served either on its own or in an omelette as *tortilla de Tudela*. Cardoon, so beneficial to Martin the Humane, is boiled and served in a white sauce with ham as *cardón a la Navarra*.

Snails are popular in Navarra, and you may encounter them on menus as *caracoles a la corellana* (cooked with garlic, parsley, cloves, bay leaves, thyme and lemon juice) or as *caracolillas de Navarra* (small snails cooked in earthenware dishes with olive oil, tomatoes, green peppers, chillis, breadcrumbs and seasoning). There is first-rate trout from the mountain streams, served as *truchas a la Navarra* (first marinated and then cooked in an earthenware dish with onions, red wine, pepper, mint, thyme and bay leaves) or as *truchas con jamón*, with slices of ham either on top or sandwiched into the fish.

Navarra produces two good cheeses. The piquant *queso de Roncal* is made from ewe's milk and is a hard, slightly greenish cheese, smoked and ripened for two months. Idiazábal, also made in the Basque country further north, is another hard ewe's milk cheese, ripened for about a month in mountain caves, with a creamy texture and delicate, smoky, herbal, flavour.

Restaurants

Aragón

The four Paradores in Aragón all offer some regional dishes. They are situated in Bielsa in the Pyrenees; in Sos de Rey Católica, the birthplace of Isabella the Catholic, on the borders of Navarra; and in Alcañíz and Teruel further south. At the Parador Nacional de Teruel in particular there are some inventive dishes, such as the *berenjenas empanadas de jamón serrano* (rounds of aubergine sandwiched with cured ham, then coated with batter and fried).

Huesca

The old town of Huesca is a convenient stopping place when taking the picturesque route into Spain by the high Pyrenees and the Col de Somport, and the five-star Corona de Aragón Hotel is very comfortable.

VENTA DEL SOTON★

Fourteen kilometres from Huesca at Esquedas on the road to Pamplona, the Venta specializes in grills of lamb, *chorizo* and *longaniza* (pork sausage). Other appetizing fare includes *revuelto de trigueros con gambas* (eggs scrambled with fresh asparagus and prawns), haricot beans stewed with squid and clams, and pigeon and partridge in season. Apart from Rioja, there are some good local wines from Barbastro.

Zaragoza

LA CASA DEL VENTERO★★

Although this small restaurant offers regional dishes and local wines, it is the proprietor's wife who does the cooking, and she specializes in well-prepared French dishes, such as the delicious salmon in pastry, bass with fennel and stuffed shoulder of lamb.

COSTA VASCA★

Well-known in Zaragoza, the Costa Vasca excels in hake cooked in various ways – grilled, in cider, or as *kokotxas* (strips cut from the 'cheek').

MESÓN DE CARMEN★

This is the place to come for a wide repertoire of regional dishes, including *menestra de verduras* (mixed vegetable dish), *bacalao ajoarriero* (a creamy form of dried cod), *pollo al chilindrón* (chicken in the famous Aragonese sauce) and peaches in wine.

Navarra

Olite

PARADOR NACIONAL PRINCIPE DE VIANA

It is worth staying here for the magnificent surroundings of this restored palace of the kings of Navarra. The dining-room serves a variety of regional dishes, including *bacalao ajoarriero* (creamed salt cod), *magras con tomate* (bacon with tomato) and grilled ribs of lamb. There are wines from the Señorío de Sarría and other nearby bodegas.

Pamplona

JOSETXO★★★

Probably the most sophisticated restaurant in the region, Josetxo is best-known for its game, such as partridge with grapes, wild boar with chestnut sauce and rabbit with snails. The vegetables – aubergines, cardoons and Tudela asparagus – are first-rate, and other specialities are *bacalao al pil pil* and *bacalao ajoarriero* (different styles of dried cod), lamb in *chilindrón* sauce and fillet steak in wine. Long list of wines.

RODERO★★

An elegant restaurant offering both regional and French food. Try the *calamares en su tinta* (squid in their ink), *merluza a la Navarra* (Navarra-style hake), sea bass with orange, beans with pork, *tostadas de leche frita* (egg fritters) or the home-made *cuaja de oveja* (cottage cheese made from ewe's milk).

HARTZA★

The three Hartza sisters who run this popular restaurant near the bullring offer a delicious *menestra* (mixed vegetable dish), *marmitako* (fish stew), hake served either in cider with clams or in a garlic sauce, edible fungi with scrambled eggs, and a ewe's milk cheese from their native village of Urbasa.

Tudela

EL CHOKO★

This comfortable restaurant, halfway between Zaragoza and Logroño and just off the motorway, is known for its *menestra de verduras* (mixed vegetable dish) and magnificent fresh asparagus, locally grown. Other worthwhile dishes are the frogs' legs fried with garlic, the snails with tomato and ham, the roast leg and ribs of lamb, and game in season. There is a good light red Navarra house wine.

Bacalao al pil-pil (dried cod in spicy sauce).

Recipes

Truchas con Jamón / Trout with Ham

Serves 4

METRIC/IMPERIAL	AMERICAN
1 tablespoon olive oil	1 tablespoon olive oil
200 g/7 oz fresh streaky bacon, chopped	7 oz fresh lean bacon, chopped
4 thin slices ham or Italian prosciutto	4 thin slices ham or Italian prosciutto
4 300-350 g/11-12 oz river trout, cleaned, backbone removed and dusted with flour	4 11-12 oz river trout, cleaned, backbone removed and dusted with flour

Heat the oil in a heavy pan and fry the bacon to render the fat. Remove and discard the bacon and fry the ham in the mixed oil and bacon fat. Remove and reserve the ham, keeping it hot. Now fry the trout in the same pan until golden, then insert the slices of ham in the middle. Serve with sautéed potatoes.

One of the many excellent dishes using local trout, *Truchas con Jamón* (trout with ham).

Pollo en Chanfaina/Chicken in Chanfaina Sauce

Serves 4

Lamb may be cooked in the same spicy sauce; use the boned middle neck or cut-up loin.

METRIC/IMPERIAL	AMERICAN
Olive oil	Olive oil
3 courgettes, washed, blanched and coarsely chopped	3 zucchini, washed, blanched and coarsely chopped
2 red or green peppers, seeded and coarsely chopped	2 red or green peppers, seeded and coarsely chopped
2 onions, chopped	2 onions, chopped
500 g/1 lb 2 oz tomatoes, blanched, peeled and coarsely chopped	18 oz tomatoes, blanched, peeled and coarsely chopped
2 cloves garlic, crushed	2 cloves garlic, crushed
1 small glass/75 ml/3 fl oz dry white wine or sherry	1 small glass/$\frac{1}{3}$ cup dry white wine or sherry
1 bay leaf	1 bay leaf
Thyme	Thyme
Salt	Salt
Black pepper	Black pepper
1 $1\frac{1}{2}$-kg/$3\frac{1}{4}$-lb chicken cut into pieces	1 $3\frac{1}{4}$-lb chicken cut into pieces
Flour	Flour
Squares of fried bread	Squares of fried bread

Heat some olive oil in a pan and fry together the courgettes, peppers and onions for about ten minutes. Drain off excess oil, add the tomatoes and garlic and cook gently for another ten minutes until the tomatoes are soft. Now stir in the wine, herbs and spices, remove from the heat and transfer to a stew-pot while you prepare the chicken.

Reheat the oil in the same frying pan, adding a little more if necessary, dredge the pieces of chicken in flour, brown them and then transfer them with a slotted spoon to the stew-pot. Cook over a low heat for about an hour until the chicken is tender, then serve surrounded by the squares of fried bread and fried potatoes.

Melocotones con Vino Tinto/Peaches in Red Wine

Serves 6 to 8

METRIC/IMPERIAL	AMERICAN
$\frac{1}{2}$ litre/18 fl oz red Rioja wine	18 fl oz red Rioja wine
100 g/4 oz caster sugar	$\frac{1}{2}$ cup fine white sugar
Vanilla pod	Vanilla pod
8 large fresh peaches, blanched, skinned, halved and stoned	8 large fresh peaches, blanched, skinned, halved and stoned
100 g/4 oz roasted almonds, skinned and chopped	$\frac{3}{4}$ cup roasted almonds, skinned and chopped

Warm the wine and sugar in a saucepan, scraping a little of the vanilla pod into it (keep the pod for further use). Once the sugar is dissolved, transfer the liquid to a serving bowl and soak the peaches for four hours. Refrigerate and serve very cold, garnished with the almonds.

Catalonia

THE FOUR PROVINCES OF CATALONIA – Gerona, Lérida (or Lleida as it is called in Catalan), Barcelona and Tarragona – lie between the Pyrenees and the Ebro delta in the south, and are bounded to the west by the old kingdom of Aragón and to the east by the Mediterranean, with the holiday beaches of the Costa Brava and Costa Dorada. Apart from a narrow coastal plain, the landscape is rugged and broken and has been described as a flight of stairs rising from the coast towards the 11,350-ft peak of Mount Aneto in the Pyrenees.

The existence of passes through the eastern Pyrenees has from the earliest times made Catalonia a corridor between the Iberian Peninsula and the rest of Europe, and laid it open to successive incursions, usually short-lived as the invaders passed on, from the Carthaginians, Romans, Visigoths, Moors and the Franks to their descendants, the French.

Catalan energy and individualism are firmly rooted in history. After the union with Aragón in 1137 and under the Counts of Barcelona, the principality became the wealthiest mercantile country in the Mediterranean during the fourteenth century, trading as far afield as north Africa, Syria and Egypt, while her soldiers and sailors occupied Sicily and campaigned in Constantinople and Greece. The fortunes of Catalonia declined after the union with Castile in 1479, but the spirit of Catalan independence has never been extinguished and a nineteenth-century revival made Barcelona the commercial capital of Spain. It remains a kingdom within a kingdom, with its own language and autonomous ruling body, the Generalitat.

In many ways Barcelona *is* Catalonia. It gave its name to the ruling dynasty ; it was the seat of Catalan sea power and mercantile enterprise, the birthplace of the *Usatges*, the code of civil liberties which preceded *Magna Carta* by almost a century, and the mainspring of the nineteenth-century *Renaixença*, which gave new life to the Catalan language and literature. It was also in Barcelona that a new working class first became aware of its human rights and political influence.

It is a city of strange contrasts, with its old quarter bounded abruptly by wide avenues lined with plane trees and reminiscent of a dustier, sunnier Paris. The heart of the old city is the Barrio Gótico, where among a network of narrow streets with their antique shops, small grocers and bars, you will come upon Roman remains, the medieval cathedral and the Palace of the Generalitat. Adjoining it is the crowded *Ramblas*, a tree-lined avenue with a central promenade leading down to the port, where the stalls selling flowers, books and caged birds stand cheek by jowl with the open-air cafés.

The best panorama of the port is from the heights of Montjuich, where there is a fine museum of Catalan art and extensive exhibition halls – the biennial Salón de la Alimentaria is one of the largest international wine and food fairs. Elsewhere there are fascinating museums of modern art devoted to Picasso and Miró, and on no account to be missed are the many extraordinary buildings by that master of *Art Nouveau*, Antonio Gaudí, his great unfinished cathedral of La Sagrada Familia in particular.

PREVIOUS PAGE **A street in the Gothic quarter of Barcelona.**

OPPOSITE **The Pavilion in the Parque Guell in Barcelona, designed by Gaudí.**

A worthwhile excursion from Barcelona is to the Monastery of Montserrat, perched on a precipitous hill and surrounded by great outcrops of rounded, weatherworn rock. It houses the blackened wooden image of the Virgin of Montserrat, the patron saint of Catalonia, and its choir school is the oldest musical conservatory in Europe. From here there are long views across the wine-growing country of the Penedès below.

North of Barcelona and lying back from the Costa Brava with its rocky coastline, sandy coves and seaside resorts – Rosas, Palafrugell, San Feliu, Tossa del Mar, Lloret del Mar, Blanes and the others – is the old city of Gerona. It is a place of narrow streets, steps and arches, with a rampart of old houses along the River Oñar and a beautiful Gothic cathedral surmounting a great Baroque stairway.

Tarragona, the Roman capital of northern Spain, lies towards the other extreme of Catalonia, on the coast south of Barcelona. The walls of the old citadel were built by the Romans on the basis of much earlier monolithic blocks, and other Roman remains include an amphitheatre overlooking the sea, the relics of a forum and a fine aqueduct outside the town. The Gothic cathedral, with its great doorway and rose window, one of the largest in Europe, contains remarkable medieval sculptures and carving. The town proper, with a wide tree-lined main avenue and blue brilliance of light, lies above the port where the dusty streets are lined with bodegas given over to the blending and export of wine.

Lérida, the capital of the most westerly of the four provinces, is near the boundary with Aragón, off the motorway from Barcelona to Zaragoza. It, too, has Roman associations, but the town was much knocked about during the Civil War when many of the old buildings were destroyed; the most interesting is the old cathedral, long abandoned, but a magnificent example of Romanesque architecture with Moorish overtones.

The great monasteries of Ripoll, north of Vich on the road to Puigcerdá and the French frontier, San Cugat de Vallés, between Barcelona and Montserrat, and Poblet, in the hills north of Tarragona off the road to Lérida, are all worth a visit. Poblet, founded in 1153 and the burial place of the Kings of Aragón and Catalonia, has been meticulously restored, and with its wide courtyards, beautiful twelfth-century church and vaulted medieval wine cellars, is one of the most impressive ecclesiastical buildings in Spain.

For wine-lovers the wine museum in Vilafranca del Penedès, off the motorway from Barcelona to the south, is a must. Housed in a thirteenth-century palace of the Kings of Aragón, this tells the story of wine-making from Egyptian times onwards, with the help of tableaux, pictures and prints, examples of Greek, Carthaginian and Roman amphorae, reconstructions of bodegas of different periods, and every type of barrel, wine-press and agricultural implement used in the Penedès region. There is a large collection of wine glasses and of the *botas* and *porrones* traditionally used for drinking wine in Spain, and a bar with a wide selection of Catalan wines.

OPPOSITE Gerona, with its magnificent Gothic cathedral overlooking the old houses along the River Oñar.

The Wines

Apart from the Rioja, Catalonia is the most important producer of quality table wines in Spain. It makes some ninety-nine per cent of *cava* or Spanish sparkling wine, together with excellent still wines, the maderized *rancio* and the old *solera*-made dessert wines of Tarragona. Tarragona is also the centre of a flourishing industry making vermouth and liqueurs; and Catalan brandies made by the traditional Charentais method are among the best in the country.

Wine-making was first begun by Greek, Phoenician and Carthaginian colonists, who settled along the coast. The fishing village of Castelló de Ampurias is, in the words of Richard Ford, 'all that remains of the ancient commercial Emporiae Emporium, Εμποριαι Εμπορειον. This colony of Phocaean Greeks from Marseilles was founded in 550 BC, and became the rendezvous of Asia and Europe.' The planting of vineyards and making of wine began in earnest with the Romans, whose villas on the outskirts of their towns were the forerunners of the *masias* so typical of Catalonia from the medieval period onwards. The rapid progress of viticulture in Catalonia has been demonstrated by the discovery of enormous quantities of amphorae belonging to the *early* period of Roman occupation and used for bringing wine from Italy; but by the middle of the first century AD it was found necessary to protect the Italian growers by enforcing strict limitations on the planting of new vines in the Hispanic provinces.

With the decline of the empire and the invasions of 'barbarians' from northern Europe, wine-making fell into abeyance during the period of Visigothic rule, and even more so when Catalonia fell prey to the Moors. The revival began in early medieval times, when the great monasteries of San Cugat de Vallés, Poblet and Santes Creus re-established vineyards and constructed wineries.

The system of agriculture, with its roots in the Roman period, had a great deal to do with the very variable quality of the wine produced in Catalonia until recent decades. After the Reconquest from the Moors, the old Roman *masos* were progressively reoccupied, the custom being for a *pagès* or tenant farmer to obtain the right to cultivate a plot of land on condition that he cleared it and planted it with vines, sharing the produce with the owner. It was clearly in the interests of both to produce the maximum amount of wine, so that the emphasis was on quantity rather than quality.

A further condition of the *Rabassa Morta*, as the arrangement was termed, was that the *pagès* lost his right to cultivate the land after the death of the first-planted vines. Before the incidence of oidium, mildew and 'Black Rot' during the 1850s, and more particularly of phylloxera in 1878, the vines regularly lived for fifty years or more, so that the agreement was of long standing. The premature death of the vines and the much shorter life of the grafted ones with which they were replaced led to legal arguments between farmers and landlords and widespread unrest in agricultural areas; this resulted in a fairer allocation of responsibilities between landlords and tenants, and it is now common for small farmers to own their land.

The phylloxera epidemic was not an unmitigated disaster. Before the insatiable bug found its way across the Pyrenees, the industrious Catalans seized the opportunity to export huge quantities of wine to France, planting new vineyards on every available plot of land, even terracing the hillsides – some of these now-abandoned terraces can be seen along the motorway from Barcelona through the Penedès. Towards the end of the eighteenth century there had been very sizeable exports of Catalan brandy and wine (the best was the sturdy red from S. Pere de Ribes) to England, Russia, Italy and America, but in 1881 exports from the province of Barcelona climbed to no less than 1,269,896 hectolitres, and in 1886 exports to France alone stood at 397,427 hectolitres. The boom came to an end when phylloxera appeared in northern Catalonia in 1878, reaching the province of Barcelona in 1882 and thenceforth advancing at an inexorable twenty kilometres a year, devastating the vineyards of the Penedès.

The situation was gradually restored by replanting with vines grafted on to American stocks, but the wine industry suffered another crippling blow when many of the vineyards and wineries were destroyed during the fighting of the Civil War of 1936-9. It is only during the last twenty or thirty years, with the introduction of modern technology and the planting of vineyards with improved types of grape and noble varieties from abroad, that Catalan wines have come to be regarded as among the best from Spain.

A landmark in Catalan wines was the production in 1872 of the first bottles of sparkling wine by Don José Raventós. Don José, whose family

The dinner for King Alfonso XIII after his visit to the cellars of Codorníu in 1904.

firm of Codorníu had been making still wines in the Penedès since 1551, studied the making of Champagne in France, and his successful introduction of the *méthode champenoise* to the Penedès was the first step in establishing what is now one of the most important sectors of the Spanish wine industry, with a large and growing market world-wide for its *cava* wines.

Cava is the subject of a *Denominación específica* applying to Spanish sparkling wines in general (although this is currently being modified to provide for a VDQS applying to individual regions). The demarcated regions of Catalonia, now administered not by INDO (Instituto Nacional de Denominaciones de Origen) but by INCAVE (Instituto Catalan de Vino), an agency of the revived Generalitat, are : Penedès, Tarragona, Priorato, Terra Alta and Conca de Barberá, south-west of Barcelona ; and Alella and Ampurdán-Costa Brava to the north-east. The other main wine-growing area of Lérida, west of Barcelona, is not demarcated.

Cava (Sparkling Wine)

When Don José Raventós first began making sparkling wine in the Penedès it was known as *champaña*, but as other firms followed his example and the industry grew, the producers in Reims not unnaturally objected. The wines were thereafter referred to officially as *espumosos*; establishments making wine by the champagne method have long been called *cavas* rather than bodegas, but the use of the word *cava* for their wines is of recent origin and was introduced to emphasize that they are not imitations of Champagne or less expensive substitutes, but sparkling wines in their own right, characteristic of the region in which they are made and of its grapes.

Smaller amounts of *cava* are made in other regions of Spain, mainly in Ampurdán-Costa Brava, Lérida and the Rioja, but some ninety-nine per cent is produced in the Penedès. Production centres on San Sadurní de Noya (or, in its Catalan form, Sant Sadurní d'Anoia) some thirty kilometres from Barcelona along the motorway to Tarragona, where there are some sixty *cavas* in and around the town, ranging from small firms selling their wines on the spot to the giant Codorníu and Freixenet.

In the main, the wines are still made from the three native grape varieties used by José Raventós: the white Macabeo (or Viura of the Rioja), Xarel-lo and Parellada. The Macabeo contributes fruit and freshness; the Xarel-lo, body and alcoholic strength; and the Parellada, grown on the hill slopes of the Penedès Superior, acidity and delicacy of nose. A little of the red Monastrel is sometimes used in the interests of freshness and long life, and experiments are being made with the Chardonnay, of which there are sizeable plantations at Raimat near Lérida. Pink wines are made by using a proportion of black grapes, such as the Garnacha or Cariñena.

Although EEC regulations are phasing out the use of the term *méthode champenoise* on labels, it is precisely by this method that the wines are made. The grapes are pressed in the horizontal presses of the basket and chain or pneumatic Wilmes type, or, as at Codorníu, in a continuous band press. The must (less, of course, stalks, skins and pips) is left to stand, so that any solid matter settles out, and then cold-fermented for some three weeks. At Freixenet this is done in huge stainless steel tanks of 600,000 litres capacity, and at Codorníu in batteries of smaller tanks controlled from a central computer. The wine is then cooled to precipitate tartrate and put into stout champagne-type bottles, together with a solution of sugar in wine from the previous vintage and cultured yeasts. The bottles are closed with crown caps and left in cool underground cellars while the yeast works on the sugar, so producing the carbon dioxide which gives the wine its bubble. The next stage is very gradually to up-end the bottles so that the fine sediment falls towards the neck.

This is traditionally done by placing the bottles in a *pupitre* in the shape of an inverted 'V', allowing for the inclination of the bottle to be increased progressively so that it ends up

almost on its head. The *pupitres* have, however, largely been replaced by a device of Catalan invention, the *girasol* or 'sunflower', a large metal frame on an octagonal base holding some five hundred bottles and dispensing with the need to turn and shake them individually.

ABOVE Turning bottles of *cava* wine by hand in a *pupitre* at Freixenet.

ABOVE LEFT *Girasols* (or sunflowers), which now replace the traditional *pupitres* in the *cavas* of the Penedès.

LEFT A horizontal wine-press at Codorníu.

The final stage is to freeze the neck of the bottle and remove the temporary stopper, whereupon the plug containing the sediment is ejected by the gas pressure from inside. A *licor de expedición* containing a little sugar dissolved in brandy and old wine is added (the completely dry *natur* is topped up only with unsweetened wine) and the bottles are recorked and wired and allowed to rest before labelling and despatch.

In increasing order of sweetness *cava* is labelled:

Natur or Brut natur	extra-dry
Brut	dry
Seco	fairly dry
Semi-seco	semi-dry
Semi-dulce	semi-sweet
Dulce	sweet

Spanish tastes in sparkling wine are sweeter than those abroad, and if you like a really dry wine, you should ask for the *brut natur* or *brut*.

By no means all Spanish sparkling wines are made by the champagne method. You will also come across wines labelled *gran-vas*, in which the second fermentation takes place not in individual bottles but in pressurized tanks, known in France as *cuves closes*. These are pleasant enough for holiday drinking, but with a coarser and shorter-lived bubble than *cava*; what are to be avoided are the *gaseosos*, made simply by pumping carbon dioxide into still wine. The corks of *cava* are marked with a four-pointed star and those of *gran-vas* with a circle.

There has been a great deal of heated discussion about the relative merits of champagne and *cava*, with opinions ranging from flat assertions that they are not in the same league as champagne to the terse report of that most skilled of wine-makers, Miguel A. Torres, on a series of blind tastings, that: 'the *cava* wines of San Sadurní de Noya have frequently been judged superior to their French homologues'. As Hugh Johnson put it in a recent book:

The *cavas* of Penedès today range from the extremely deft and delicate to the fat and clumsy. The best can certainly be counted among the world's finest sparkling wines. It is only in the inevitable comparison with Champagne that they lose. Where Champagne triumphs is in the vigour of flavours that it assembles so harmoniously.

CASTELLBLANCH, S.A.
Large firm with *cavas* in the heart of Sant Sadurní d'Anoia. Formerly part of the Rumasa group, it now belongs to Freixenet. The best of its wines are the 'Brut Zero' and the slightly sweeter 'Cristal Seco'.

CASTILLO DE PERELADA
Situated in the foothills of the Pyrenees in the demarcated region of Ampurdán-Costa Brava, not far off the motorway from the French frontier to Barcelona, this is one of the most picturesque wineries in Catalonia. The medieval castle houses a library, collections of ceramics and glass, an interesting wine museum and also a casino; and the cellars lie beneath the fourteenth-century church of Carmen de Perelada. Best of the wines is the dry, round and flowery 'Gran Claustro', kept for five to six years in the cellars.

The associated company of CAVAS DEL AMPURDÁN, S.A., makes *gran vas* wines by the *cuve close* method (see above). Its premises lie across the road from the castle, since establishments making *gran vas* and *cava* must by law be separated by a public highway. The very drinkable 'Perelada' is one of the best-known Spanish wines of this type and was the subject in 1960 of the legal action (known in France at the time as the 'second battle of the Marne') in which the French Champagne companies obtained a ruling from the English courts banning the use of the term 'Spanish Champagne'.

CAVAS MASCARÓ
This family firm also makes liqueurs and a good brandy. Its *cavas* in Vilafranca del Penedès are small and traditional in their methods, and produce fresh and fragrant 'Cava Reservada' and 'Brut' wines containing a high proportion of Parellada.

CODORNÍU, S.A.

The first surviving record of the Codorníu family dates from 1551; an inventory of the effects left by Jaime Codorníu to his heirs details wine cellars, presses, casks and much other wine-making equipment. It is evident that the family had been making wine for long years before, and it continued to do so until 1659 when matters took a new direction. The last of the line was a woman, 'La Pubilla', María Anna Codorníu, and when she married Miguel Raventós, of another well-known wine-making family, the interests of both houses were merged. The business continued, making wines along traditional lines, until, in the mid-nineteenth century, Don José Raventós hit upon the idea of making a sparkling wine in the manner of Champagne.

The time was ripe. Barcelona was going through a time of commercial expansion, and a new mercantile class had emerged with the taste and money for luxuries. Don José prepared the ground by travelling to Reims and studying the methods of the Champagne houses. On his return to Sant Sadurní d'Anoia he made a selection of the most suitable types of grape, and in 1872 uncorked the first bottles of his Spanish sparkling wine. His son, Manuel Raventós, carried on and extended the work begun by his father, travelling extensively and employing French technicians to help in the construction and operation of the large new winery and underground cellars which he put in hand.

From 1888 onwards his sparkling wines, named 'Codorníu' in honour of his ancestors, began winning gold medals at international exhibitions in Barcelona, Antwerp, Bordeaux, Brussels and elsewhere, and in 1897 he received a royal warrant from the Queen Regent, María Cristina, for the supply of sparkling wine to the court, replacing the Champagne until then served at state banquets. Foreseeing the importance of advertising, Don Manuel organized a competition in 1898: colourful posters by such outstanding artists as Casas, Utrillo, Tubilla and Junyent, depicting ladies in long evening dresses and monocled gentlemen in top hats and tails, were soon to make Codorníu a household name all over the world.

The *cavas* of Codorníu in Sant Sadurní d'Anoia are now the single largest establishment in the world making sparkling wine by the Champagne method. The original buildings and house of the Reventós family were designed in *fin de siècle* style by José María Puig i Cadalfalch, and are set in ornamental grounds with water gardens, fountains and beds of flowers, under which five tiers of cellars extend for seventeen kilometres. The former labelling hall, declared a National Monument, has been converted into a reception centre for the 160,000 visitors who visit the *cavas* each year; the old press house is now a spacious and well-arranged wine museum; and one of the old cellars has been remodelled and serves as the headquarters of a Catalan wine fraternity, the Serenísimo Capítulo de Caballeros del Vino.

The equipment and installations are of the most modern, comprising continuous band presses, temperature-controlled fermentation tanks, and a computerized system for retrieving bottles from the distant reaches of the vast underground cellars. During harvest time, from mid-September to late October, Codorníu processes a million kilos of grapes daily; its reserves amount to some seventy-five million litres; and it sells thirty-five million bottles a year, four million of which are exported.

The wines range from the simple and fruity to the highly refined, and include the 'Première Cuvée', light, pale in colour and very dry, made from forty-five per cent Xarel-lo, forty-five per cent Parellada and ten per cent Macabeo; 'Anna de Codorníu', made from thirty per cent Macabeo, thirty per cent Parellada and ten per cent Chardonnay; the famous 'Non Plus Ultra'; and the delicious 'Gran Codorníu' which gains in depth and complexity from longer age in bottle. There has been some discussion between us about the relative merits of the older and younger Codorníu wines. Eventually it comes down to personal preference. The fresh 'Anna de Codorníu' has a

ABOVE A poster designed for Codorníu by R. Casas in 1898.

BELOW *Pupitres* in the eleven-mile underground cellars of Codorníu.

OPPOSITE The house of the Raventós family in the grounds of Codorníu.

youthful charm quite different from the deeper flavours of 'Gran Codorníu'. One is better for refreshment or as an aperitif; the other has more body and flavour and would go better with food. The associated company of Raimat, S.A., with vineyards and *cavas* near Lérida, also makes a range of sparkling wines, some of them containing a proportion of Chardonnay, under such labels as 'Rondel', 'Carta Dorada', 'Carta Oro', 'Raimat' and 'Delapierre' (named after a French oenologist formerly working for Codorníu).

By the purchase of the famous Masía Bach in the Penedès (see p. 149) and extensive planting at Raimat near Lérida (see CONIUSA, p. 155), Codorníu is now also a large producer of still wines.

CONDE DE CARALT

Made in the *cavas* of Segura Viudas, the 'Reserva 1980 Brut Nature' and 'Conde de Caralt Brut' have recently been commended by British tasters for their full fruit, freshness and good balance – and were, in fact, preferred to the wines from Freixenet, the firm's new owners.

FREIXENET, S.A.

Between them, Codorníu and Freixenet make at least eighty per cent of all the *cava* wine from the Penedès, both firms exporting very large amounts to the United States. Since the acquisition by Freixenet of the *cavas* of Segura Viudas, Conde de Caralt, Renée Barbier and Castellblanch, formerly within the expropriated Rumasa group, the two concerns are about equal in size.

The company was founded in 1915, and its massive winery lying close to the motorway from Barcelona is one of the most modern in its equipment in Sant Sadurní d'Anoia. Unlike Codorníu, it believes in vinifying the wine in tanks of the largest possible size, of which it possesses ten of 600,000 litres, temperature-controlled and made of stainless steel. It pioneered the use of *girasols* (see p. 141) in place of the traditional *pupitres*, and its bottling line is a miracle of automated ingenuity. It is, in fact, by technical innovations of this kind that the large houses in the Penedès have been able to keep down the prices of their sparkling wines without loss of quality.

Its less expensive wines are the 'Carta Nevada', 'Cremant Rosé' and fresh dry non-vintage 'La Sirena'. 'Brut Nature' and the rounder and very slightly sweeter 'Cordón Negro' are both most attractive wines, and there are also special vintage releases such as the 'Cuvée D.S. 1969', named in honour of Doña Dolores Sala, widow of the company's founder, Don Pedro Ferrer Bosch.

GONZALEZ Y DUBOSC, S.A.

The company is owned by the great sherry firm of Gonzalez Byass. Until recently its wines, labelled as 'Jean Perico' in the United Kingdom, were made by Segura Viudas, but they are now produced in the firm's own *cavas*. The 'Jean Perico Brut' is a clean, straightforward wine with good mousse and finish, very reasonably priced.

JUVE Y CAMPS

Family firm founded in 1916, priding itself on the unhurried care with which it makes its excellent *cava*, mostly from grapes grown in its 130 hectares of vineyards in the Penedès Superior. The firm also makes a fresh young 'Blanc Flor Ermita d'Espiells', named after the Romanesque hermitage on the estate.

SEGURA VIUDAS, S.A.

Once the maker of prestige wines for the Rumasa group, but now owned by Freixenet, Segura Viudas shares premises with Conde de Caralt and René Barbier, and its modern winery adjoins a picturesque old house outside Sant Sadurní in the direction of Montserrat, part of the grapes coming from the surrounding vineyards. 'Reserva Heredad', belying its ornate and clumsy bottle, is one of the best of *cavas*, dry, light and delicate.

The following two firms in the Rioja also make good *cava* wine:

BODEGAS BILBAÍNAS, S.A.

This old Rioja firm has for years been making small amounts of *cava* by thoroughly traditional methods in cellars underneath its bodega in Haro, using Viura and Malvasía grapes. The 'Royal Carlton Cuvée Especial' and 'Royal Carlton Brut Nature' are dry and full-flavoured.

BODEGAS MUGA, S.A.

Isac Muga, well-known for his red wines, some years ago revived an old Riojan tradition for making sparkling wine (at the height of the phylloxera epidemic the Rioja actually supplied grapes to the producers in Reims). With advice from the Estación de Viticultura y Enología in Haro and using mainly Viura grapes and cultured yeasts, he has produced a very light and refreshing 'Conde de Haro', bone-dry because no *licor de expedición* is added.

Penedès

Cava apart, the Penedès, with its limestone soils and temperate climate, produces the best of the Catalan wines. The classical dessert wines from Sitges on the coast, made from Malvasia and Moscatel grapes allowed to wrinkle on the vine, no longer exist in significant amount; but modern technology and the planting of improved vines, some of them 'noble' varieties from abroad, has resulted in the production of a wide range of refreshing white wines and fruity reds, some of them up to Rioja standards.

With some twenty-five thousand hectares under vines, the region extends south-westwards of Barcelona along the Mediterranean coast and inland towards the mountains of the interior. Of the three sub-regions the hottest is the Bajo Penedès, lying back from the rugged coast and growing mainly red grapes; the Medio Penedès, at an average height of two hundred metres, produces more than half of the wine, especially the white used for *cava*, while the cooler Penedès Superior, rising to some seven hundred metres in the hills of the interior, is planted mainly with the white Parellada.

VINTAGE CHART FOR PENEDÈS WINES

Year	Whites	Reds
1966	Very good	Good
1967	Good	Excellent
1968	Average	Bad
1969	Excellent	Average
1970	Average	Excellent
1971	Average	Good
1972	Bad	Bad
1973	Very good	Excellent
1974	Good	Very good
1975	Very good	Good
1976	Excellent	Good
1977	Very good	Good
1978	Very good	Excellent
1979	Good	Average
1980	Good	Excellent
1981	Excellent	Very good
1982	Very Good	Very good
1983	Good	Good
1984	Excellent	Good
1985	Good	Good

The Consejo Regulador, or official regulatory body, approves five varieties of grape for the white wines: the Garnacha blanca, Macabeo (or Viura of the Rioja), Xarel-lo, Subirat-Parent and Parellada. Perhaps the most typical of the region is the Parellada, which makes delicately fruity and somewhat acidic wines with a greenish cast and appley nose. The approved black grapes are the Garnacha tinta, Ull de Llebre (Tempranillo), Cariñena, Monastrel and Samsó.

The best wines are made from acclimatized foreign grapes, or from a blend of foreign and native. The planting of foreign varieties has been pioneered by Miguel Torres, and on a smaller scale by Jean León. Torres grows white varieties accustomed to the cooler climate of northern Europe, such as the Chardonnay, Sauvignon Blanc and Gewürztraminer, in the hills of the Penedès Superior, while the extensive plantations of Cabernet Sauvignon, Cabernet Franc, Merlot and Pinot Noir are in the Medio Penedès.

The production of still wines centres on Vilafranca del Penedès, off the motorway from Barcelona to Tarragona, on which Richard Ford supplied the interesting note that: 'it was founded by Amilcar [Hamilcar Barca], and was the earliest Carthaginian settlement in Catalonia; it was retaken from the Moors in 1000, by Ramon Borel, and, being a frontier of a disturbed district, was declared free, and highly favoured, in order to attract settlers – hence its name.' A pleasant market town full of bodegas large and small, one of its main attractions is the splendid wine museum (see p. 137).

With an average annual temperature of 14.4°C (and maximum and minimum of 27.8°C and 2.6°C), some 2550 hours of sunshine and 20.2 inches of rain, the climate is so mild that it is only in exceptional years that there is a poor vintage.

CONDE DE CARALT, S.A.

Apart from *cava*, Caralt makes a range of still wines, including a dry white, a very light and crisp rosé, and reds, of which the best is the 'Conde de Caralt Tinto Reserva', containing fifty per cent Cabernet Sauvignon.

JEAN LEÓN, S.A.

This tiny bodega belongs to an expatriate Spanish restaurateur in Los Angeles who began planting Chardonnay and Cabernet Sauvignon even before Torres. The wines, most of which are exported to the United States, are made entirely with grapes grown in its own vineyards (ten hectares of Chardonnay and one hundred hectares of Cabernet Sauvignon). The Chardonnay is excellent, with good 'buttery' flavour, and the Cabernet Sauvignon is a huge, fruity and tannic wine which will repay years of storage in bottle. There can be no doubting the exceptional quality of these wines, nor the potential that they, along with the great Torres reds, represent.

León's Cabernets are made for the long haul:

OPPOSITE **A selection of labels of wines from the region.**

a decade and more has not yet resolved the intense flavours of the 1974 and 1975, while the 1978 and 1979 in 1986 are still children. The indications are that they will make magnificent adults.

MARQUÉS DE MONISTROL, S.A.

Better-known for its *cava*, Monistrol also produces a refreshing and slightly *pétillant* young 'Vin Natur Blanc de Blancs', made with sixty per cent Parellada and forty per cent Xarel-lo, and smooth red *reservas*.

MASÍA BACH, S.A.

The history of Masía Bach dates from the years just after the 1914–18 war, when a couple of elderly bachelor brothers from Barcelona, who had made their fortune by selling army uniforms to the British and French, built a Florentine-style mansion near Sant Sadurní d'Anoia and began making wines as a hobby. The bodega, acquired some years ago by the

The vineyards of Masía Bach, with Montserrat in the background.

cava giant, Codorníu, is now one of the largest in the Penedès, with a storage capacity of more than three million litres and some ten thousand oak casks for maturing the wines (many of them passed on to Bach by Codorníu after the use of barrels for fermenting the *cava* wine was discontinued in favour of stainless steel).

Bach has been known best in the past for its luscious and very oaky white 'Extrísimo', one of the best Spanish dessert wines. It is now making a dry and fresh young white wine without age in oak, the 'Extrísimo Seco Bach', and also produces fruity and full-bodied red wines made from a blend of sixty-five per cent Tempranillo, twenty per cent Cabernet Sauvignon and fifteen per cent Garnacha, labelled as 'Tinto Bach' and 'Extrísima Tinta'. The latest vintages of Masía Bach reds have shown considerably more depth and complexity than the previous, fairly simple, wines. These are wines to follow closely.

MIGUEL TORRES

Largest and most important of the bodegas in Vilafranca with a world-wide reputation for its wines, the firm remains firmly in the control of the Torres family which has been making wine in the Penedès since the seventeenth century. The company was founded in 1870 by Miguel Torres Vendrell. In partnership with his younger brother, Jaime, who had made his fortune in the petroleum business in Cuba, he built it up into the largest wine concern in Vilafranca, constructing a huge wooden vat of 450,000 litres inside which King Alfonso XIII of Spain and a company of fifty were entertained to dinner in 1909.

Its enormous success dates from the period after the Spanish Civil War, when its present head, Miguel Torres Carbó, travelled the world selling its wines. He has been ably abetted by his son, Miguel A. Torres, who began by improving the quality of the grapes, both by clonic selection of the best native varieties and by large-scale acclimatization of 'noble' grapes from abroad (see p. 147). At the same time the winery was completely modernized. Torres was

one of the first concerns in Spain to vinify its wines in temperature-controlled stainless steel tanks; and huge underground galleries, which now hold some eleven thousand casks for maturing them, were excavated beneath the vineyards. The new outdoor, gravity-fed vinification plant looks more like a refinery than a winery and is one of the most advanced in the world.

Miguel A. Torres, who trained as an oenologist in Dijon, has been much influenced by French wine-making methods and does not believe in ageing the red wines for more than a year or eighteen months in oak, after which the best are given extended periods in bottle. Apart from the 'Gran Viña Sol Green Label', which

The new fermentation plant of Miguel Torres.

spends a few months in cask, the white wines are not matured in oak. No other bodega in Spain even attempts to produce such a wide range of top-quality wines. One must look to California for the only true parallels.

Torres' base white wine is made from Parellada grapes and sold as 'Viña Sol'. The young 'Viña Sol' is exceptionally lively, its striking acidity backed up with plenty of vividly fruity flavour rather in the manner of a young 'Chenin Blanc' from the Loire. 'Gran Viña Sol' has a proportion of about one-third of Chardonnay added and is aged briefly in French oak barrels – not so long as to give it the typically Spanish oak imprint, but enough to hint at the connection with white burgundy. The unblended (and still experimental) Chardonnay is extremely rich, and clearly still benefits from the acidity of Parellada in a blend.

Torres grows Rhine Riesling in the high Penedès, at an altitude of seven hundred metres, to produce the very clean, slightly sweet, spicy and tempting Waltraud, certainly the best Riesling grown on or near the shores of the Mediterranean. Gewürztraminer is still at an experimental stage, but a blend of Gewürztraminer and Muscat d'Alsace makes the very successful 'Viña Esmeralda', clean, intense, aromatic, with rich but not over-sweet flavours and good length: an original and memorable addition to Spain's white wine repertoire.

'Gran Sangre de Toro' is Torres' most traditionally Catalan red, made of Garnacha and Cariñena and aged eighteen months in American oak. It is certainly one of earth's red wine bargains, remarkably complex to smell: dusty, oaky, spicy and mushroomy at once, with both 'cut' and follow through in the mouth.

'Coronas' is also a true native, made of Tempranillo and a little Monastrel, also well oak-aged, rather meatier and more forceful both to smell and taste than 'Gran Sangre de Toro', with more tannin and acidity, still closed and balanced at three years old.

Pinot Noir is made both alone and in a blend with Tempranillo under the name 'Viña Magdala'. The Pinot Noir vines are still young but already give a hint of the high-toned violet-like aromas in store.

In 'Gran Coronas' Cabernet Sauvignon is blended with Tempranillo in the proportion of about two to one to achieve a very attractive, almost floral scent, and flavours that at five years are still young and vital with mint-like freshness.

The top of the Torres range is the tremendous 'Gran Coronas Black Label', a pure Cabernet wine that has been compared with Château Latour. Old vintages of Black Label back to 1970 confirm its extraordinary quality, with a bouquet compounded of oak, blackcurrants, tobacco, cinnamon and a hint of tar, and long deep sweet flavours that remain firm (all the press-wine is added to give tannic grip) into a long plateau of splendid maturity. The 1978 is a triumphant example.

Torres also makes a maderized *rancio* wine, sherry-like in taste and matured in glass carboys (or '*bombonas*') with access to air, and an excellent range of brandies. It has begun making wines in Chile and has recently acquired vineyards in California.

RENÉ BARBIER

Founded in 1870 by Leon Barbier, an immigrant French wine-maker, the firm was bought by the Rumasa conglomerate in 1978, and operations were transferred to the *cavas* of Segura Viudas near Sant Sadurní d'Anoia. It has since been acquired by Freixenet, which has discontinued the René Barbier *cava*, but maintains production of the range of still wines. They are made with modern equipment, the grapes being pressed in Wilmes or Vaslin presses and fermented in steel or cement vats coated with vitrified epoxy resin. The reds are matured in 225-litre oak *barricas* and further aged in bottle.

The white 'Kraliner' is very pale with a greenish cast, very light and fresh with a flowery nose. Best of the red wines is the *reserva*, made with forty per cent Cabernet Sauvignon, thirty per cent Garnacha and thirty per cent Tempranillo.

Tarragona

The largest of the demarcated regions in Catalonia, Tarragona, to the south-west of the Penedès, is divided into the sub-zones of Camp de Tarragona, Falset and Ribera d'Ebre, with 25,000 hectares of vineyards between them. The wines, mainly cooperative-made, lack the delicacy of those from the Penedès : sturdy reds and earthy whites, they are sold for everyday consumption or blending.

Tarragona itself is an important centre for the blending and export of inexpensive beverage wines. It is best-known for its *clásicos* or sweet dessert wines, made by the *solera* system (see p. 18) and containing up to 23° of alcohol. The 'Tarragona' once sold in English pubs, also known as 'poor-man's port' or 'red biddy' and popular with lemon, was a cheap *clásico* of this sort. Tarragona and the neighbouring Reus are also large-scale producers of vermouth and liqueurs (see p. 156).

The most famous of Tarragona's bodegas is

The laboratory at the Vinícola Iberica in Tarragona, where customers' samples are 'matched'.

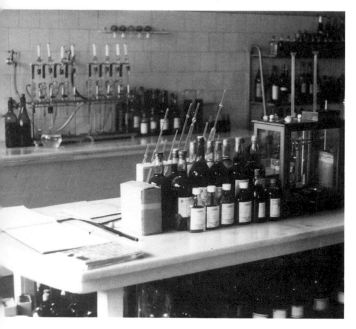

the old-established firm of DE MÜLLER, founded in 1851 and celebrated as makers of 'altar wine', which it sends not only to the Vatican but all over the world. The Church is, incidentally, as rigorous in its requirements as many a *denominación de origen*, forbidding the baptizing of the wine with water, sugar, citric acid or additives in general. De Müller's historic old bodegas by the port were the first in Spain to clarify wine by refrigeration, and house more oak casks for maturing them than all the other bodegas in Tarragona put together. The white wines are now fermented in stainless steel.

Apart from a range of inexpensive 'Solimar' table wines, De Müller produces some quite remarkable old *solera*-made *clásicos*, including a mahogany-coloured 'Pajarete' and 'Moscatel Muy Viejo, Solera 1926', reminiscent of first-class Málaga or fine old sweet *oloroso* sherry, and also magnificent *rancios*, made with wine from its bodega in Priorato, such as the 'Dom Juan Fort Solera 1865' and 'Priorato Dulce Solera 1918'. In their intensely aromatic sweetness these splendid wines must, one feels, relate to the sort of wine that was made in Tarragona when it was a great Roman city. They certainly equal or excel even the best of the Vins Doux Naturels which represent a similar tradition just north of the Franco-Spanish border in Roussillon and Rivesaltes.

Priorato

Priorato means 'priory', and this small demarcated region in the mountains due west of Tarragona takes its name from the great Carthusian monastery of Scala Dei. After the anticlerical reforms of Juan Alvarez Mendizábal in 1836 the monastery was abandoned, and all that remains is a great roofless church and crumbling walls and arches choked with trees and shrubs. According to legend, it was founded on the spot where angels had been seen ascending and descending a long ladder into the heavens, and this at least is preserved in the seal of the Consejo Regulador.

There is very little level ground, and the vines are grown in small plots on the terraced mountain sides in a volcanic soil consisting of decayed lava with a high content of silica. The climate is more extreme than in other parts of Catalonia, and the scorching summers produce wines containing as much as 18° of alcohol. They are of high quality despite their strength, however, the most typical being the deep, full-bodied reds made from the Garnacha and Cariñena. Some white wine is also made from the Garnacha blanca, Macabeo and Pedro Ximénez grapes, and both types are used for making the maderized *rancio* wines so typical of the region. Peasant-made *rancios* are often much oxidized and sour, but those from the *soleras* of De Müller are quite outstanding.

The best Priorato is made by DE MÜLLER and CELLERS DE SCALA DEI, both in the village of Scala Dei, dramatically situated at the foot of a great natural amphitheatre formed by the surrounding mountains. The 'Legitimo Priorato de Müller' has upheld the reputation of Priorato for years and is a third-year wine, dark, full-bodied, intense in flavour and of 15°. The Cellers de Scala Dei occupy an old stone building almost monastic in appearance, but well-equipped with stainless steel tanks for vinification, epoxy-coated storage vats, oak *barricas* and a small modern bottling line providing for the topping up of the bottles with carbon dioxide. Its young 'Novell Scala Dei' is dark purple, fresh-tasting with an intense blackberry flavour and of 13.8° strength. The 'Cartoixa Scala Dei', bottled after eighteen months in oak, is almost black in colour, chewy and full-bodied to a degree, a little sweet to begin with but dry and tannic in finish: a good wine, but one for strong heads.

Conca de Barberà

This hilly region to the west of the Penedès has a history of wine-making dating from the twelfth century, when vineyards were planted by the Knights Templars and Cistercians. The cellars where the monks of the noble monastery of Poblet made their altar wines still survive.

Fairly recently demarcated by INCAVI (Instituto Catalán de Vino), it has 9,900 hectares under vines and produces an average 250,000 hl of wine, much of it made from the Parellada and Macabeo, going to the *cavas* of Sant Sadurní d'Anoia for elaboration as sparkling wine. The only concern to bottle the wines with *Denominación de Origen* is the large UNIÓ AGRÀRIA COOPERATIVA DE REUS in the adjoining region of Tarragona, which sells a rosé 'La Conca de Barberà' made from Garnacha, Ull de Llebre and Trepat.

After careful investigation, Miguel Torres has found that the clay soils are well suited to the cultivation of foreign vine varieties, and has embarked on extensive plantations of Cabernet Sauvignon, Pinot Noir and Chardonnay around the old castle of Milmanda, close to the monastery of Poblet.

Terra Alta

The remote and mountainous Terra Alta, with its Romanesque churches and ruined castles, is the most westerly of the Catalan wine areas. The predominant vines are the white Macabeo and Garnacha blanca, and the best of the wines are those made *en virgen* with only the lightest pressing of the grapes. The traditional reds are robust and astringent, but some attractive *tintos de yema* are now being made with musts obtained without mechanical pressing. PEDRO ROVIRA, a firm with branches elsewhere in Catalonia, bottles a dry young 'Blanc de Belart', a sweet white 'Alta Mar' and a red 'Vinya D'Irto' matured in oak.

Alella

The wines from Alella, just north of Barcelona, known even in Greek and Roman times, enjoy a reputation out of proportion to the tiny size of the area, the smallest demarcated region in Spain, with only 350 hectares under vines. They have long been favourites in Barcelona, but it is Barcelona which threatens their continued existence with urban encroachment and a motorway driven through the heart of the vineyards. Wine-making might well have disappeared but for the energetic action of the Cooperativa Vinícola, which has obtained a ban on further building in the demarcated area.

The principal grapes are the white Garnacha blanca and Xarel-lo (known here as the Pansà blanca), and the best is the Pansà grown in the granitic soils of the hills above the town of Alella, which makes delicate and aromatic wines with a refreshing acidity. Smaller amounts of the red Ull de Llebre (Tempranillo) and Garnacha tinta are grown in the coastal strip.

Until recently the wines were made in only two establishments, the COOPERATIVA ALELLA VINÍCOLA, founded in 1906, and the bodega of VINOS JAIME SERRA. They were traditionally made by continuous addition of fresh must to the cement vats, so as to prevent undue rise of temperature; both red and white wines were then aged for two years in large barrels of Canadian oak. The Cooperative has now, however, begun using temperature-controlled stainless steel tanks. Its wines are known all over Spain under the name of 'Marfil' ('Ivory') and include a dry white, a rounder and fruitier semi-dry, white *reservas*, a rosé and red wines.

In 1981 a new company, ALTA ALELLA, S.A. entered the field. With 45 hectares under vines, mostly Pansà, and a modern winery equipped with stainless steel fermentation tanks and refrigeration machinery, it makes a cold-fermented white in new style without time in oak. The 'Marqués de Alella' is the palest straw colour, light, fruity and delicate. Under the name of 'Parxet', the firm also makes a *cava* wine.

Ampurdán-Costa Brava

Back from the holiday coast and in the foothills of the Pyrenees, this is one of the more recently demarcated regions, but probably the first in Catalonia to make wine. The earliest Catalan treatise on wine-making was written by Father Ramón Pere de Novás from the monastery of Sant Pere de Roda.

One of the problems with which the growers have to cope is the high winds, which blow in one direction or another almost every day of the year, sometimes reaching velocities of 100 m.p.h., and for this reason the vines are staked. Some seventy per cent of the wines are rosés made with the Cariñena and Garnacha tinta, but the region also makes full-bodied and fruity reds and some white wine from the Garnacha blanca (known locally as Lledoner) and Macabeo. A speciality is the delicious dessert 'Garnacha' made by adding grape spirit to the must, so arresting fermentation and leaving the wine with residual grape sugar and some $15°$ of alcohol. A new departure is the *vi novell*, a young red wine made by *macération carbonique* in the manner of Beaujolais Nouveau. Good examples are those from the cooperatives of

Espolla, Mollet de Perelada and Garriquella.

The best-known winery in Ampurdán-Costa Brava is the CAVAS DEL AMPURDÁN, S.A., a sister ship of the Castillo de Perelada (see p. 142), which apart from producing the well-known *cuve close* sparkler, makes a range of worthwhile still wines, including a three-year-old red 'Tinto Cazador', the rosé 'Perelada' and a well-balanced and fruity 'Reserva Don Miguel', aged in cask and bottle. The refreshing white 'Pescador' is halfway between a still and a *cuve close* wine, being made in tanks pressurized to less than the normal degree.

The bodega at Raimat, designed by Rubió i Ors for Codorníu and completed in 1922. Running water over the crow-stepped gable kept the building cool in summer.

Lérida

Wine-making in the Comarca del Segrià had declined until the Raventós family of the sparkling wine firm of Codorníu bought the Castle of Raimat and its estates in 1918, and commissioned a magnificent bodega from the well-known architect Rubió i Ors. Completed in 1922, it embodied such novel features as provision for running water over the crow-stepped roof so as to cool the building in summer.

Although the district is not demarcated, it is now making some of the best Catalan wine since Don Manuel Raventós Domenech of Codorníu embarked on the replanting of the three thousand-hectare estate (of which some one thousand hectares are now under vines) and the modernization of the winery. The larger part is planted with the native Tempranillo, Parellada, Xarel-lo and Macabeo, but Don Manuel has also obtained virus-free vines from California, and there are 180 hectares of Cabernet Sauvignon, 20 hectares of Merlot and 200 hectares of Chardonnay, some of it used for making *cava*. Because the rainfall is low, the vineyards are irrigated both with a system of fixed pipes and with perforated tubes which are moved forward by what look like huge bicycle wheels. This is unusual in Spain, but the vines have certainly not suffered.

CONIUSA produces a range of wines, including a delicate and fruity white 'Raimat Pinot Chardonnay'; a dry white 'Clos Casal' made with a blend of Macabeo, Parellada and Chardonnay; the sweeter white 'Clos de la Dama'; a fresh rosé; a fruity and well-balanced 'Can Abadia' containing fifty per cent Cabernet Sauvignon, thirty per cent Tempranillo and twenty per cent Garnacha; and a Cabernet Sauvignon with ten per cent Merlot. The relatively short recent history of the Raimat wines gives every reason to think that this area has enormous potential. Its Cabernet Sauvignon in particular has a richness of flavour balanced with good acidity that bodes excellently for the future.

Brandy and Liqueurs

Although most Spanish brandy is now made in Jerez de la Frontera (see p. 30), there is a much longer history of brandy-making in Catalonia, which was shipping it to England as long ago as the seventeenth century. It was made, of course, by the traditional method of distilling the wine in pot stills, and the tradition has been continued by two firms in particular, MIGUEL TORRES and ANTONIO MASCARÓ, in Vilafranca del Penedès. The excellent Mascaró brandies are made by double distillation in copper Charentais-type stills, rather than from spirit produced in a steam-heated column, and aged, not Jerez-style in a *solera*, but in individual oak casks. The best of the Torres brandies, the 'Miguel Torres Black Label', is made in similar fashion. Both are very similar in style to Cognac or Armagnac, and it is difficult to tell them apart at a blind tasting.

Mascaró, which for long made Cointreau under licence, produces a very similar 'Gran Licor de Naranja' by steeping dried orange peel from Spain, Algeria, Haiti and Italy in alcoholic solution and then distilling it (Cointreau now has its own establishment in Vilafranca).

The most famous of liqueurs from Catalonia is, however, Chartreuse made in Tarragona. It is often thought that the Tarragona-made Chartreuse is an imitation. This was once put to me dogmatically by a German connoisseur, but nothing could be further from the truth. I found that the Chartreuse which he had been drinking for years had been made during the period when the fathers from La Grande Chartreuse, expelled from France in 1903 by an anti-clerical government, set up their distillery in Tarragona, resuming production in Grenoble only in 1940. The famous liqueurs, yellow and green, are today made both in France and Tarragona from the same recipe, the three initiates who possess the closely guarded secret of compounding the herbs dividing their time between Voiron and Tarragona. The old distillery in the port area of Tarragona, built around a courtyard planted with palm trees and fragrant with herbs, is well worth a visit, which ends with a tasting in a tiled *salón de degustación* lined from floor to ceiling with bottles containing fraudulent imitations.

The Cuisine

In gastronomy, as in other matters, Catalonia is one of the richest and most individual regions in Spain, and Spanish books on cooking keep returning to the magic figure of some hundred different regional specialities.

It was only to be expected that a state as rich and inventive as medieval Catalonia should not be backward in the culinary arts, which received further stimulus from the large-scale importation of spices from the East; it was, in fact, the spice trade which motivated Catalan maritime expansion in the eastern Mediterranean.

A most important event in Spanish cooking was the publication in 1477 of the *Llibre de Coch* (Book of Cookery) in Barcelona. Its author, a Maestre Rubert de Nola, was reputedly chef to Alfonso the Magnanimous of Aragón-Catalonia (1416-58) and accompanied him on the expedition which led to the conquest of Naples. The book was originally written in Catalan, but was revised and translated into Castilian on the initiative of that great gourmet, the Emperor Charles V of Spain. It subsequently ran to some twenty editions, and circulated very widely outside Spain. It is one of the earliest compilations of recipes dating from the medieval period: of very considerable variety and sophistication, they ran to 243 in the Castilian edition. Maestre Rubert also includes detailed instructions for the carving of meat and game and the serving of food and drink. He adds some pithy remarks on the functions of the different household officials :

There are three officials in noble houses who are never at peace : the carver, the steward and the chef. If the steward brings the meat without properly breaking the bones or provides meat of poor quality, the chef says that he does not know how to buy and that he is a poor steward, and at times they quarrel. Similarly the carver tells the chef that his food is uneatable and that he has no talent for cooking because the meat is overdone and impossible to carve, with the result that the master loses patience and it is he who is blamed for it. This is the reason why these three officials are never at peace ; and if they are to settle their differences among themselves, it is essential that the steward is a good

The title page of the 1529 edition of Rubert de Nola's *Llibre de Coch* ; one of the earliest European cookbooks, it was first published in Barcelona in 1477.

cook and carver, that the chef is a good carver as well as cook, and that the carver is a good steward and chef . . .

The *Llibre de Coch* was only the first of a series of treatises on cooking. It was succeeded by works such as the anonymous *La cuynera catalan o sian reglas utils, facils, seguras y economicas per cuynar bé* (Catalan Cooking, or Useful, Easy, Reliable and Economical Rules for Cooking Well) ; *Avisos o sian reglas sensillas a un principiant cuyner o cuynera, adaptadas a la capacitat dels menos instruits* (Instructions or Sensible Rules for a Learner Chef or Cook, Adjusted to the Capabilities of the Less Knowledgeable), written by Felip Cirera, probably a functionary of the episcopal palace at Vich ; and the *Magnific manual de cuina práctica catalana* (Magnificent Manual of Practical Catalan Cooking) by Ignacio Doménech, doyen of Spanish chefs during the early decades of the present century, in the heroic mould of an Escoffier.

Spanish writers stress that each small locality in Catalonia has its individual way of preparing traditional dishes, for example singling out the Costa Brava for its seafood. The difficulty with the Costa Brava, as with other intensely developed holiday areas, is that there is now hardly a village without its quota of hotels and restaurants laid out for foreign tourists, and in the seas of fish-and-chips and prawn cocktails authentic Catalan dishes have often sunk without a trace. If you want to sample regional cooking, go inland to Gerona or some small town such as Sta Coloma de Farnés, or better still start your adventures with the knife and fork in Barcelona. Here, as in the Basque country, cooking in the many sophisticated restaurants has been much influenced by the *nouvelle cuisine*, and there has been a return to simpler forms of cooking, so as to lighten the sometimes heavy and oversubstantial native dishes and bring out the flavours of the ingredients. The most rewarding area for typical regional food is in the streets off the *Ramblas* or in the harbour area at their lower end. It was the boast of that noted Spanish epicure, Luis Antonio de Vega, that you could walk into almost any small restaurant in Barcelona with your eyes shut and not be disappointed.

Catalonia possesses five basic sauces, of which pride of place must go to *alioli*, a Roman invention originally made by beating up garlic and olive oil to which Virgil gave the name *moretum*, and corresponding to the *aïoli* of Provence. The others are *picada*, containing almonds and toasted hazelnuts; *chanfaina*, made with peppers, onions, tomatoes and garlic and akin to the *chilindrón* sauce of Aragón; *sofrito*, the Catalan version of *salsa española*, used the length and breadth of Spain; and *romesco*, which takes its name from the small, hot, dried red peppers used in making it.

Catalans often begin a meal with *pan con tomate y jamón* (country bread rubbed with fresh tomato, salt and garlic, and sometimes served with slices of cured ham). Other popular starters are vegetable dishes, such as *espinacas a la catalana* (boiled spinach with pine kernels and raisins), *calcotada* (made only in spring with sliced spring onions, grilled over a wood fire and served with a *romesco*-like sauce) or *habas a la catalana* (fresh broad beans with Catalan black sausage and other ingredients).

As might be expected of a region with a long Mediterranean seaboard, fish soups like the

Shelling hazelnuts, which are one of the ingredients of *picada*, a traditional Catalan sauce.

sopa de mejillones catalana (made with mussels and flavoured with *aguardiente*, a form of *marc*, and garlic) are legion; and two fish dishes deserve special mention. *Bullabesa* is akin to the Provençal *bouillabaisse* (the dishes are of common origin). *Zarzuela*, which takes its name from a Spanish word meaning a variety show, is a truly magnificent dish, containing a variety of shellfish and firm white fish, cooked in a rich sauce with onions, garlic and tomatoes.

Other favourite fish dishes are *langosta a la catalana* (stewed lobster with onions, carrots, garlic, herbs, chocolate, nutmeg and brandy), *parrillada de pescado con salsa romesco* (mixed grill of fish with *romesco* sauce and mayonnaise) and *rape a la Costa Brava* (monkfish cooked with fresh peas, red peppers, mussels, saffron, garlic, parsley and white wine, with a little lemon).

Chicken in *chanfaina* sauce and turkey are favourites with the Catalans, and there is no shortage of game like quail and partridge. Another intriguing dish is *conejo con caracoles* (rabbit cooked with snails). The substantial *escudella i carn d'olla* is one of the most traditional of dishes and, like the *ollas* from La Mancha, is served in parts: first the *escudella*, a meaty soup with pasta, and then the *carn d'olla*, a rich stew containing veal, chicken, ground pork, blood sausage, egg, breadcrumbs and vegetables, both fresh and dried.

Best-known of the sweets is *crema quemada a la catalana*, a baked custard topped with a thin

layer of brittle caramel. Other specialities are *mel y mató* (fresh cream cheese with honey), *panellets* (a marzipan-like confection made with almonds or pine kernels, sugar and eggs) and *postre de músico*, almonds, raisins, walnuts, hazelnuts, figs and other dried mixed fruits.

The old cathedral town of Vich in the foothills of the Pyrenees makes a range of charcuterie, including *chorizos* (paprika sausage), *morcilla* (blood sausage), *jamón serrano* (highly cured ham) and the delicate white *butifarra*, typical of Catalonia and the Balearics, prepared from minced pork, spices and a little of the blood, put into sausage skins and hung up to dry. It may be eaten raw, cooked on its own or used in other dishes such as *butifarra amb mongetes*, in which it is stewed with the local haricot beans.

Restaurants

Arenys de Mar

HISPANIA★★★
This busy roadside restaurant run by the redoubtable Rexach sisters serves some of the best traditional fare in Catalonia. The long menu lists such things as *gambas al estilo Denia* (prawns boiled in salt water and iced), *lubina con russinyols* (sea bass with mushrooms, hollandaise sauce and fish *fumé*), *buñuelos de bacalao* (dried cod fritters), *suquet de almejas* (clam chowder), grilled sea snails, roast shoulder of kid, and a delicious *crema catalana* (baked caramel custard topped with brittle caramel). Red and white house wine from Ampurdán.

Barcelona

Any list of the scores of good restaurants in Barcelona must be highly selective and personal. If you are in search of fresh seafood, head for the port area and chance your arm.

ELDORADO PETIT★★★
See San Feliú de Guixols.

FLORIÁN★★★
The reputation of this small and intimate restaurant is based on its Catalan food, but it also serves dishes from the rest of Spain and a few from Italy. Typical are the salad of *angulas* (small eels), *papillottes* of red mullet, hake with a seaweed sauce, *magret* of duck and the Riojan tripe with *chorizo*. There are good home-made sorbets and ice creams and well-selected Spanish and French wines.

JAUME DE PROVENÇA★★★
The imaginative Jaume Bagués is equally at home with the *nouvelle cuisine* and traditional dishes, and his restaurant is one of the best in Barcelona and Spain. Start with one of the salads, such as *níscalos y verduras 'al dente'* (fungi with vegetables) or with river crabs or lobster. The choice is then between Catalan dishes like the baby cuttle fish with broad beans or those in the new style like suprême of hake with *nécoras* (crabs) or mousse of *bacalao* (dried cod) with scallops. The emphasis is on fish, but the fillet steak with anchovy sauce is delicious, and there is a good selection of sweets and sorbets, as also of wines, Spanish and French.

NEICHEL★★★
Jean Louis Neichel is the leading exponent of the *nouvelle cuisine* in Barcelona, which he has brilliantly adapted to the cooking of local ingredients in the cold cream of sea crayfish with saffron, medallions of monkfish and fresh salmon, chicken liver pie, truffled pigeon and many others.

RENO★★★
Established for thirty years, Reno has unfailingly maintained its reputation for good cooking both of traditional Catalan dishes and international fare, such as the goose liver terrine, brochette of langoustines, truffle soufflé and sole in pastry with sauce aurore. Good French and Spanish wines.

AGUT D'AVIGNON★★

In the heart of old Barcelona, this is one of the city's best-known and most popular restaurants. It offers a wide range of both Spanish and international dishes including game terrines, belly of pork with *mongetes* (beans), beans with herring, and goose with pears or caper sauce. It is essential to book a table.

VÍA VENETO★★

An elegant restaurant where the emphasis is on Catalan dishes such as *brandade de bacalao* (dried cod), *jarrete con níscalos* (oxtail with mushrooms), leg of lamb and baked gilthead. Other sophisticated dishes include marinated salmon with coriander and cream of radishes, lobster cardinal and *magret* of duck. Long wine list.

CASA COSTA★

This large restaurant facing the sea is the best-known of those in the port area, and the place to come for fresh seafood, either plain boiled or in the form of a mixed grill (*parrillada de pescado*) or rich stews, such as *bullabesa* or *zarzuela*.

Cambrils

CA'N GATELL★★

Like the other two restaurants in Cambrils (on the coast near Tarragona) belonging to the Gatell family, this serves a splendid variety of fish and shellfish, and the *entremeses especiales* (hors d'oeuvres) are famous for their diversity; the succession of shellfish, both hot and cold, seems endless. If, after the *entremeses*, you wish to continue, there is a range of interesting dishes from Tarragona, including sole with almonds, fish in spicy *romesco* sauce and *arroz abanda* (rice with fish).

CASA GATELL★★

With an agreeable terrace overlooking the sea, Casa Gatell serves food very much along the same lines as Ca'n Gatell.

EUGENIA★★

The charming service and simple cooking of fish in its natural juices has gained this third of the Gatell establishments the same high reputation as the others.

Figueras

AMPURDÁN ★★★

Off the motorway on the old road to France, the Motel Ampurdán offers the best hotel cooking in Spain. It was opened by Josep Mercader, originator of the new Catalan cuisine, and his pupil Jaime Subirat continues in the same tradition. Much to be recommended are the salad of broad beans with mint, prawn mousse with cucumber salad, and aubergines stuffed with anchovies. Delicious fish dishes are the *ragôut* of monkfish and fresh salmon with saffron, and baked gilthead. There is meat from the charcoal grill and first-rate stuffed leg of lamb. The ices and sorbets, as one would expect in an establishment founded by Mercader, are outstanding. Good local wines, including a *vi novell*.

DURÁN★★

The Hotel Durán has been serving good Catalan, Spanish and French food for almost a century and remains in the hands of the same family. It serves such dishes as crêpes of cuttle fish and cabbage, sole with orange, *bacalao* (dried cod) with *chanfaina* sauce, *magret* of duck, quail stuffed with foie gras, together with good home-made sweets and sorbets, and a selection of Spanish and French cheeses. Good list of local wines.

Lérida

FORN DEL NASTASI★★

The cooking is straightforward, and the menu, based on the excellent local vegetables and top quality fish and meat, always includes some Catalan specialities. Typical are the *menestra* (mixed vegetable dish), fish soups, hake in its juice, leg of pork with snails and duck with pears or figs.

San Feliú de Guixols

ELDORADO PETIT★★★

From small beginnings in 1972, Luis Cruañas, with the help of his family, has made Eldorado Petit the most sophisticated restaurant on the Costa Brava. He is currently rated among the top ten restaurateurs in Spain. He has travelled extensively in France and Italy and has been much influenced by the *nouvelle cuisine*, but tempers it with the traditions of Ampurdán. Examples of his dishes are cream of broad bean soup, steamed monkfish à la vinaigrette, turbot with sea urchin sauce or fillet steak with mushrooms and onion sauce – but the names convey little of the delicacy of the cooking. He has recently opened a second Eldorado Petit with similar standards in Barcelona.

S'Agaro

HOSTAL DE LA GAVINA★★

The Hostal is the most fashionable (and expensive) hotel on the Costa Brava, and its restaurant offers sophisticated international food, with a few Catalan dishes such as the fish soup Costa Brava, the local *butifarra* sausage with black pepper, Palamos prawns with garlic and *crema catalana* (baked cream caramel with brittle top). Long wine list.

Tarragona

SOL RIC★★

Sol Ric, with its pleasant garden, has an extensive repertoire of Catalan and Tarragonese dishes, including grilled fish, *bacalao* (dried cod) fritters, squid and clams, game in season, *romesco* (fish stews), Catalan stuffed turkey, steak with Roquefort sauce and *menja blanca* (a sweet made from ground almonds, cream, kirsch and lemon).

Recipes

Espinacas a la Catalana/ Catalan-Style Spinach

Serves 4

METRIC/IMPERIAL

4 tablespoons olive oil

2 cloves garlic, chopped

6 anchovy fillets, chopped

2 kg/4½ lbs spinach, washed, boiled, drained and chopped

50 g/2 oz pine kernels

50 g/2 oz raisins, tailed if necessary and chopped

Salt and freshly ground pepper

AMERICAN

4 tablespoons olive oil

2 cloves garlic, chopped

6 anchovy fillets, chopped

4½ lbs spinach, washed, boiled, drained and chopped

¼ cup pine nuts

¼ cup raisins, stemmed if necessary and chopped

Salt and freshly ground pepper

Heat the olive oil in a heavy pan and add the garlic, anchovies, spinach, pine kernels and raisins. Cook for about fifteen minutes, stirring with a wooden spoon. Season with salt and pepper and serve hot.

Rape a la Costa Brava/Monkfish Costa Brava Style

Serves 4

METRIC/IMPERIAL	AMERICAN
2 onions, peeled and cut into rings	2 onions, peeled and cut into rings
1 kg/2¼ lbs monkfish, boned and cut into thin slices	2¼ lbs monkfish, boned and cut into thin slices
200 g/7 oz fresh peas, shelled and boiled (or frozen)	1¾ cups fresh green peas, shelled and boiled (or frozen)
12 mussels, scraped, boiled to open, shells removed (reserve stock)	12 mussels, scraped, boiled to open, shells removed (reserve stock)
4 tablespoons chopped parsley	4 tablespoons chopped parsley
4 canned red peppers, drained and cut into strips	4 canned red pimientos, drained and cut into strips
275 ml/10 fl oz dry white wine	1¼ cups dry white wine
Salt	Salt
3 cloves garlic, chopped	3 cloves garlic, chopped
Few strands saffron	Few strands saffron
1 level tablespoon flour	1 level tablespoon flour
4 tablespoons mussel stock	4 tablespoons mussel stock
2 lemons cut into wedges	2 lemons cut into wedges

Cover the bottom of an oven dish with the onion. Put on top the fish, defrosted peas, mussels, parsley, peppers and wine. Season with salt and cook in the oven (350°F/180°C/Gas Mark 4) for twenty minutes.

Meanwhile pound the garlic and saffron in a mortar, add the flour and mussel stock so as to make a smooth paste, and add it to the fish after the first ten minutes of cooking. Decorate with lemon and serve with a salad.

The Basque Country

THE GREEN AND MOUNTAINOUS Basque country in the north-eastern corner of Spain, bounded by the Atlantic and by the Pyrenees and French frontier to the east, has always been a region apart. Richard Ford describes it as the 'corner of water' and remarks that when the grey clouds roll in from the Bay of Biscay it rains 'contrary to all reason and experience, κατα δοξως, which we take to be the true etymon of our "cats and dogs"'.

The Basques themselves are as much of an historical enigma as their strange language. The most generally accepted theory is that they are the last survivors of the original Celtiberian inhabitants of the Peninsula. A Soviet historian and philologist, Alexander Kihnadze, claims to have catalogued some 360 Basque words similar or identical to those used in the Caucasus or present-day Georgia (*Iveria*). As further evidence he cites an ancient tablet excavated in Bilbao, bearing an inscription recently deciphered by Georgian scholars. This purports to describe a mass immigration from the east after a natural cataclysm in prehistoric times.

Be that as it may – and the idea has been considered worthy of investigation by the Society for the Defence of the Basque Language – the Basques have always displayed a lively independence, and still do. From the Romans and Moors to Napoleon's conquering armies, no foreign invader has established a lasting foothold. In Spain's internal struggles the Basques have always favoured the side that promised local autonomy, and thus supported the pretender Don Carlos during the Carlist Wars of the nineteenth century and the Republicans during the Civil War; their desire to rule themselves remains unabated today. The Basque country nevertheless makes a most important contribution to the Spanish economy: it is the headquarters of the country's steel-making and shipbuilding industries and of many of the important banks.

Apart from industrial Bilbao, crouching at the mouth of the Nervión River like some Spanish Newcastle, the largest city is San Sebastián. Most elegant of Spanish seaside resorts and the favourite of the Spanish court and well-to-do Madrileños until it became the fashion to head south for the Costa del Sol in summer, it faces a magnificent bay, and the great curving beach of La Concha is fringed by the old houses of the aristocracy, restaurants, shops and hotels. Along the precipitous Atlantic coast between San Sebastián and Bilbao, there is a string of picturesque fishing ports and smaller resorts, such as Zarauz, Guetaría, Zumaya, Motrico and Bermeo.

No one has written more poetically of these places and the mystique of the sea than Pío Baroja in stories such as 'The Restlessness of Shanti Andía'; and the Basques are hardy fishermen and sailors. Having braved their own stormy waters, they often turned to exploration and sometimes to piracy; it was a Basque, Juan Sebastián Elcano, who first circumnavigated the globe.

PREVIOUS PAGE **The port of San Sebastián, centre of the Basque fishing industry.**

The Wines

Some ninety-seven per cent of the wine from the Basque country is made in the province of Alava, of which the southern tip forms part of the Rioja. This is described with the other Riojas in Chapter 4.

Because of the mountainous terrain and a rainfall amounting to some fifty-three inches annually, the provinces of Guipúzcoa and Vizcaya make only very limited amounts of Chacolí (or *txakolí* in its Basque form), *pétillant* young wines in the style of the Portuguese *vinhos verdes*.

The grapes are of two types, the white Ondarrubi zuria (akin to the Courbut blanc) and the red Ondarrubi beltza. They are grown without grafting, because the pools of water which form around the base of the stocks in winter prevent aeration of the soil and roots and kill the phylloxera insect. The vines are grown high, and this necessitates a great deal of manual labour in tending them, in draining away the water in spring and in combatting the plant diseases brought on by the damp climate.

The wines, either white or *rosado* (rosé), are low in alcohol (9-11°), *pétillant* and acidic, but at their best, fresh and fragrant with good finish. The Basques toss them down as an aperitif from a small thick glass known as a *chiquito*, but they also go well with the local shellfish when drunk in more leisurely fashion.

Among the best of the Chacolís are those from BODEGAS HERMANOS EYZAGUIRRE in Zarauz, labelled as 'Monte Gárate' and 'Hilbera', and the 'Txacolí Txomin Echániz' from TXOMIN ECHÁNIZ in Guetaría.

The Cuisine

It is generally accepted in Spain that the best and most varied cooking is to be found in the Basque provinces. Spanish writers often refer

The Pyrenees near Roncesvalles, the scene of Roland's death and Charlemagne's defeat by the Basques.

to Bilbao as the country's gastronomic capital. As long ago as 1549, Pedro de Medina wrote in his *Libro de grandezas y cosas memorables de España* : 'Bilbao is a noble city of much quality, because three things are to be found there : pleasant situations, *abundance* of food and the good conduct of its people and merchants.' Both Bilbao and San Sebastián have long been renowned for their *cofradías* or dining societies, where food is prepared by both men and women *socios* (or members). Gastronomes such as the Marqués de los Andes and Luis Antonio de Vega are quick to point out that these gatherings are notable not only for the abundance of the fare, but for its sophistication. Good cooking stems from the quality of the materials, and the Basque country is blessed with dairy produce, vegetables and fruit from its green meadows, good meat from its mountain pastures and splendid fish from the cold waters of the Bay of Biscay.

The fishermen are themselves no mean cooks and trenchermen ; at the beginning of the anchovy season in the spring, it was formerly the custom of the crews to seal their compact with the owners of the boats not in writing but by sitting at table with them and sharing a copious meal. The famous *marmite*, made by stewing tuna with onion, garlic and potatoes, was often prepared on board the fishing craft and took its name from the pot, concave in shape to prevent the contents slopping over, in which it was cooked.

Among more elaborate feasts, one worth recording was that given in 1623 by the Duke of Buckingham in his flagship off Santander, when he escorted the Prince of Wales (the future Charles I) to Madrid in fruitless pursuit of the hand of the Spanish *infanta*. According to tradition, no fewer than 1600 dishes were served, and when the moment came for the royal toast the guns of the fleet fired a thunderous salute – resulting in the immediate destruction of the glass and crystal.

Merluza a la vasca (Basque-style hake), one of the best-known dishes from the region, is also one of the very few of which the origin and date

are known. In his *Viaje por la cocina española*, Luis Antonio de Vega recounts how he came upon a letter written during the first week of May 1723 by Doña Plácida de Larrea of Bilbao to a namesake living in Navarra. Doña Plácida specifies that the fish must be caught from a small boat by hook and line and describes how she stewed it in an earthenware *cazuela* and served it with cockles and crabs in a green sauce made from parsley and with a garnish of asparagus, a present from friends in Tudela.

Basque fish dishes are so numerous that it is a question of picking out some of the best-known. High on the list must come *bacalao a la vizcaína* : with its sauce containing garlic, red peppers, onion and breadcrumbs, this is a revelation to people who imagine that the salted and dried cod so popular in Spain, and even more so in Portugal, is necessarily insipid. Squid is perhaps another specialized taste ; it is at its best and most tender when cooked in a black sauce made from its own ink as *calamares en su tinta*. Other delicacies at their best in this region are *angulas*, the tiny freshwater eels, and

Guindillas, a variety of chilli, hung out to dry in the sun. It is used in a variety of spicy dishes all over Spain.

kokotxas, a dish made from strips cut from the 'cheek' or throat of the hake and cooked in an earthenware *cazuela* with a little olive oil, parsley and garlic. *Paella marinera*, though of Valencian origin, is at its best in these parts because of the variety and magnificent quality of the shellfish.

Santander, strictly in Old Castile, lies on the western fringe of the Basque country, of which its food is typical: notable are the luscious *percebes*, a form of edible barnacle served as an aperitif; spider crab, from which the meat is removed, cooked in white wine and replaced in the shell; or the homely but delicious fresh sardines, grilled over charcoal in the cafés flanking its wide beaches. A more ambitious restaurant, serving one of the best selection of *tapas* in the country, is the Riojano, stone-flagged and supported by great timber baulks. Formerly a fishermen's *taberna*, it is now atmospherically decorated with wine casks, with the ends painted by some of the best artists in Spain. Its menu was designed by Picasso.

The Vascongadas is also a region of mountains and rivers, like the Deva, Nansa, Asón, Pas and Saja, renowned for their trout and salmon. Among the wealth of fish, it is easy to forget that the Basque country also produces excellent beef, lamb and pork, and do not overlook the most individual *piperada* or Basque omelette (also popular in the Basque region on the French side of the Pyrenees), made by breaking and stirring eggs into a mixture of onions, tomatoes, peppers and chopped ham. This is one of the few parts of Spain where fresh cream is readily available and is used in making sweets. Incidentally, it is a misconception that cream plays a significant part in the national cuisine. In southern Spain, what cream there is can be bought only in cans, largely produced by the Nestlé factory in Santander. The Basque cheeses, of which the best are the hard and semi-hard Gorbea, Orduṇa and Idiazábal, are made from ewe's milk.

When Paul Bocuse launched the *nouvelle cuisine*, among his most talented disciples were a group of chefs from the Basque country, who in 1976 formed the *Grupo de la Nueva Cocina Vasca*, dedicated to the cooking of the best prime materials in such a way as to bring out their natural flavours to the full. Juan María Arzak, Pedro Subijana and Jesús María Oyarbide (who migrated to Madrid to open Zalacaín, arguably the best restaurant in Spain) are now famous beyond their homeland: and the movement which they started has swept the more sophisticated restaurants of Spain.

Arzak and his Basque colleagues, much as they admired and were influenced by Paul Bocuse and Raymond Oliver, were never, however, slavish imitators of the *nouvelle cuisine* – and how many of us, in less inspired restaurants from London to Los Angeles, have become inured to those dainty little plates of steamed vegetables – five French beans, three broccoli sprouts, three tiny potatoes and the same number of miniature carrots – or of a small portion of white fish poached in its own juices, but accompanied by a sauce hollandaise so rich, one suspects, as to engender at best a sleepless night, and at worst a heart attack?

The Basque chefs welcomed the *nouvelle cuisine* as a bold step in breaking loose from the set forms and complications of *Le Guide Culinaire* or *Le Répertoire de la Cuisine*, and in reverting to simpler methods of cooking which enabled them to make the most of the splendid fish and vegetables of Spain's north coast. Arzak's devotion to inherent flavour is typified by the Case of the Disappearing Pea. His suppliers began selling him small and tender peas of the sort that look so well on those fastidiously arranged vegetable 'garnishes' – their only drawback being that they did not taste of peas. He then discovered that the local growers were planting a high-cropping pea from Madagascar, and he is at present campaigning for at least a proportion of the fields to be planted with the more flavoursome native variety.

The attitude of these chefs who have spearheaded a renaissance of Spanish cookery is perhaps best put by Pedro Subijana, of the renowned Akelarre in San Sebastián:

People go to France, or to Japan if necessary, and in most cases they simply copy recipes to the last possible detail. This, as I see it, is profoundly wrong; the important thing is to understand why things are done and to know how to adapt them without losing one's own personality . . .

He goes on to define the aims of the *nueva cocina vasca* as:

The return to simple cookery and the respect for tradition and its rehabilitation. You therefore have on your menu: old dishes, some included more for nostalgic reasons than for their flavour; traditional dishes, but very carefully cooked; and, finally, some new ones.

You may judge the results by visiting some of the restaurants listed below.

Restaurants

Bilbao

GOIZEKO KABI★★★
Under its young management team this is a restaurant which has greatly contributed to the renaissance of Basque cooking. Ask for the warm salad of mange-touts and foie gras, the *ragôut* of scallops with mushrooms and truffles, crab crêpes, *cogete* (hake in a sauce with red peppers), fillet steak with puff pastry or leg of kid with mushrooms. The lemon crêpes with hot chocolate are delicious.

GURIA★★★
Installed in a charmingly decorated house in old Bilbao, Guria is perhaps the city's most famous restaurant. Excellently prepared Basque dishes include the smooth and creamy *bacalao del chef*

OPPOSITE **An open market in Guernica, with a typically wide range of local produce.**

(dried and salted cod), hake in different styles, *ijada de bonito* (tuna) and *lubina neguri* (sea bass). In the hands of Jenaro Pildain rice pudding emerges as a masterpiece. There is an excellent selection of local cheeses.

Fuenterrabía

The old walled town of Fuenterrabía, with its baronial houses and a castle (now a Parador), overlooks Hendaye and the Bidasoa estuary and is only a few miles from the frontier post of Irún.

RAMÓN ROTETA★★★
Ramón Roteta was one of the founders of the *nueva cocina vasca*. After contributing much to the success of El Amparo in Madrid, he returned to his native country to open his own restaurant. Among many immaculately prepared dishes are fresh salmon with river crabs, sea bass with barnacle sauce, turbot with clams, *cordero guisado al estilo de la abuela* (stewed lamb), Basque-style lobster and entrecôte in red wine. There is a first-rate Idiazábal cheese and sorbets in season. Excellent Chacolí from Guetaria and a five-year-old Rioja house wine.

San Sebastián

ARZAK★★★★
The much-decorated Juan María Arzak, one of the founders of the *nueva cocina vasca*, runs one of the best restaurants in Spain, varying the menu according to season. Specialities are the *confit* of goose, the sea bass steamed with seaweed and served with a sauce fines herbes, Bidasoa salmon in pastry, the red sea scorpion pie and *cocochas* (strips from the 'cheek' of the hake). Game in season includes woodcock, wild boar and venison, and there is excellent roast lamb. The 'new cooking' is represented by dishes such as the vegetable salads with walnut oil and the escalopes of duck with pastry and pears. Comprehensive wine list, both French and Spanish.

AKELARRE★★★

Beautifully situated on the slopes of Monte Igueldo overlooking the sea, Akelarre is the creation of Pedro Subijana, who is both owner and *maître de cuisine* and in 1979 won the title of Best Chef in Spain for his contributions to the *nueva cocina vasca*. Sample his cooking with steamed tuna in a sauce flavoured with peppers, escalope of milk-fed veal with foie gras and mushrooms, endive salad with apple and nuts or fillet of sole with Chacolí. Meats include tournedos in red wine and entrecôte au poivre, and the sweets, strawberry tart and sorbets of lemon and champagne.

NICOLASA★★★

One is made welcome with a glass of Chacolí at this famous and thoroughly traditional old Basque restaurant. The *menestra* (mixed vegetable dish) is outstanding, and other favourites include *txangurro* (crab), line-caught squid, scrambled eggs with sea crayfish, roast capon with chestnut purée, chicken stuffed with truffles and guinea fowl in Armagnac. Among the first-rate sweets are *tocino de cielo* (egg-yolk sweet), *huevos moll* (another egg sweet) and an apple pudding. The wine list is particularly strong on Riojas but also includes some good French wines.

Zarauz

KARLOS ARGIÑANO★★★

It was in Zarauz that Luis Irizar conducted a school of cookery which evolved the *nueva cocina vasca*. One of its most brilliant students was Karlos Argiñano, who now prepares a wide range of imaginative dishes in his own kitchens. They include prawn and leek pie, peppers stuffed with fish, crêpes with salmon and scallops, entrecôte with watercress and marrow sauce, and also more traditional Basque fare, such as kidney beans with blood sausage and line-caught squid in their ink. There are good home-made sweets and sorbets, and local Chacolí wines.

Recipes

Angulas en Cazuela/ Elvers (Young Eels) in Ramekins

This is best cooked in individual earthenware *cazuelas* (see p. 54); otherwise use small Pyrex or similar flameproof dishes.
Per person:

METRIC/IMPERIAL

2 tablespoons olive oil

1 clove garlic, chopped

$\frac{1}{2}$ dry chilli pepper, seeds removed, and chopped

150 g/5 oz elvers, boiled

Salt and pepper

AMERICAN

2 tablespoons olive oil

1 clove garlic, chopped

$\frac{1}{2}$ dry chili pepper, seeds removed, and chopped

5 oz elvers, boiled

Salt and pepper

Heat the oil in the *cazuela* and add the garlic and chilli; when the garlic changes colour, add the elvers and shake the dish rather than stir – if you wish to stir a little, use a wooden fork. Cook for only two minutes until they are hot, but not fried, then cover with a lid and serve with all speed, so that they are still bubbling when brought to the table. Serve with warm French bread and eat with wooden forks.

Pisto a la Bilbaína/Ratatouille Bilbao Style

Serves 4

METRIC/IMPERIAL	AMERICAN
4 tablespoons olive oil	$\frac{1}{4}$ cup olive oil
200 g/7 oz boiled ham or Italian prosciutto, chopped	7 oz boiled ham or Italian prosciutto, chopped
2 large onions, peeled and chopped	2 large onions, peeled and chopped
1 large potato, peeled and very thinly sliced	1 large potato, peeled and very thinly sliced
4 courgettes, blanched and cut into thin rounds	4 zucchini, blanched and cut into thin rounds
4 green peppers, washed, seeds and core discarded, chopped	4 green peppers, washed, seeds and core discarded, chopped
2 cloves garlic, peeled and chopped	2 cloves garlic, peeled and chopped
Salt and pepper	Salt and pepper
6 fresh tomatoes, blanched and skinned	6 fresh tomatoes, blanched and skinned
1 tablespoon concentrated tomato purée	1 tablespoon concentrated tomato paste
4 large eggs	4 large eggs

Heat the oil in a heavy pan and fry the ham, then add the onions, potato, courgettes, peppers, garlic, and a little salt and pepper. Cover and leave to cook slowly for about half an hour until the mixture is soft. Now add the tomatoes and tomato purée and leave on the heat a little longer, uncovered so as to evaporate the tomato liquid. The vegetables may be cooked in advance; before serving, break the eggs on top and cook until the whites are set. Bring to the table with fresh bread.

Merluza en Salsa Verde/Hake in Green Sauce

Serves 4

METRIC/IMPERIAL	AMERICAN
4 tablespoons olive oil	¼ cup olive oil
2 cloves garlic, chopped	2 cloves garlic, chopped
4 slices hake, about 150 g/5 oz each	4 slices hake, about 5 oz each
300 ml/½ pint mussel or fish stock	1 cup mussel or fish stock
6 tablespoons chopped parsley	6 tablespoons chopped parsley
1 tablespoon fresh mint	1 tablespoon fresh mint
Salt and freshly ground pepper	Salt and freshly ground pepper
12 mussels, scraped, boiled, opened, shells discarded (keep stock)	12 mussels, scraped, boiled, opened, shells discarded (keep stock)
450 g/1 lb canned asparagus tips	1 lb canned asparagus tips

If possible in an earthenware *cazuela* or otherwise in a flameproof dish, fry the garlic until it begins to colour, then remove and discard it. Fry the hake in the same oil and reserve it. Drain and return the hake to the pan, and add the fish stock, parsley, mint and a little salt and pepper. Shake and cook gently for fifteen to twenty minutes. Decorate with the mussels and asparagus tips and serve.

Asturias and Galicia

*A*STURIAS AND GALICIA lie in the far north-western corner of Spain. Probably because of the mountainous terrain and wet climate, which had little appeal for the invaders from north Africa, this was the one part of the country never to be occupied by the Moors (and proved to be their Achilles heel). It was King Pelayo of Asturias who, according to legend, defeated a Moorish army at Covadonga in 718, so striking the first blow in the centuries-long Reconquest.

During the Middle Ages, Galicia became the spiritual rallying point for the hard-pressed Christians. Santiago de Compostela (*campus stellae* or 'the field of the star') was the furthest point reached by St James the Apostle in his missionary travels and his remains are buried there. The defeat of the omnipotent 'Abd-al-Rahman III at Simancas in 939 was attributed to the miraculous intervention of the saint on the field of battle, and from the eleventh century the pilgrimage to his shrine was the most famous in Europe. After the Benedictines from Cluny built a cathedral to house the shrine and constructed staging posts along the route from France, the pilgrimage formed the single most important link between Spain and Christian Europe.

Much later in Spain's history, the far north was to play a crucial role in organizing resistance to another invader. In May 1808 the Supreme Junta of Asturias sent deputies to London with an urgent plea for help in the struggle against Napoleon; and La Coruña, at the northernmost tip of Galicia, was the end-point of the tragic retreat which culminated in the death of Sir John Moore and the evacuation of the British expeditionary force during the early stages of the Peninsular War.

Perhaps the best way to gain an overall impression of this unspoilt and picturesque part of Spain is to take the long road from Santander through Asturias. After leaving Gijón, surprisingly the largest port in the country, and passing the huge steel mills of that Asturian Sheffield or Pittsburg, Avilés, the route winds among hills and apple orchards, eventually emerging on to a green coastal strip between the snow-capped mountains and the rocky coves of the Atlantic coast. Over the mountain border with Galicia the scenery changes and gives way to granite mountains, falling away towards the coast to the myriad *Rías*, somewhat resembling the fjords of Norway, whose dark blue waters are the source of much of Galicia's splendid shellfish.

Apart from Santiago de Compostela, the historic cities of Galicia, La Coruña, Vigo and Pontevedra lie along the coast. Particularly interesting is the great Atlantic seaport of Vigo. Upstream of the harbour the waters of the estuary, with their green mountain backdrop, are dotted with what at first appear to be small black houseboats, but are in fact *mejilloneras*, or floating platforms for fishing cultured mussels.

PREVIOUS PAGE The *calzada* or pilgrim's way to Santiago de Compostela, winding over the Pass of Piedrafita.

OPPOSITE The cathedral of Santiago de Compostela, to which pilgrims from the ends of Europe travelled to visit the shrine of St James.

The best time to visit Galicia is in the early summer, when the rain relents and the mountain slopes, fragrant with pine and eucalyptus and strewn with flowers, are a vast natural rock garden. Along the coasts of both Asturias and Galicia you will find secluded coves with clean sand and unpolluted Atlantic water.

OPPOSITE The picturesque little town of Redondela on the River Vigo.

BELOW *Mejilloneras*, or floating platforms, for the breeding of cultured mussels.

The Wines

Asturias produces no wine, but makes the best cider in Spain, formerly drunk from the barrel, but now bottled and aerated and sent both to other parts of Spain and abroad. The best-known brand, 'El Gaitero', is considerably more expensive than any but the more select wines. Cider is often used to advantage in Asturias for cooking fish, and parallels have been drawn with the cider-producing areas of Normandy and Brittany in France.

Despite its wet winters and short summers, Galicia produces wines resembling the *vinhos verdes* or 'green wines' of northern Portugal in very sizeable amounts. They were much drunk by John of Gaunt's soldiers in 1386, when, as Froissart records in his *Chronicles*, an English army was incapacitated for two days by imbibing them; and they were also the bane of Sir John Moore's troops during the retreat to La Coruña, when his half-tipsy soldiers were cut down in droves by the pursuing French dragoons. Until the end of the eighteenth century there was, in fact, a considerable export trade to Portugal and northern Europe.

That they are not better known abroad is probably because they did not travel well until modern methods were introduced for stabilizing them. Added to this, the great bulk of the wine continues to be made by small proprietors who sell it locally (there are only six cooperatives in the whole area). Galicia in fact consumes rather more wine than it produces, and some of the commercial firms 'stretch' the characterful but somewhat acidic local wine with neutral white wine from La Mancha so as to meet the demand.

The soils are granitic, and the outstanding vine variety is the white Albariño, the subject of a *Denominación específica*, applying not to a region but to the wines made from the grape.

OPPOSITE **High-growing vines in Galicia.**

However, upwards of a hundred different varieties are grown in Galicia, among the best of them being the white Treixadura, Torrontés, Godello, Macabeo, Albillo and Loureira; and the red Sonsón and Mencía. It was from the Mencía that the village of Amandi made the *clarete* which, according to legend, was such a favourite with Caesar Augustus as an accompaniment to his spiced lamprey.

Like the Portuguese in the Minho, the hard-working Galicians found an answer to their wet climate by training the vines clear of the damp ground in pergolas or on wires strung between granite pillars or wooden posts. This results in the grapes receiving less reflected sunshine than those grown low and without support, *a la castellana*, as in other parts of the country (and also in the easterly Galician regions of Verín and Valdeorras). The wines would be unacceptably sharp and acid if they did not (after normal fermentation is finished) undergo a prolonged secondary fermentation, converting the malic acid in the unripe fruit to the smoother-tasting lactic acid, and at the same time leaving them with a subdued and refreshing *pétillance*. White, red or rosé, they are ready for drinking in the late spring following the harvest. The red wine, though much appreciated by Galicians, is generally too tart for foreign palates. The whites, on the other hand, are delicate and flowery and because of their slight bubble often display a tingle on the tongue.

The largest production of Galician wine is in the demarcated region of Ribeiro in the province of Orense, centring on the township of Ribadavia near the confluence of the Rivers Sil and Miño. The great modern Cooperativa de Ribeiro, numbering some 1,600 *socios* or partners, produces an average of seven million litres of wine annually and is equipped with a modern bottling plant and refrigeration machinery.

Much of the most characterful wine comes from the small undemarcated districts of the Condado de Salvatierra and El Rosal, in the extreme south-west of the province of Pontevedra bordering the River Miño and the Portuguese frontier. It is made in small private bodegas, however, and is difficult to come by except in the bars and restaurants to which they sell directly.

By general agreement, the very best Galician wine is made from the white Albariño grape – just as the best of the Portuguese *vinhos verdes* are the Alvarinhos made from the same grape in Monção across the River Miño (or Minho in its Portuguese form). Dry, flowery and delicate, it has been compared to Moselle, and there is good reason to believe that the vines were in fact

The courtyard of the Parador Nacional Casa del Barón at Pontevedra, typical of a Galician *pazo*, or baronial house.

brought to Galicia from the Rhine and Moselle by Cluniac monks in the twelfth century. Production centres on the area around Cambados, north of Pontevedra and opposite the island of La Toja, where an annual Fiesta de Albariño is held in mid-August when the wines from different growers may be sampled. Their cult is such that Xosé Posada writes in his book *Os viños de Galicia* of a friend who 'married in Cambados so as to have better opportunities of drinking them', adding 'I think the sacrifice was well worthwhile'!

It is not normal in Spain for brandy and spirits to be made in the same establishment as wine, but the Bodega Cooperativa del Ribeiro produces a very potent *aguardiente*, akin to the French *marc de Bourgogne* or Portuguese *bagaceira*, by distilling the skins and pips of the grapes. This is described in its brochure as:

> A drink which taken by itself requires three men to a glass: one to drink it and two friends to support him, since it is one of the strongest drinks in the world. If drunk in the form of 'QUEIMADA', it is transformed into a deceptively mild nectar, dangerous in the extreme by virtue of the spell it then casts.
>
> The *Cooperativistas* of Ribeiro recommend that before drinking it, you pin a card with your address on the lapel of your jacket.

Queimada is prepared by pouring a little of the *aguardiente* into a white china bowl (also used in Galicia for red wines) and setting light to it to burn off some of the plentiful alcohol. When the blue flame subsides, the liquid, surprisingly, is stone-cold. More elaborate *queimadas* are made by pouring a bottle or half-bottle of *aguardiente* into a large earthenware *cazuela*, adding slices of lemon, roast coffee beans and maraschino cherries and setting fire to the brew (leaving plenty of headroom for the resulting blaze). The grateful liquid is then ladled out into glasses. Without going to Galicia, you may obtain a good *queimada* at any of the Galician restaurants in Madrid, and most cheering it is on a cold winter's day.

ALBARIÑO DEL PALACIO

Don Joaquín Gil Armada occupies a separate wing of the palace of Fefiñanes, where, like his brother the Marqués of Figueroa, he makes an excellent wine, the 'Albariño del Palacio', growing his own grapes in a small vineyard to the rear of the palace.

BODEGAS CHAVES, S.L.

Founded by José Cándido Chaves Chaves some thirty years ago, this small family firm owns vineyards and a bodega equipped with stainless steel fermentation tanks and refrigeration machinery, outside Cambados. It makes a light, fresh rosé and a one hundred per cent white Albariño, young, flowery and somewhat acidic, labelled as 'Castel de Fornos'. This is one of the very few Galician wines, and probably the only Albariño, available in the United Kingdom (from Laymont & Shaw of Truro).

COOPERATIVA DEL BARCO DE VALDEORRAS

The cooperative bottles very drinkable red and white wines with *Denominación de Origen* Valdeorras, fuller-bodied, without *pétillance* and higher in strength than most Galician wine. Apart from its 'Valdeorras Tinto' and 'Valdeorras Blanco', it markets a very fresh young 'Moza Fresca' and two very superior wines from vineyards replanted with the best of the traditional grapes, 'Godello' and 'Revival'.

COOPERATIVA DEL RIBEIRO

Founded some fifty years ago, this cooperative with its modern equipment and storage capacity of eleven million litres is by far the largest in Galicia. The best of its wines are *vinos de yema* made without mechanical pressing of the grapes. Production of the white 'Pazo' amounts to some four million bottles annually, and this is the Galician wine most widely encountered both in Spain and abroad. English consumers will be intrigued by the label of the lighter and somewhat *pétillant* 'Xeito', which bears a reproduction of Hogarth's 'Shrimp Girl'. The recently launched 'Viña Costeira' is made with a blend of Treixadura, Torrontés and Palomino;

while the pride of the cooperative is its 'Bradomin', made with ungrafted Treixadura and Torrontés in the style of the classical Galician wines of the past.

PALACIO DE FEFIÑANES

A part of the old palace of Fefiñanes on the outskirts of Cambados is given over to a small bodega, where the Marqués de Figueroa makes the most famous of Albariño wines, the 'Albariño de Fefiñanes'. Made from grapes grown in his own vineyards, the younger wines are aged in oak for two years and the *reservas* for six. Dry, delicate and fruity, they are not *pétillant* like most Albariños, and the *reserva* is a deeper yellow and fuller in flavour.

Trellised Albariño vines at the palace of Fefiñanes.

SANTIAGO RUIZ

The best of the bodegas in El Rosal, bordering Portugal in the south-west of Galicia, where few of the producers sell the wines under their own label. The excellent Albariño wine is sold as 'Vino de el Rosal'.

The Cuisine

In culinary terms Asturias is best known for its vegetables and fish. The most famous dish from these parts is *fabada asturiana*, a nourishing stew made with a basis of *alubias* or butter beans (the Asturians maintain that a good *fabada* can be made only with beans from the province) and *morcilla*, the local blood sausage, of which the

An *horreo*, used in Asturias and Galicia for storing grain and cheeses away from damp.

nearest British equivalent is the Scottish black pudding which is prepared, however, with oatmeal instead of rice. Variations on *fabada* include *fabes con almejas* (butter beans with clams) and *alubias estofadas* (bean stew).

The fish and methods of preparing it are legion. Fresh tuna is cooked with tomatoes as *ventesco de bonito con tomate*; monkfish is served in a green sauce as *pixin con salsa verde*; and the *crema de andaricas* (cream of crayfish) is particularly delicious. Fish is often cooked in the local cider instead of wine, as with *chopa a la sidra* or the sumptuous *merluza a la sidra* (hake in a sauce made from cider, brandy, mussels, flour, hard-boiled eggs and red peppers). A piquant starter, incidentally, is the *chorizo a la sidra* (cured pepper sausage in cider).

With such a range of fish, meat figures less on the menu, but try the tender *chuletón de ternera* (veal chop) or the *chuletón de buey* (beef chop), sometimes daringly served with figs in vinegar. To finish with, there is a particularly delicious milky rice pudding, *arroz requemado asturiana*, flavoured with aniseed, cinnamon and lemon and topped with brittle caramel.

Asturias makes Spain's major veined cheese, the blue Cabrales, reminiscent of Roquefort and indeed so fully flavoured that there is a *canard* that it is matured in heaps of manure! This is, of course, quite untrue. The curd is first skimmed from the whey with a hollow circle of bark like that used by the Homeric Greeks, and then dried in front of a fire. It is subsequently transferred to an *horreo* (from the Latin *horreum*), a wooden shed on stone stilts, typical of Asturias and Galicia and used generally to store grain away from damp or rats. When the blue mould makes its appearance the cheeses are taken to the famous cave of Jouz del Cuevu to complete their maturation among the great stalactites, and must be eaten within a few weeks after being removed. Cabrales is not the only cheese from Asturias. Also made from cow's milk, sometimes with the addition of

OPPOSITE ***Pulpo a feira*** – **stewed spiced octopus.**

ewe's or goat's milk, is the very similar Gamonedo; while the the *Queso de los Bellos* is hard and made from ewe's milk.

Even the critical Alexandre Dumas *fils* favoured Galicia with a few words of praise: 'It is in Galicia that one eats the best fish, particularly fresh cod, eels, both from the rivers or the sea, lamprey and finally octopus...' He goes on to commend its clams and oysters and *marrons glacés*, 'the most exquisite confection known to the civilized world', and was so impressed by *caldo gallego*, a rich meat and vegetable potage, that he took the recipe back to France.

Galicia is first and foremost famous for its magnificent shellfish (*mariscos*), which include lobsters, scallops, prawns and scampi in all shapes and sizes, clams, cockles, oysters, *percebes* (edible barnacles resembling a detached clump of lobster's claws) and *nécoras* (a species of spider crab). All of this magnificent assemblage may be eaten (at a price) in the shellfish bars or *marisquerías*, where they are now sold by weight. Both shellfish and white fish are regu-

larly flown from Galicia to the leading Madrid restaurants.

The scallop shells worn as a badge by the medieval pilgrims are commemorated today in the name of a well-known Galician dish, *conchas de peregrino*, akin to the French *coquilles St Jacques*. Scallops, or *vieiras* as they are called in Galicia, are also prepared by marinating them in the local Albariño wine, then seasoning them with parsley, garlic and nutmeg, and sprinkling them with breadcrumbs before browning in the oven or under the grill. Among the best of Galician fish dishes is the *caldereta de pescado*, a rich fish stew almost identical with the *caldeirada* from across the frontier (there are many similarities between the cooking of Galicia and that of northern Portugal) and with a strong family likeness to *bouillabaisse*. This northern part of the peninsula was once a historical whole, and links with Portugal are again evident in the *caldo a la gallega*, a soup with a strong affinity to the famous *caldo verde* of the Minho, or in *callos a la gallega*, in which tripe is highly spiced and served with haricot beans in the style of the justly famous *tripas à moda do Porto*.

The *empanada gallega*, a thick tart with a filling of onions, tomatoes and peppers, together with sardines or loin of pork, is very characteristic of Galicia, as is *lacón con grelos*, knuckle end of pork cooked with *chorizo* and sprouting turnip tops. All of this is hearty but extremely appetizing fare, appropriate to the cold and wet winters. There are some good sweets, including *filloas* (cream-filled pancakes cooked in liqueur) and *flan de manzanas*, a variation on the baked cream caramel so universally popular in Spain, made with apple purée. You should have no difficulty in finding these dishes, or such popular favourites as *paella* and *zarzuela*, or simple grilled meat, which is of excellent quality, in the local restaurants or the Paradors.

Galicia makes cheeses in some variety, all from cow's milk, the main types being the hard or semi-hard Cebrero and smoked San Simón, and the soft Tetilla and Ulloa for immediate consumption.

Restaurants

In this, as in the other more inaccessible parts of Spain, the Paradors are comfortable and convenient stopping places. Especially to be recommended for their regional dishes are the Parador Nacional Molino Viejo in Gijón and the Parador Nacional Condes de Villalba, a most useful staging post on the borders of Asturias and Galicia. The palatial Parador Nacional Conde de Gondomar at Bayona boasts a *marisquería* (shellfish bar) in its beautiful grounds overlooking the sea.

There are any number of good restaurants specializing in fish and seafood, and only a few can be listed.

Cambados

CHOCOLATE★★★
Between Cambados and Villagarcía de Arosa, this is often rated the best restaurant in Galicia. Its splendid fish is bought in markets up and down the coast. Among its specialities are *empanada de vieiras* (scallop pie), *caldeirada de pescado* (fish stew), *empanada de maíz con berberechos* (savoury pie with sweetcorn and cockles) and *lacón con grelos* (knuckle end of pork with turnip tops). It also offers first-rate grilled and barbecued meat, and there is a good Albariño house wine and a long wine list.

Gijón

LAS DELICIAS★★
Since it was founded as a modest eating house by the grandmother of the present young and enthusiastic proprietor, Valentín Villabona, standards have so improved that it is now one of

A gateway in the grounds of the Parador Nacional Conde de Gondomar, Bayona. The Hapsburg double eagle on the shield is that of Philip IV (1605–65).

the most exciting restaurants in Asturias. Delicious fish dishes include *lenguado relleno* (stuffed sole), *rape con marisco* (monkfish with shellfish), *ventreska de bonito con tomate* (tuna fish in tomato sauce) and *pastel de tiñosu* (rock fish pie). Of the meat dishes, the *chuletón de ternera* (veal chop) is particularly good. Homemade tarts and apple, almond and walnut ice creams.

Oviedo

LA GOLETA★★
The decor in the form of a schooner's interior and the display of fresh shellfish at the entrance underline that this is first and foremost a seafood restaurant. Choose from *crema de nécoras* (bisque of spider crabs), *fideos con almejas* (clams with vermicelli), *aprillada de mariscos* (assorted grilled seafood), *caldereta* (seafood stew) or the sea bass, monkfish and red mullet. The house wine is an Albariño from Cambados.

TRASCORRALES★★
The charming use of stone and wood in the decor and the interesting antiques enhance the pleasures of the table. The menu combines traditional Asturian dishes and others created by the inventive Fernando Martín. They include *merluza con cocochas y almejas* (hake with clams), *revuelto de oricios* (scrambled eggs with sea urchins), spider crab with a delicious vegetable cream, and entrecôte with Cabrales cheese.

Santiago de Compostela

VILAS★★
Founded in 1915, Vilas offers Galician cooking at its best. Choose from *lamprea al vino tinto* (lamprey in red wine), *merluza a la gallega* (Galician-style hake), *pulpo guisado con patatas* (stewed octopus with potatoes) and *vieiras al horno* (scallops baked in their shells). There is a memorable *jarrete de ternera guisada* (stewed

veal) and a delicious *tarta de Santiago* (almond tart) to finish with. Good Galician wines.

HOTEL LOS REYES CATÓLICOS
Any visitor to Santiago will want to stay or to eat in this luxury hotel facing the cathedral, if only because it is housed in a magnificent sixteenth-century palace, beautifully decorated and furnished in period.

Villagarcía de Arosa

LOLIÑA★★
On the quayside of a charming fishing village on the Ría de Arosa, this is the place to come for Galician shellfish at its fresh and splendid best, boiled within hours of being caught. Wonderful oysters, scallops, clams, langoustines and lobster – and try the *santiaguiños*, a large crayfish, so-called because the marking on the head resembles the cross of St James.

Empanada de Santiaguiños – a tart made with large crayfish.

Recipes

Empanada Compostelana/Savoury Tart from Santiago de Compostela

Serves 4

METRIC/IMPERIAL	AMERICAN
Pastry	*Pastry*
350 g/12 oz plain flour, sieved	3 cups all-purpose flour, sifted
1 teaspoon salt	1 teaspoon salt
6 tablespoons melted margarine	$\frac{1}{3}$ cup melted margarine
6 tablespoons olive oil	$\frac{1}{3}$ cup olive oil
6 tablespoons cold water	$\frac{1}{3}$ cup cold water
Flour for rolling out	Flour for rolling out

Sift the flour and salt together into a large bowl, and add the margarine, olive oil and water to make a stiff dough, taking it out and kneading it until smooth. Wrap it in foil and let it rest in the refrigerator for one hour.

Meanwhile make the filling.

Filling	*Filling*
2 tablespoons olive oil	2 tablespoons olive oil
1 large onion, peeled and chopped	1 large onion, peeled and chopped
2 green peppers, seeded, cored and finely chopped	2 green peppers, seeded, cored and finely chopped
6 fresh tomatoes, blanched and skinned	6 fresh tomatoes, blanched and skinned
2 cloves garlic, peeled and chopped	2 cloves garlic, peeled and chopped
2 tablespoons freshly chopped parsley	2 tablespoons freshly chopped parsley
1 teaspoon fresh thyme	1 teaspoon fresh thyme
1 tablespoon tomato purée	1 tablespoon tomato paste
Salt and freshly ground pepper	Salt and freshly ground pepper
1 kg/2¼ lbs fresh sardines, cleaned and fried, or equivalent amount of canned sardines, drained	2¼ lbs fresh sardines, cleaned and fried, or equivalent amount of canned sardines, drained
1 small beaten egg for brushing	1 small beaten egg for brushing

Manzanas Fritas del Ferrol/Fried Apples from El Ferrol

Serves 4

METRIC/IMPERIAL	AMERICAN
2 tablespoons flour	2 tablespoons flour
2 tablespoons *oloroso* sherry	2 tablespoons *oloroso* sherry
4 large eating apples, peeled, cored and cut into rounds	4 large eating apples, peeled, cored and cut into rounds
Olive oil for frying	Olive oil for frying
50 g/2 oz caster sugar	$\frac{1}{4}$ cup fine white sugar
2 teaspoons ground cinnamon	2 teaspoons ground cinnamon

Make a batter with the flour and sherry, adding a little more sherry if necessary. Coat the rounds of apple with the batter and fry them in hot olive oil. Sprinkle with the mixed sugar and cinnamon ground and serve hot.

Heat the oil in a frying pan and fry the onion and peppers until soft. Drain off the oil and reserve for further use, then add the tomatoes, garlic, parsley, thyme, tomato purée and a little salt and pepper, and cook uncovered until the water has evaporated and the mixture is smooth and thick.

Divide the pastry into two equal parts, rolling out the first and lining a pie dish of 20 to 25 cm/8 to 10 in diameter. Spread some sauce on the bottom and cover with a layer of sardines, repeating with more sauce and sardines until both have been used up. Roll out the remaining pastry and put it on top, sealing the edges with your fingers. Brush with beaten egg and bake in the oven (375°F/190°C/Gas Mark 5) for thirty to forty minutes until golden.

The *empanada* can be eaten hot or cold, cut into squares. Instead of sardines, you may use canned tuna, or cooked lean pork or chicken.

Caldeirada Gallega/Sailor's Soup

Serves 6

METRIC/IMPERIAL	AMERICAN
3 tablespoons olive oil	3 tablespoons olive oil
2 onions, finely chopped	2 onions, finely chopped
3 cloves garlic, finely chopped	3 cloves garlic, finely chopped
4 tablespoons freshly chopped parsley	4 tablespoons freshly chopped parsley
2 bay leaves	2 bay leaves
250 g/9 oz hake, boned and skinned	9 oz hake, boned and skinned
250 g/9 oz conger eel, boned and skinned	9 oz conger eel, boned and skinned
250 g/9 oz monkfish, boned and skinned	9 oz monkfish, boned and skinned
150 ml/5 fl oz dry white wine	$\frac{2}{3}$ cup dry white wine
2 litres/$3\frac{1}{2}$ pints fish stock, made with the bones and skins of the fish. Ask the fishmonger to give you some additional trimmings	7 cups fish stock, made with the bones and skins of the fish. Ask for some additional trimmings
1 tablespoon potato flour	1 tablespoon potato flour
Few strands saffron, ground	Few strands saffron, ground
Salt and freshly ground pepper	Salt and freshly ground pepper
200 g/7 oz thin toasted bread	7 oz thin toasted bread

Put the olive oil, onions, garlic, parsley, bay leaves, fish and white wine into a deep saucepan, cover and let it marinate for thirty minutes. Dissolve the potato flour and saffron in a little hot stock and add to the saucepan together with the rest of the fish stock. Simmer for fifteen minutes, then serve with toasted bread on top.

Extremadura

THE EXTREMADURA, from the Latin *Extrema Ora*, lies on the western extreme of Spain bordering Portugal. A region of rolling sierras, cork oaks and wandering herds of sheep and pigs, it was largely depopulated after the Reconquest from the Moors, and its impoverished inhabitants, among them Cortés and Pizarro, swelled the ranks of the Conquistadores who sought their fortunes in Spanish America.

In Roman times Augusta Emerita, the present Mérida, was the capital of Lusitania, which embraced most of modern Portugal. It was the headquarters of Augustus's legions and the ninth city of the empire. On the main route from Madrid to Lisbon, it is among the most rewarding of Spanish cities to visit: its remarkable Roman remains include a magnificent theatre, an aqueduct, the great bridge across the River Guadiana, a triumphal arch of Trajan, splendid tesselated pavements, an amphitheatre and vestiges of a circus.

Guadalupe, in the mountains on the eastern fringe of the Extremadura, owed its foundation to the unearthing of a statue of the Virgin, buried during the Moorish occupation towards the end of the thirteenth century. The Virgin of Guadalupe subsequently became the patron saint of the Conquistadores, while the monastery was frequented by generations of Spanish royalty, including the Catholic Monarchs (it was here that they authorized Columbus to undertake his first voyage of discovery), and soon rivalled Santiago de Compostela as the object of pilgrimage. Despite its sack by Napoleon's troops,

PAGE 189 Vineyards near Almendralejo, the centre of wine production in Extremadura.

OPPOSITE ABOVE The Roman bridge over the River Tagus at Alcántara.

OPPOSITE BELOW Ploughing in the traditional fashion near Mérida in the province of Badajoz.

BELOW LEFT The Virgin of Guadalupe, blackened by the kisses of countless pilgrims.

BELOW RIGHT The great Hieronymite monastery at Guadalupe, founded by Alfonso XI in 1340 and dedicated to the Virgin. The main façade dates from 1349–69.

the monastery is still a storehouse of treasures. The series of scenes from the life of St Jerome painted for its sacristy are among Zurbarán's finest works ; the wooden image of the Virgin, blackened by the kisses of countless pilgrims, still survives, as do its marvellous collections of jewelled vestments and illuminated choir books.

The monastery of Yuste, cool and secluded among its overgrown gardens and groves of towering eucalyptus on the southern slopes of the Sierra de Gredos, will always be associated with Charles V, who spent his last years there after abdicating as Holy Roman Emperor in 1555. His apartments, still hung in black from ceiling to floor in memory of his mother, contain many of his personal belongings, including his invalid chair – to judge from its size, he must have been of diminutive stature. His original tomb was constructed immediately below the high altar of the chapel, so that even the most humble of priests would in effect step on him when celebrating Mass.

Trujillo was the birthplace of Francisco Pizarro, and its Plaza Mayor, flanked by arcades, enclosed by a rampart of baronial houses and dominated by the bulk of the castle, is one of the most evocative in Spain. At the centre is a statue of Pizarro, mounted on one of those horses which so astonished and terrified the Incas as to allow the conquest of their country by a handful of bold adventurers. In nearby Medellín, with its fine seventeenth-century bridge and towering castle, there is a bronze of its illustrious son, Hernán Cortés, in the dusty, sun-bleached square. The remote little town of Jerez de los Caballeros near the Portuguese frontier was the birthplace of yet another of the Conquistadores, Vasco Núñez de Balboa, explorer of the Pacific. It was also the last stronghold of the Knights Templars in Spain (the *caballeros* of its name), and the ruins of their castle are approached through a maze of steep and winding Moorish alleys impassable to motor traffic.

In short, the far-flung Extremadura is a fascinating and little-known part of Spain. Hotels are few and far between, but it is well served by the Paradors installed in historic castles and monasteries at Guadalupe, Mérida, Trujillo, Ciudad Rodrigo, Zafra (near Jerez de los Caballeros) and Jarandilla (adjoining Yuste).

LEFT **The statue of Francisco Pizarro, conqueror of Peru, at his birthplace, Trujillo.**

BELOW **The Parador Nacional Carlos V, Jarandilla, near Yuste, where the Holy Roman Emperor spent his last years.**

The Wines

Although none of the wines from the Extremadura are demarcated, they have a long and honourable history. When the Emperor Charles V, that great enthusiast of Valdepeñas, settled in Yuste, he was still as keenly interested in his wine as in his food. Hearing that the best in the region was made in the bodegas of Pedro Acedo de Berrueza in Jarandilla, he sent a trusted German retainer to investigate. Much flattered, the *bodeguero* offered two hogsheads of his best, one for the Emperor and the other for his emissary, who, in the words of the original story, 'went happily to the palace and told the Emperor what had transpired with the said Pedro. The Emperor, too, was pleased, and the German overjoyed when the promised consignment of wine arrived at the palace.'

The area around Jarandilla and the historic town of Plasencia still makes some light red wine, but the vineyards are very scattered, and in some places (like Miajadas) disappearing, and the best wines from the province of Cáceres are now made around Montánchez in its extreme south and Cañamero on its eastern border.

The wines from the remote village of Montánchez, high in the hills north of Mérida, are as remarkable as its famous hams. They are fermented in earthenware *tinajas* (see p. 67), and the whites, made from the Borba, Pedro Ximénez and Cayetana grapes, develop a *flor* or layer of yeasts in the manner of sherry or the traditional Rueda, which they somewhat resemble in nose and flavour.

Even more remarkable was the traditional *red* Montánchez, made from the Garnacha, Bején and Monastrel; unlike all other red wines, it too developed a *flor*, which gave it a very special nose and flavour and has been the subject of investigation by foreign oenologists. The red wine currently being made is deep in colour with fragrant nose and slight *goût de terroir*, like the whites.

The only wines to be sold outside the area are those of BODEGAS GALÁN Y BERROCAL, S.A., labelled 'Castillo de Montánchez', 'Viña Valdemantilla' and 'Tambil'. The three-year-old 'Trampal' is matured in oak. Traditional, slightly turbid Montánchez from the *tinajas* (or *conos* as they are called locally) of the small family bodegas may be sampled in the bars of Mérida.

The wines from Cañamero, in the mountains near Guadalupe, also grow a *flor*. Vines were first planted there in the early 1920s by a group of enthusiasts, including the local doctor and priest; by the 1950s the wines were being much sought after by connoisseurs, but production is so small that they are only available locally.

The typical Cañamero is a light red, made by fermenting together white grapes (mainly Palomino) and the red Garnacha in small concrete vats. A layer of yeasts develops on the surface of the new wine in the manner of sherry; it is subsequently transferred to oak casks and becomes turbid after some fourteen to eighteen months, but later clears.

The only sizeable firm in the village of Cañamero is that of FELIPE RUIZ PARRALEJO. It bottles its wines as the two-year-old 'La Cepa de Cañamero' and the seven-year-old 'Reserva Felipe Ruiz', which are available in the bars of Guadalupe and in the Parador, whose pleasant carafe wine is orange-coloured, fragrant and slightly turbid, with a pronounced sherry-like flavour. Some of the bars also sell a peasant-made young *pitarra* – albeit of very variable quality and sometimes excessively maderized.

Much the largest production of wine in the Extremadura is in the Tierra de Barros in the province of Badajoz, further south, of which the wine centre is Almendralejo, whose dusty main street is lined with bodegas and distilleries. *Barro* means 'clay' (the clays from the district were, in fact, much used for making domestic utensils), and the vines grow in clays deeply coloured with iron, but becoming lighter and chalkier on the hilly fringes. Some seventy-five per cent of the area is planted with the white Cayetana, which yields somewhat neutral wines, most of them despatched to Jerez,

Asturias and Galicia for blending. The wines are produced more cheaply than in any other part of Spain and in such bulk that it is the only region in the country not to import wine from other areas.

Smaller amounts of red wine are made from the Morisca Mollar, some of the best, deeply coloured and aromatic, in the remote village of Salvatierra de Barros towards the Portuguese border.

Since 1980, probably the best wine from the Tierra de Barros has been made by INDUSTRIAS VINÍCOLAS DEL OESTE, S.A. of Almendralejo, though not from the typical local grapes. It is bottled as 'Lar de Barros'; both the white (made from Macabeo) and the red (made with a blend of Tempranillo and Garnacha) are fresh, fruity and not over-alcoholic.

The Cuisine

In times past the Extremadura was renowned for its ample fare. For the sustenance of the pilgrims the ecclesiastical authorities of Guadalupe provided an annual fifteen thousand bushels of wheat, fifty thousand gallons of wine,

Drying red peppers in the sun for milling near Jarandilla.

and six or seven thousand head of cattle, in addition to veal, kids, chicken and game.

Of the gastronomic Charles v, the Spanish historian Emilio Castelar writes:

The mail coaches from Lisbon to Valladolid went far out of their way to deliver fish to Yuste, and the *Corregidor* of Plasencia received the strictest orders from Valladolid to provide the Emperor with all the meat that he demanded . . . Valladolid presented him with eel pies, Zaragoza with veal, Ciudad Real with game, Gama with partridge, Denia with sausages, Cádiz with anchovies, Sevilla with oysters, Lisbon with sole, the Extremadura with olives, Toledo with marzipans and Guadalupe with stews devised by its numerous and inventive chefs.

The repositories of the culinary arts were the great monasteries, and during the Peninsular War the French invaders paid passing tribute to the survivals of a highly developed cuisine. When General Junot sacked the monastery of Alcántara near the Portuguese border in 1807 and ordered its medieval parchments to be used for making cartridges, one of the precious manuscripts which he preserved was the monastery's recipe book. His wife, the Duchess of Abrantes, reproduced parts of it in her *Mémoires*, and the famous Escoffier was later to comment that: 'It was the major trophy, the only positive advantage which France reaped from that war.' The remark was justified, because the centuries-old manuscript contained the first known references to consommé (under the name of '*consumado*' or '*consumo*'), early directions for the use of truffles, and a recipe for *pâté de foie gras*.

The area was laid waste during the war and the great monasteries were stripped and declined from their former glory; but if the Extremadura can no longer boast culinary profusion, it still furnishes a variety of interesting regional dishes.

Gazpacho extremeño is a variant of the cold soups so popular in Andalucía. *Coliflor al estilo de Badajoz* is prepared by dividing cauliflower into florets, then dredging them in egg and breadcrumbs and frying them crisp in olive oil. *Bacalao al estilo monacal*, described by Dionisio Pérez as a 'delicious mortification for a day of fast' and one of the old monastic recipes, is one of the many ways of preparing the dried and salted cod so popular in Spain. *Migas*, or fried breadcrumbs, are again popular as in rural districts all over Spain. *Huevos a la extremeña* are prepared by making a sauce with olive oil, onions and tomatoes and adding boiled potatoes, *chorizo*, ham and seasoning. The eggs are broken on top and the dish is finished in the oven.

Typical meat dishes include *cochifrito* (lamb cooked and served in an earthenware dish with onions, garlic, paprika, freshly ground pepper, parsley and lemon juice); *frito típico extremeño* (fried and seasoned kid); *riñonada*, made with a mixture of lamb's kidneys and sweetbreads; and *solomillo de cordero* (lamb stewed slowly in a marinade of salt, pepper, olive oil and red wine).

Game is plentiful and prepared in a variety of ways (try the excellent partridge pie), and the *pièce de resistance* of Extremaduran cooking is *faisán al modo de Alcántara* (pheasant Alcántara style). This elaborate recipe was among those pillaged by General Junot; the bird is stuffed with a purée of fried duck's livers spiked with truffles, marinated in port for three days, then roasted and served with a sauce made by reducing the marinade and adding truffles.

One of the glories of Extremadura is its *embutidos* or charcuterie, in the form of cured ham (*jamón serrano*) and spiced pepper sausage (*chorizo*). Richard Ford wrote of them: 'Those of Galicia and Catalonia are also celebrated, but are not to be compared for a moment with those of Montanches, which are fit to set before an emperor,' adding that 'His grace the Duke of Arcos used to shut up the pigs in places abounding with vipers, on which they fattened. Neither the pigs, dukes, nor their toad-eaters seem to have been poisoned by these exquisite vipers . . .'

Neither *jamón serrano*, which resembles Parma and Bayonne ham but is perhaps even fuller in flavour, nor *chorizo* is cooked; both, after salting and spicing, are hung up to dry. *Jamón serrano* is best cut very thin and may be eaten on its own or with melon; *chorizo* is often served raw among the dozens of small dishes that make up Spanish *entremeses* (or *hors d'oeuvres*); it is frequently added to *cocidos* and stews of dried vegetables to lend them flavour and piquancy; it makes savoury *tortillas*, and is also the basis for dishes such as *huevos a la flamenca*.

The last word may be left to the dramatist Lope de Vega:

> *Toda es cosa vil*
> *a donde falta un pernil.*

> Life is but an empty sham
> Where there is lacking Spanish ham.

Restaurants

When touring in this region, the most convenient eating places are usually the strategically located Paradors, and the Parador in Mérida has won awards for its cooking.

Badajoz

EL SÓTANO★

Probably the best restaurant in the whole region, despite uninspired surroundings. It serves *bacalao* (dried and salted cod) in various forms, excellent cured ham, good veal stew and an outstanding *riñonada*, made from lamb's kidneys and sweetbreads. The four-year-old red wine from Almendralejo is full-bodied and soft.

Guadalupe

HOSPEDERÍA DEL REAL MONASTERIO

In centuries-old tradition the monastery maintains a guest house and large restaurant for its many pilgrims and visitors. Well-prepared and modestly priced regional dishes include Extremaduran hors d'oeuvres, cured ham and charcuterie, fried pork, *cochifrito* (stewed lamb), roast kid and *muegado* (a typical sweet from Guadalupe).

Mérida

PARADOR NACIONAL VÍA DE LA PLATA★
The Parador is housed in an old convent with a beautiful interior patio and Moorish-style garden. Regional dishes include Extremaduran hors d'oeuvres (fifteen separate dishes and virtually a meal in itself); *gazpacho a la extremeña*; trout served with ham; *alcachofas con jamón* (artichoke hearts sautéed with ham); *caldereta de cordero* (a classic lamb stew); and *torta del convento* (sweet pancake).

HOTEL EMPERATRIZ
The hotel is installed in an old palace of the Mendoza family, incorporating Roman masonry. The tables are set in a great patio with fountains and tiered rows of arches, screened from the sun by a high awning overhead, and it is worth eating here if only for the surroundings. There is a good selection of local wines from Almendralejo and elsewhere.

Plasencia

HOTEL ALFONSO VIII
The hotel restaurant offers local trout from the River Jerte, *caldereta extremeña* (lamb stew) and other Extremaduran dishes, also wines from Cañamero and Montánchez.

Trujillo

CASA LA PATA
Best for its *tapas* and aperitifs, this restaurant also serves regional dishes such as fried lamb, *moragas* (barbecued meats) and the local truffles. It is open for lunch only.

Recipes

Ensalada de Boquerones/ Fresh Anchovy Appetizer

Serves 4

METRIC/IMPERIAL

1 kg/$2\frac{1}{4}$ lbs *boquerones* or sprats, middle and other bones removed, split in two

Vinaigrette sauce

150 ml/5 fl oz white wine vinegar

6 cloves garlic, very finely chopped

4 tablespoons virgin olive oil

6 peppercorns

Freshly ground sea salt

4 tablespoons freshly chopped parsley

AMERICAN

$2\frac{1}{4}$ lbs *boquerones* or sprats, middle and other bones removed, split in two

Vinaigrette sauce

$\frac{2}{3}$ cup white wine vinegar

6 cloves garlic, very finely chopped

$\frac{1}{4}$ cup virgin olive oil

6 peppercorns

Freshly ground sea salt

4 tablespoons freshly chopped parsley

Lay the fillets of fish in the bottom of a Pyrex dish. Make a vinaigrette sauce with the other ingredients, pour on top and keep in the refrigerator covered with plastic wrap for a day or two before serving.

Huevos a la Extremeña/Eggs Extremaduran Style

Serves 4

METRIC/IMPERIAL	AMERICAN
4 tablespoons olive oil	$\frac{1}{4}$ cup olive oil
2 onions, finely chopped	2 onions, finely chopped
225 g/8 oz tomatoes, blanched, skinned and chopped	8 oz tomatoes, blanched, skinned and chopped
1 kg/2$\frac{1}{4}$ lbs potatoes, peeled, boiled and diced	2$\frac{1}{4}$ lbs potatoes, peeled, boiled and diced
150 g/5 oz *chorizo*, skinned and diced	5 oz *chorizo*, skinned and diced
150 g/5 oz smoked ham or Italian prosciutto	5 oz smoked ham or Italian prosciutto
8 large eggs	8 large eggs
400 g/14 oz cooked peas	2 cups cooked green peas
Salt and pepper	Salt and pepper

Heat the olive oil in a frying pan and fry the onions until soft, but not brown. Drain off any remaining oil, add the tomatoes and cook for a further twenty minutes. Make a fine purée in a food processor or by passing through a sieve and transfer to an oven dish, adding the potatoes, *chorizo*, ham, salt and pepper, and mixing well together. This can be done in advance. Before serving, break the eggs on top, garnish with the peas and cook in the oven (450°F/230°C/Gas Mark 8) for about five to six minutes until the egg whites are set, the yolks remaining soft. Serve in the same dish.

Ternera a la Extremeña/Veal Extremaduran Style

Serves 4

METRIC/IMPERIAL	AMERICAN
1 kg/2¼ lbs loin of veal in one piece	2¼ lbs loin of veal in one piece
6 cinnamon sticks	6 cinnamon sticks
4 tablespoons olive oil	¼ cup olive oil
1 onion, chopped	1 onion, chopped
2 cloves garlic, chopped	2 cloves garlic, chopped
4 tomatoes, blanched, skinned and chopped	4 tomatoes, blanched, skinned and chopped
1 large glass *fino* sherry	1 large glass *fino* sherry
300 ml/½ pint meat stock	1 cup meat stock
Salt and pepper	Salt and pepper

Insert the cinnamon sticks into the meat. Heat the oil in a heavy frying pan and brown the meat, then add the onion and garlic and cook for ten minutes. Now incorporate the tomatoes, sherry, stock, salt and freshly ground pepper. Cover and cook slowly for an hour or a little longer depending on the tenderness of the meat.

Put the meat on a carving dish, remove cinnamon sticks, cut into thin rounds and replace in original shape. Meanwhile make a smooth sauce by passing the contents of the pan through a food processor or sieve. Pour this on top of the meat and serve.

Balearics and Canaries

*S*TANDING IN THE GREAT HALL of Palma airport, thronged with visitors in their thousands waiting to take off for Hamburg or Manchester in their jumbo jets, it is difficult to realize that until the tourist boom of the early 1950s, Majorca and the smaller islands of Minorca, Ibiza and Formentera were deserted and impoverished, a haven for romantics such as George Sand and Chopin.

Today, with every beach flanked by hotels and high-rise apartments, there are still long stretches of coast too rocky for development; and in the mountainous interior of Majorca the foreign invasion has actually resulted in depopulation as the younger people migrate to Palma to work in the shops and hotels. All too frequently the solid stone houses of their forebears stand roofless, the olives, figs and almonds go unpicked, and the only noise to break the silence of the surrounding mountains is the will-o'-the-wisp jingle of a goat bell.

The islanders are of very mixed origin. Majorca in particular was a regular port of call for Greeks, Phoenicians, Carthaginians and Romans. The Jews arrived in strength after their expulsion from Rome and the Holy Land and were for long the backbone of the professional and commercial classes, as are their Christianized descendants today. One of the great

PREVIOUS PAGE **Fishing boats drawn up at Arrecife in Lanzarote; some of the varieties of fish from the Atlantic waters are unknown elsewhere.**

BELOW **San Torrella de Santa María, a baronial house near Binisalem in Majorca.**

Melons ripening in the sun on the roof of a cottage in Minorca.

formative influences was the Moorish occupation of the Balearics in AD 902, and it was not until 1229 that James the Conqueror arrived off the western tip of Majorca with a large fleet and after stubborn fighting around Palma claimed the islands for the Crown of Aragón. Cultural and linguistic ties with Catalonia and the bordering provinces of France, which were also for long dominated by the house of Barcelona, remain close; and the Mallorquín spoken in the islands today is very similar to Catalan and the dialect of the Languedoc.

Though sharing the same mild climate and beaches with fine white sand and transparent water, each island has its own character. In contrast to Majorca, Minorca is almost without hills, and the British who occupied it from 1708-82 have left their mark on its architecture, especially in the capital, Port Mahón. Ibiza, which became a byword for trendy holidays, remains a surpassingly beautiful island, with its hilly countryside and groves of pines, almonds, figs and olives, while the ever-present palms are a reminder of the nearness of Africa.

The most memorable town in the Balearics is the capital, Palma de Majorca. Its thriving port is dominated by a magnificent Gothic cathedral, while in the steep and narrow streets of the old town the restaurants stand side by side and there are charming glimpses of the arcaded patios of the old baronial houses.

The Canary Islands lie some five hundred miles off the Atlantic coast of north Africa. Known to the ancients as the Gardens of the Hesperides, they were once thought to be part of the lost continent of Atlantis, but they are in fact of volcanic origin. The Arabs, Moors, Genoese, Portuguese and Spaniards all at one time or another tried to establish themselves in the islands, but it was not until 1402 that a French adventurer, Jean de Béthencourt, enlisted the help of Henry III of Castile and, beginning with the conquest of Fuerteventura, claimed the whole group for Spain and became the first ruler.

With their mild Atlantic climate, the islands are sometimes called the Land of Eternal Spring and, apart from growing sugar cane, vines, bananas, tobacco and spring vegetables, are a favourite with visitors in search of sun and bathing.

The largest of the seven islands, Tenerife, is one of contrasts, with a mountain chain flanked by lush and fertile valleys and with the great crater of Las Cañadas del Teide at the centre. Gran Canaria, the site of the capital Las Palmas and the centre of a thriving cigar industry, possesses every type of scenery: sandy deserts, mountains clothed with tropical vegetation, steep ravines descending to the coast and smiling banana plantations. Lanzarote, swept by torrid winds from the Sahara, is completely different in character. Covered with lava and pock-marked by more than three hundred volcanoes, it is encircled by tranquil coves and beaches with red, black or startlingly white sand. The beaches of Fuerteventura, an island of wide plains and gentle streams, are a sunbather's paradise.

LEFT The Canary Islands make excellent cigars; here a girl inspects leaves for use as outer wrappers in a factory in Las Palmas.

RIGHT Palma de Majorca, the harbour and the cathedral.

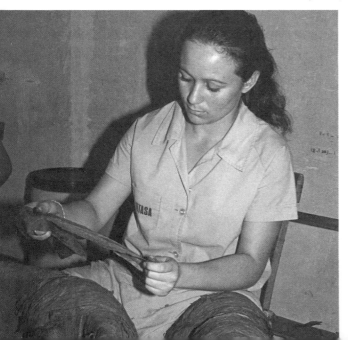

The Wines

Balearics

There is a long history of wine-making in Majorca dating from Roman times, and Pliny mentions its wines as being among the best from the Mediterranean. Viticulture survived the Moorish occupation, and in the Middle Ages the sweet Malvasía was a favourite at the court of the Crown of Aragón.

Majorca was the last area in Europe to be affected by the phylloxera epidemic of the late nineteenth century, and profiting from the devastation of the French vineyards the Majorcans planted thousands more hectares of vines and began exporting their wines in a big way. With the onset of the plague the wine industry suffered a blow from which it has never recovered: exports from the port of Palma fell from 300,000 hectolitres in 1889 to 32,000 in 1893, and by 1907 the area under vines had decreased from its peak of 30,000 hectares to less than 3000. Today, the islands are net importers of wine, and it is much easier to obtain a bottle of Rioja or Catalan wine than of the local growths.

More than ninety-six per cent of the wine, most of it red, is produced in Majorca, most of it around Binisalem to the north-east of Palma and Felanitx and Manacor to the south-east. The soils are mainly ferruginous clays, and the most important vine variety is the Manto negro, which gives rise to fruity and intensely coloured wines, well-suited to ageing in oak but lacking somewhat in acidity. Other native black grapes are the Callet, Fogoneu and Fogoneu francés, while small amounts of white wine are made from the Sumoll. The famous Malvasía has all but disappeared.

The number of concerns making good quality bottled wine is very limited.

BODEGAS JAUME MESQUIDA, CA'N XENOY

Jaume Mesquida has experimented with the planting of Cabernet Sauvignon at Porreras in the east of Majorca and is making a good red wine with a blend of Cabernet and native grapes.

BODEGAS JOSÉ L. FERRER, FRANJA ROJA, S.A.

Situated in Binisalem and owned by the skilled and informed Don José L. Ferrer, with some 150 hectares of vineyards under the Manto negro this is the most important producer in Majorca. The well-made and attractive wines include the young red 'Autentico' and excellent 1976 and 1978 *reservas*. There is also a fresh young 'Blanc de Blancs' made from the white Sumoll. The wines are readily obtainable in hotels and in the shops and restaurants of Palma, but exports are very limited.

SOCIEDAD COOPERATIVA DE FELANITX LTDA.

Founded in 1919, this is the largest winery in Majorca and makes worthwhile red wines from the Fogoneu, Calop and Callet grapes.

Canaries

Canary is a wine more famous for its past than its present. Both Sir John Hawkins and Richard Hakluyt, the geographer, put in at the islands during the sixteenth century and reported enthusiastically on its Malvasía ('Malmsey') grapes and sweet 'sack', that 'marvellous searching wine' mentioned by Shakespeare in *Henry IV*, Part 2 and *The Merry Wives of Windsor*. Shipments to England reached a peak of 682,000 gallons in 1815, after which there was a steady decline; today, the Canaries export no wine and produce little more than young wines for local consumption, none of them demarcated and most sold in bulk. Even in the capital, Las Palmas, it is almost impossible to find local wines, and to taste them you must go to the small restaurants on the islands where they are made.

The soils are volcanic; because of their geographical isolation the Canaries were never affected by phylloxera, and the vines are therefore planted ungrafted. The main white

Vines on the island of Lanzarote, sunk into pits in the volcanic soil to protect them from the Sahara winds.

varieties are: Listán blanca, Malvasía, Blanca común and Pedro Ximénez; and the red: Listán negra, Vijiriego, Negramoll and Negra común. Cultivation is often very difficult. For example, in the Orotava valley in Tenerife, the vines are planted on steep terraces difficult of access, while in Lanzarote they are sunk individually in pits surrounded by stone walls to shelter them from the Sahara winds. Mechanical cultivation is therefore impossible and they must be tended individually by hand. Another problem is that vines require a resting period during winter if quality wines are to be produced, but the climate is so warm that, left to themselves, they would fruit twice a year. Dedicated wine-makers like Don Miguel González Monje of El Sauzal in Tenerife combat this by removing the stakes after the harvest, bending over the vines and burying the tips in the ground so as to protect them from the heat.

Others resort to an extra pruning to prevent the plants budding in winter. The low yields in face of such difficulties are highlighted by Miguel A. Torres when he writes in *Los vinos de España – Cata* of a visit to a small proprietor, who invited him to taste his new vintage, informing him that the 500-litre barrel represented the total yield from six hectares of vineyards.

Red wines are made mainly in Tenerife, where the largest vineyards are around Tacoronte, west of Santa Cruz and near the north coast, and Monte Lentiscal on the island of Gran Canaria. They are strong and spicy, but honest enough.

White wines, which predominate, are made near Fuencaliente at the southern tip of the island of La Palma; in Lanzarote, which produces the best of the white Malvasías; in Frontera on the island of Hierro; in Arafo, Fasnia and Vilaflor on Tenerife; and in minuscule quantity on the small island of Gomera.

Most of the wine is made by small proprietors for sale in bulk, and only ten bodegas bottle their wines. They include:

BODEGA DE MIGUEL GONZÁLEZ MONJE
Señor Monje is an impassioned enthusiast of the wines of his native Tenerife, of which an excellent example is his red 'Mi bodega' made in Santa Ursula.

BODEGAS EL GRIFO
Located in La Geria on Lanzarote, with its own vineyards and modern equipment embracing stainless steel fermentation tanks and refrigeration machinery, Bodegas El Grifo probably makes the best wines from the Canaries. Its white 'Malvasía El Grifo', labelled as *seco* (dry), *semiseco* (semi-dry) and *dulce* (sweet) has been much praised.

BODEGAS MOZAGA
Also located in La Geria on Lanzarote, Mozaga has done much to revive vineyards in the area, at one time abandoned. It bottles a red, rosé and white 'Mozaga' and also makes good Malvasías.

BODEGAS TENEGUÍA

This sizeable firm in Fuencaliente on the island of La Palma takes its name from the volcano which erupted in 1949. It makes good quality white and rosé wines, labelled as 'Blanco Teneguía', and 'Rosado Teneguía', and also a sweet Malvasía.

The Cuisine

Balearics

Ties with Catalonia are reflected in the native cooking, which is basically peasant in character and dependent on local ingredients.

To begin with breakfast, *ensaimadas*, eaten with coffee or chocolate, are one of the few Majorcan specialities to be served in the holiday hotels. Light, fluffy, a little sweet and halfway between a bun and a pastry, they resemble a Moorish turban in shape. It seems that *ensaimadas* cannot properly be made except in the islands, and large consignments are regularly shipped to Barcelona and the mainland.

The basis of many native dishes is the excellent vegetables. Good examples are the famous *supa mallorquina*, made with onions, cabbage or spring vegetables, garlic and paprika; *acelgas con pasas y piñones*, a Spanish variant on spinach, boiled and served with a sauce made with pine kernels, raisins, toasted bread and garlic; and *tumbet*, an egg and vegetable pie made with potatoes, red peppers, onions, courgettes (zucchini) and tomato sauce.

The seafood is so fresh as to be magnificent in any guise, as for example *caldereta de datiles de mar* (a soup made from the small brown *datil de mar* or 'sea date'); *calamares a la mallorquina* (squid stuffed with pine kernels, raisins and other ingredients); or *langosta a la mallorquina* (hot lobster). There seems little reason to doubt that mayonnaise, with which this lobster is served, was a Minorcan invention, taking its name from Port Mahón – though other less convincing derivations have been put forward.

Arenques, or salt herrings, from Palma de Majorca.

Meat is much less varied than fish; the best is pork in its different forms. The *embutidos*, made by salting, spicing and smoking the various cuts and innards of the animal, include *chorizo* (see p. 195), the delicate white *butifarra* (see p. 159) and the soft orange-coloured *sobrasada*, which may be spread on bread, or when stirred into a stew forms a ready made and piquant sauce.

A well-known speciality is *coca mallorquina*, resembling the Italian *pizza* and made from a pasta with embedded strips of onion, pepper and tomato, sometimes with the addition of anchovies or tuna. It is cooked by the country people in outdoor ovens of stone or brick, fired with wood or almond shells, but may be bought

A selection of Majorcan seafood – crayfish, spiny lobsters and mussels.

in the *confiterías* (confectioners' shops) to take away for a picnic.

The Balearics produce splendid almonds and olives, and grow beautiful figs and oranges and the more exotic prickly pear and pomegranates, of which the flesh may be eaten fresh with a little sugar and sherry. The islands, especially Minorca, make a good semi-hard cheese with full flavour from cow's milk, the *queso de Mahón*, in the form of large rectangular cakes with rounded corners.

Canaries

You will find few native dishes in the holiday hotels, but the islanders themselves, as perhaps in no other part of Spain, have lovingly conserved dishes inherited from the original inhabitants, the Guanches. South American and North American influences are also evident, but traditional food is served only in small country restaurants.

One such Guanche survival is *gofio*, the bread made in the shape of a large ball and eaten all over the islands. It is made from the flours of various ingredients (wheat, barley, maize and dried chick-peas) sometimes blended, but always toasted before milling, and mixed with either water or milk.

Most famous of vegetable dishes is *papas arrugadas*, new potatoes boiled in their skins in sea water, then baked and served with the spicy *mojo colorado*, a sauce containing garlic, olive oil, cayenne pepper, chillis and cumin seeds. A favourite soup, the *sopa del Teide*, is made with rice, garlic, tomatoes, onions, lemon and olive oil. Fish and shellfish – including lobster, clams, sole, hake, anchovies and other varieties, such as *vieja*, unknown elsewhere – is plentiful and is cooked in Canarian style. Other typical dishes are: Canary-style tripe, boiling fowl and turkey, and *cabrito al salmorejo* (kid in spicy sauce). The *puchero canario* resembles the *cocido* of La Mancha and is known in its most elaborate form as the 'stew of seven meats', since it contains beef, chicken, veal, boiling fowl, pigeon, rabbit and partridge, stewed with potatoes, pulses and fresh vegetables. It is served as three courses: soup, green vegetables, and meat with potatoes and beans.

There is a variety of original sweets, including an intriguing baked Alaska laced with Cointreau and Grand Marnier and shaped like the crater of the famous volcano of Teide; delicious *buñuelos de dátiles* (date rolls); and, as might be expected of islands which grow such good ones, a range of unusual desserts made with bananas, sometimes fried, or with other ingredients such as pineapple, semolina, eggs and liqueurs.

Restaurants

Balearics

Ibiza

SAN RAFAEL

GRILL SAN RAFAEL★
A pleasant restaurant with terrace garden and views of the bay. Specialities are the *bacalao* (dried, salted cod), baked gilthead, hake with Calvados and *crema catalana* (baked caramel cream).

Majorca

FELANITX

VIOLET★
Set in an old house with a beautiful garden, Violet is well worth a visit. The menu changes daily and includes such seasonal specialities as marinade of fresh salmon, melon consommé with crème de menthe, hare with snails and cabbage, sole with avocado mousse, entrecôte with mustard sauce and home-made sweets.

INCA

CELLER C'AN AMER★

Housed in an old wine cellar, the Celler specializes in traditional Majorcan dishes such as a good meat soup, *frito mallorquín* (mixed fried fish), roast sucking pig and home-made sweets.

PALMA DE MAJORCA

EL GALLO★★

El Gallo has been one of the best restaurants in Palma since it was opened by Juan Gual in 1979, and can only improve with the recent appointment of the inventive José Ramón Farín from Barcelona as *maître de cuisine*. Examples of Majorcan dishes are the *gratinado de berenjenas con sobrasada* (grilled aubergines with *sobrasada* sausage), *calamarcitos rellenos de verduras estofadas a la mallorquina* (stuffed squid) and *tarta de pasta de almendra* (almond tart).

ANCORA★

This comfortable restaurant, with its light and airy dining room, serves a variety of imaginative dishes, including puff pastries with langoustines and asparagus, sweetbreads with pears, fillets San Pedro with *datiles de mar* (a small brown mussel), marinated meat with mustard and marjoram sauce, and attractive sweets such as gâteau with fresh figs and puff pastry with bananas.

Minorca

PORT MAHÓN

ROCAMAR★

Established for more than thirty years, Rocamar is now known as one of the best restaurants in the Balearics. Facing the sea, it is renowned for its fish and seafood, especially the *caldereta de langosta* (lobster stew), mixed grills of fish, baked gilthead and *arroz con pescado* (rice with fish).

Canaries

Gran Canaria

LAS PALMAS

ACUARIO★

The most elegant restaurant in the capital of the Canaries, specializing in fish and seafood. You may choose from a tank with live fish.

PLAYA DEL INGLÉS

LA CAVE★

This bistro-style restaurant in the fashionable seaside resort does not serve regional food, but its cooking is probably the most sophisticated in the islands.

Lanzarote

TEGUISE

LAS SALINAS

There are beautiful views over the gardens of this five-star hotel overlooking the sea. Its restaurant serves pleasant international food, but one may enjoy regional Canary dishes in the buffet.

Tenerife

TACORONTE

LAS CUEVAS DE TACORONTE

This is the place to sample a wide range of well-cooked native dishes; it also runs to a good selection of the local wines.

The Paradors at Las Cañadas del Teide (Tenerife), Cruz de Tejeda (Gran Canaria), San Sebastián de la Gomera (Gomera), Puerto del Rosarion (Fuerteventura) and Santa Cruz de La Palma (La Palma) also make a point of including some regional dishes on their menus.

Recipes

Sopa Mallorquina/Majorcan Soup

Serves 6

METRIC/IMPERIAL	AMERICAN
4 tablespoons olive oil	$\frac{1}{4}$ cup olive oil
2 onions, peeled and very finely chopped	2 onions, peeled and very finely chopped
2 large peppers, green or red, seeded, cored and very finely chopped	2 large peppers, green or red, seeded, cored and very finely chopped
$\frac{1}{2}$ kg/1 lb 2 oz tomatoes, blanched, skinned and finely chopped	1 lb 2 oz tomatoes, blanched, skinned and finely chopped
3 cloves garlic, chopped	3 cloves garlic, chopped
2 tablespoons freshly chopped parsley	2 tablespoons freshly chopped parsley
1 kg/$2\frac{1}{4}$ lbs cabbage, washed and finely chopped	$2\frac{1}{4}$ lbs cabbage, washed and finely chopped
2 litres/$3\frac{1}{2}$ pints meat stock	7 cups meat stock
Salt and pepper	Salt and pepper
200 g/7 oz toasted stale French bread cut into thin rounds	7 oz toasted stale French bread cut into thin rounds

Heat the oil in a heavy pan and fry the onions and peppers together for about twenty minutes until soft, covering with the lid. Add the tomatoes, garlic, parsley and cabbage and cook for another ten minutes. Finally, add the stock, season with salt and pepper and boil for about fifteen minutes.

Place some of the slices of toast on the bottom of a hot soup tureen and ladle on the soup. Add more toast and more soup, leave for a few minutes for the toast to absorb the broth, then garnish with a little more parsley and serve.

Calamares a la Mallorquina/Majorcan-Style Squid

Serves 4

METRIC/IMPERIAL	AMERICAN
150 ml/5 fl oz olive oil	$\frac{2}{3}$ cup olive oil
1 small onion, peeled and finely chopped	1 small onion, peeled and finely chopped
1$\frac{1}{2}$ kg/3$\frac{1}{4}$ lbs squid, cleaned, blanched and cooled	3$\frac{1}{4}$ lbs squid, cleaned, blanched and cooled
100 g/4 oz raisins, soaked and drained	$\frac{1}{2}$ cup raisins, soaked and drained
50 g/2 oz pine kernels	$\frac{1}{4}$ cup pine nuts
50 g/2 oz fresh breadcrumbs	$\frac{1}{4}$ cup fresh breadcrumbs
2 small eggs, lightly beaten	2 small eggs, lightly beaten
1 tablespoon chopped parsley	1 tablespoon chopped parsley
Salt and pepper	Salt and pepper
Flour for dusting	Flour for dusting
2 glasses/300 ml/10 fl oz dry white wine	2 glasses/1$\frac{1}{3}$ cups dry white wine

Heat half of the oil in a heavy pan and sauté the onion for ten minutes. Meanwhile chop the tentacles of the squid and cook with the onion for a further five minutes. Drain excess oil and transfer to a bowl. Add the raisins, pine kernels, breadcrumbs, eggs, parsley, salt and pepper, stirring to achieve a thin consistency. Cool.

Now, one by one, take the bodies of the squid in your hand and stuff them with the mixture, securing with a fine skewer or with needle and thread to prevent it coming out. Dust the stuffed squid with flour, then fry them very briefly in a clean pan in the rest of the olive oil. Add the wine and a little more parsley and cook slowly for ten minutes, shaking from time to time. Serve with boiled rice.

In Majorca, this dish is made with tiny squid about 8 cm/3 inches in length. Ask for the smallest available and do not overcook or they will get tough.

Papas Arrugadas/Canary-Style Potatoes

Serves 4

In the Canary Islands these are boiled in seawater and served with the spicy *Mojo* sauce.

METRIC/IMPERIAL	AMERICAN
16 new potatoes, washed but unskinned (old potatoes are not suitable)	16 new potatoes, washed but unpeeled (old potatoes are not suitable)
Salt	Salt

Boil the potatoes in a large saucepan for twenty minutes with salty water. Drain and bake in a very hot oven (450°F/230°C/Gas Mark 8) for ten minutes.

Mojo sauce

150 ml/5 fl oz wine vinegar	$\frac{2}{3}$ cup wine vinegar
3 tablespoons olive oil	3 tablespoons olive oil
3 cloves garlic	3 cloves garlic
$\frac{1}{4}$ of a dried chilli, seeded	$\frac{1}{4}$ of a dried chili, seeded
1 teaspoon hot paprika	1 teaspoon hot paprika
1 teaspoon cumin seeds	1 teaspoon cumin seeds
Salt and pepper	Salt and pepper
2 teaspoons of freshly chopped parsley	2 teaspoons of freshly chopped parsley

Pour the vinegar and oil into a glass jar. Grind the garlic, chilli, paprika and cumin in a mortar, then transfer to the jar, season with salt and add the parsley. Close the lid and shake well together.

Cut the potatoes in half and serve with the sauce. In the Canaries it is also used with fish.

Pastelitos Mallorquines/ Majorcan Cupcakes

Makes 12 cupcakes

METRIC/IMPERIAL

3 large eggs

3 tablespoons caster sugar

50 g/2 oz rice flour, sieved

Grated zest of 1 lemon

AMERICAN

3 large eggs

3 tablespoons fine white sugar

$\frac{1}{2}$ cup rice flour, sieved

Grated zest of 1 lemon

In a big bowl, beat the egg-whites stiff, add the yolks, and using a wooden spoon work the sugar, rice flour and lemon zest to make a smooth dough. Roll out and cut into rounds with a pastry cutter or smooth into a 12-hole non-stick bun or cupcake tin. Bake in the oven for ten to twelve minutes at 350°F/180°C/Gas Mark 4.

Plátanos Canarios Fritos/ Fried Bananas Canary Style

Serves 4

METRIC/IMPERIAL

8 small Canary bananas (or 4 larger bananas)

Olive oil for frying

Caster sugar

Dash of Spanish brandy or lemon juice

AMERICAN

8 small Canary bananas (or 4 larger bananas)

Olive oil for frying

Fine white sugar

Dash of Spanish brandy or lemon juice

Peel the bananas and cut them lengthwise, then fry for ten minutes in hot oil. Drain and dry them on kitchen paper, sprinkle with sugar and brandy or lemon juice, and serve hot.

Tomates al Estilo de Las Palmas/Las Palmas-Style Tomatoes

Serves 4

METRIC/IMPERIAL	AMERICAN
4 large or 8 small tomatoes (choose large if possible)	4 large or 8 small tomatoes (choose large if possible)
50 g/2 oz cooked breast of chicken, finely chopped	$\frac{1}{2}$ cup cooked breast of chicken, finely chopped
25 g/1 oz smoked ham or Italian prosciutto, finely chopped	$\frac{1}{4}$ cup smoked ham or Italian prosciutto, finely chopped
100 g/4 oz freshly toasted breadcrumbs	2 cups freshly toasted breadcrumbs
2 tablespoons freshly chopped parsley	2 tablespoons freshly chopped parsley
Salt and black pepper	Salt and black pepper
50 g/2 oz unsalted butter	$\frac{1}{4}$ cup unsalted butter

Cut the tomatoes in half, scoop the pulp and juice on to a plate and mix with the chicken meat and ham. Stuff the empty tomatoes with the mixture, place them in an ovenproof dish, sprinkle with breadcrumbs and parsley, season and dot with butter. Bake in the oven (350°F/180°C/Gas Mark 4) for about fifteen minutes.

Further Reading

For a detailed bibliography of books on Spanish wine, readers are referred to Read, Jan, *The Wines of Spain*, 2nd ed., London 1986.

Blue Guide to Spain, ed. Ian Robertson, London 1980.

Ford, Richard, *Gatherings from Spain*, London 1846 (available in Everyman's Library).

Gonzalez Gordon, Manuel Ma., *Sherry, the Noble Wine*, London 1972.

Jeffs, Julian, *Sherry*, 3rd ed., London 1982.

Macpherson, Lalo Grosso de, *Cooking with Sherry* (trans. Maite Manjón), Madrid 1983.

Manjón, Maite, *Spain – International Gourmet Series*, London and New York 1987.

(with Read, Jan), *Flavours of Spain*, London 1978.

Michelin Guide to Spain and Portugal, pub. yearly.

Peñin, José, *Manual de vinos españoles*, Madrid 1981.

Manual de los vinos de Rioja, Madrid 1982.

Read, Jan, *Pocket Guide to Spanish Wines*, London and New York 1983.

Wines of the Rioja, London and San Francisco (The Wine Appreciation Guild) 1984.

The Moors in Spain and Portugal, London 1974.

Russell, P.E., ed. *Spain: A Companion to Spanish Studies*, London 1973.

Torres, Miguel A., *Wines and Vineyards of Spain*, Barcelona 1982.

Manual de los vinos de Cataluña, Barcelona 1983.

Torres, Marimar, *The Spanish Table*, New York 1986.

Index